other recent books on similar topic

THE HINDUS. *Bestseller*
Encyclopaedia of Hinduism in 5 Volumes
Edited by Subodh Kapoor

INTERNATIONAL ENCYCLOPAEDIA OF TRIBAL RELIGION.
in 12 Volumes
Edited by S. M. Channa

INTERNATIONAL ENCYCLOPAEDIA OF ANTHROPOLOGY.
in 12 Volumes
Edited by S. M. Channa

ENCYCLOPAEDIA OF INDIAN HERITAGE. in 90 Volumes
A Descriptive Work of Indological Research in Philosophy, Religion, Sacred Literature, Society, Thought, Traditions, and Ancient Sciences.
Edited by Subodh Kapoor

THE INDIAN ENCYCLOPAEDIA *Bestseller*
Biographical, Historical, Religious, Administrative, Ethnological, Commercial and Scientific
in 25 large Volumes
Ed. Subodh Kapoor

ANCIENT HINDU SOCIETY.
in 6 Volumes
Edited by Subodh Kapoor

Also Available . . .

INDIAN HISTORICAL RESEARCHES *Bestseller*
By Several Authors of International Repute
in 78 Volumes

LANDMARKS IN INDIAN ANTHROPOLOGY
By Several Indologists of International Repute
in 74 Volumes

THE PEOPLES OF INDIA
By Several Writers
in 36 Volumes (Continuing Series)

THE ECONOMIC HISTORY OF ANCIENT INDIA

BY

SANTOSH KUMAR DAS

PROFESSOR OF HISTORY AND ECONOMICS,
TRIBHUBAN-CHANDRA COLLEGE, NEPAL;
FORMERLY PROFESSOR OF HISTORY AND ECONOMICS,
BAGERGHAT COLLEGE, KHULNA

COSMO PUBLICATIONS

2006 New Delhi

THE ECONOMIC HISTORY OF ANCIENT INDIA

First published by COSMO 2006

ISBN 81-307-0423-4

Published by
CÓSMO PUBLICATIONS
for
GENESIS PUBLISHING PVT. LTD.
24-B, Ansari Road, Darya Ganj,
New Delhi-110 002,
INDIA

Printed at
Mehra Offset Press

Dedicated
To
the sacred memory
of
the late Sir Ashu Tosh Mukherji
in humble appreciation
of
all that he has done
for
the cause of
Ancient Indian History and Culture.

PREFACE.

At the beginning of the session 1922-23 I delivered a series of lectures on the "Economic History of Ancient India" to the students of the Kalikātā Vidyāpiṭh. The Vidyāpiṭh is now no more and therefore as a token of my humble connection with that noble institution I now publish these lectures.

In doing so, I have necessarily to make some additions and alterations but these have not modified the general scope and plan of the lectures. I have avoided on principle all theoretical disquisitions throughout this work. It has been my aim rather simply to present the facts in a connected manner with a view to illustrate, as far as possible, the gradual development of the economic conditions from the earliest times. I have always indicated the sources of my information in order that my conclusions may be tested with reference to the authorities on which they are based.

A few words must be said regarding the dates of the various literary authorities which have supplied the materials for this work. I have avoided, as far as possible, all discussions about them in the body of the book, as that would have disturbed the harmony of the subject matter dealt therein. As will be noticed I have principally relied upon two classes of works, Brahmanical and Buddhist. The principal Brahmanical texts, besides the Saṃhitās and the Brāhmanas are the Dharma-sūtras and the Dharma-śāstras. Of the Saṃhitās the Rig-Veda is undoubtedly the oldest and marks an epoch by itself. Its age was subjected to a searching and exhaustive scrutiny by Prof. Winternitz whose views have nowadays to be accepted. Says he "It seems more probable that the initial date falls in the third rather than in the second millenium" (Geschichte Indischen Litteratur, Part I. p. 258). Definitely later in date are the rest of the Vedas, the Brāhmanas and the Upanishads for which also no specific dates can be proposed which command general acceptance but they may be roughly placed in a period beginning from the middle of the second millenium down to the 7th century B. C. As regards the relative chronology of the Dharma-sūtras and Dharma-śāstras, I have been guided by the opinions of Jolly. I differ from him only about the date of Manusmṛiti, the composition of which I have placed on the authority of Bühler between second century B. C. and second century A. D. (S. B. E. Vol. XXV.

p. CXVII.). Jolly's views may be summed up in the following tabular form :—

	Texts arranged in alphabetical order.	Probalc date.	Reference to "Recht und Sitte."
Dharma-sūtras.	Āpasthamba	4th or 5th Cent. B.C.	page 3
	Baudhyāyana	5th or 6th Cent. B.C.	page 4
	Gautama	Do.	pages 5-6
	Vaśistha	4th or 5th Cent. B.C.	page 7
Dharma-śāstras.	Bṛihaṣpati	6th or 7th Cent. A.D.	page 27
	Kātyāyana	Do.	page 28
	Manu-Smṛiti	Not later than 2nd or 3rd Cent. A.D.	page 16
	Nārada	C. 500 A.D.	page 32
	Viṣhnu-Smṛiti	Nor earlier than 3rd Cent. A.D.	page 7
	Yājnabalkya	4th Cent. A.D.	page 21

Of the other Brahmanical texts, the kernel of the Rāmāyana was composed before 500 B.C. although the most recent portions were not probably added till the 2nd cent. B.C. and later (Macdonell, Hist. of Sans. Lit. p. 309) while the

Mahābhārata, very much in its present form existed at about 350 A. D. [Macdonell, Hist. of Sans. Lit. p. 207 ; Bühler places it between 300-500 A.D. (Bühler and Kriste, Contribution to the History of the Mahābhārata]. As regards the date of Pāṇinī I accept the views of Dr. R. G. Bhāṇdārkar who places him in the 7th century B. C. (Bombay Gazetteer 1896, Vol. I. Part II. p. 142). The Arthaśāstra has been referred by competent critics to the time of Chandragupta Maurya (320 B. C.) [Jolly's article in Z. D. M. G. Vol. 67, pp. 49-96 ; R. Shyām Sāstrī's Arthaśāstra pp. V.—XXV.]

The allusions which the jātaka stories in Buddhist literature contain to social and economic conditions have been referred by Fick to the time of Buddha and by Rhys Davids even to an anterior period [Fick, pp. VI-VII ; Buddhist India, p. 207.] On the authority of these two scholars I have assumed 7th and [illegible]th centuries B.C. to be the period represented by the jātakas. The canonical Buddhist texts like the Vinaya and the Sutta Pitakas have been referred by Oldenburg and Rhys Davids to about 4th century B. C. (S. B. E. vol. XIII. p. XIII ; *Ibid.* Vol. XI. p. X.)

I beg to point out that I have utilised the researches of Professors Zimmer, Macdonell and Keith, Drs. Fick and Rhys Davids and Professor Hopkins who have dealt with the economic data on the basis respectively of the Vedas, the

Jātakas and the Epics. I am no less indebted to the researches of Mrs. Rhys Davids and Drs. Rādhā Kumud Mukerji, Rameśh Chandra Mazumdar and D. R. Bhāṇḍārkar.

My thanks are due to my friend Bābu Rākhohari Chatterji, M. A. who has taken infinite pains in supplying me with books and journals whenever required and to His Honour Lieutenant-general Sir Kaiser Shum Shere Jung Bāhādur Rāṇā K. B. E. and Major Shivaprotāp Thāpa B. Sc., Asst. Director of Public Instruction, Nepal, for their kind encouragement and sympathy which it is alike my pleasure and duty to gratefully acknowledge.

The method of transliteration followed in this work is substantially that of the Indian Antiquary.

Tribhuban-Chandra College, Nepal, — SANTOSH KUMAR DAS.

List of Authorities Consulted.

A Comparative Grammar of the Dravidian Languages—Dr. Caldwell.

Aitareya Brāhmana.

Amarkoṣha.

Ancient India as Described by Megasthenes and Arrian—McCrindle.

Ancient India as Described by Ktesias—McCrindle.

Ancient India as Described by Ptolemy—McCrindle.

Ancient India as Described in Classical Literature—McCrindle.

Ancient Ceylon—H. Parker.

Ancient Khotan—Dr. Stein.

Ancient and Mediæval India—Mrs. Manning.

Ancient Geography of India—Cunningham.

Ancient Egyptians—Wilkinson.

Antiquity of Hindu Medicine—Dr. Royle.

Antiquities of India—Barnett (1913).

Ancient India—Professor S. Kriṣhṇaswāmi Iyengar (1911).

An Account of Buddhist Regions—Tao-sün.

Ancient Indian Numismatics—Professor D. R. Bhāṇḍārkar.

Anglo-Indian Studies—S. M. Mitra.

Arthaśāstra, Kautilya's—Eng. Trans. by Dr. R. Shyām Śāstri.

Asiatic Researches—Heeren.

Aśoka—V. A. Smith (Rulers of India Series).

Atharva Veda—Eng. Trans. by Whitney in the H. O. Series.

Atthakathā.

Altindischen Leben—Zimmer.

B. M. Catalogue of the Coins of the Gupta Dynasty, The—John Allan (1914).

Baudhyāyana—Eng. Trans. in the S. B. E. series.

Beginnings of South Indian History—Professor S. Krishnawāmi Iyer (1918).

Bhilsa Topes—Cunningham.

Bodhisattābadāna Kalpalatā—Kshemendra.

Bombay Gazetteer

Brihaspati Samhitā—Eng. Trans. in the S. B. E. series.

Brihat Samhitā—Dr. Kern.

Buddhist India—Rhys Davids (1903).

Buddhist Records of the Western World—Beal.

Cambridge History of India Vol. I—Edited by Rapson.

Caste in India—V. A. Smith in the "East and West" June, 1913.

Catalogue of Gupta Inscriptions—Dr. Fleet.

Cathay and the Way Thither—Yule.

Catalogue of Coins in the Indian Museum—V. A. Smith.

Chānakya's Land Revenue Policy—Dr. R. Shyām Sāstri in Indian Antiquary, 1905.

Characteristics of Ancient Indian Trade—A pamphlet by Professor J. C. Coyajee.

Chinese Buddhism—J. Edkin.

Chips from a German Workshop—Max Müller.

Chinese Topography—Cosmos Indicopleustes.

China and the Roman Orient—G. Hirth.

Citizen of India—Lee Warner.

Coins of Ancient India—Cunningham.

Commerce and Navigation of the Ancients—Dr. Vincent.

Coins of Southern India—Sir W. Elliot.

Corporate life in Ancient India—Dr. R. C. Mazumdar (second edition).

Ctesias—Indica.

Da Alte Indien Vol. I.—Von Bohlen.

Disquisitions concerning Ancient India—Dr. Robertson (1792).

Early History of the Deccan—Dr R. G. Bhāṇdārkar.

Early History of India—V. A. Smith.

Eastern and Indian Architecture—Ferguesson.

Economic and Political conditions in Ancient India—N. S. Subbarao, Mysore, 1917.

Economic Geology of India—Dr. Ball.

Economic Review.

Economic Condition in Ancient India—J. N. Samaddar.

Epitome of Roman History—Florus.

Epic India—C. V. Vaidya.

Epigraphia Indica.

Evolution of Caste, The—a pamphlet by Dr. R. Shyām Shāśtri,

Fine Arts in India and Ceylon—V. A. Smith.

Gautama—Eng. Trans. in the S. B. E. series.

Geography—Ptolemy.

Gabila Grihya Sūtra.

Growth and Vicissitudes of Commerce—Dr. Yeats.

Great Epic of India, The—Hopkins (1901).

Gujrat—Bird.

Gujrat—Sir C. Bayley.

Harṣhacharit—Bāna.

Hindu Architecture—E. B. Havell (1913).

Hindu Positive Sciences—Professor Benoy Kumar Sarkar.

Hindu Superiority—Harabilas Sarda.

Historians History of the World.

History of Antiquity—Max Dunker.

__________Burma—Sir A. Phayre.

History of India—Mill.

__________Civilisation in Ancient India—R. C. Dutt.

History of Hindu Chemistry—Dr. P. C Roy.

History of India—Sir H. Elliott.

__________Indian Shipping and Maritime Activity from the earliest times—Dr. Rādhā Kumud Mukerji.

History of Mediæval Hindu India—C. V. Vaidya.

History of Indian Literature—Weber (Eng. Trans.).

History of Java—Raffles.
History of Pegu—Sir A. Phayre.
History of Sanskrit Literature--Macdonell.
Imperial Gazetteer (New edition) Vol. II.
Imperial and Asiatic Quarterly Review.
Inscriptions of Aśoka—Professor D. R. Bhāṇdārkar and S. N. Mazumdar.
Indian Coins—E. J. Rapson.
Indian Antiquary.
India and the Western World—Rawlinson.
India as known to the Ancient World—Dr. G. N. Banerji.
Indian Pre-historic and Protohistoric Antiquities (Foote Collection, Madras, 1906) 2 Vols.
Industrial Arts of India, The—Sir George Birdwood.
Indian Craftsman, The.—Dr. Coomārswāmī.
Indian Arts and Crafts—Dr. Coomārswāmī.
Indian Architecture—Cunningham.
Invasion of India by Alexander the Great McCrindle.
India and What it can teach us—Max Müller.
Indo-Chinese Relations—H. C. Chākladār in the Dawn Magazine.
India as known to Ancient and Mediæval Europe—P. C. Ghosh.
India in Greece—Pococke.
Indica—Arrian.
India Old and New—Hopkins.
Industrial Competition of Asia—E. Daniell.

Indian Sculpure and Painting—E. B. Havell.
Introduction to the History of Religion—Jevons.
Indische Studien—Weber.
Ideals of the East—Kakasu Okakura.
Jātakas, The—Eng. Trans. by Cowell and Rouse 6 Vols. 1898 (Cambridge University Publication).
Journal Asiatique.
———of the Asiatic Society of Bengal.
———of the Bangiya Sāhitya Parishad.
———of the Department of Letters, Calcutta University.
———of the Royal Economic Soceity
———of the Royal Asiatic Soceity.
———of the Indo-Japanese Association.
———of the Bombay Branch of the Royal Society.
Kwai-Yuen Catalogue of the Chinese Tripitaka.
Life in Ancient India—Mrs. Spier.
Life of Godama—Bishop Bigandet.
Life of Hiuen Tsang—Beal.
Little Clay Cart, The—Ryder.
Local Government in Ancient India—Dr. Rādhā Kumud Mukerji.
Mahābhārata (Eng. Trans.)—M. N. Dutt.
———Wheeler.
———Pratap Chandra Roy.
Mahāwanso—Turnour.
Maitrāyani Saṃhitā.

Manu—Eng. Trans. by Bühler in the Sacred Books of the East Series.

Medhātithi.

Mitramiśra.

Mythology of the Hindus—Coleman.

Nārada—Eng. Trans. in the S. B. E. Series.

Natural History—Pliny.

Original Sanskrit Texts—Muir.

Origin of the Brāhmi Alphabet—Bühler.

Orissa—Hunter.

Oxford History of India—V. A. Smith.

Paintings in the Buddhist Cave temples of Ajantā—Griffiths.

Panchabiṃśha Brāhmana.

Parthia—Rawlinson.

Periplus of the Erythrean Sea (Eng. Trans.)—Schoff.

Positive Back ground of Hindu Sociology—Professor Benoy Kumar Sarkar (Pāṇinī Office Publication).

Positive Sciences of the Hindus—Dr. Brojendra Nath Seal.

Provinces of the Roman Empire—Mommsen.

Pre-historic India—Panchanon Mitra.

Purāṇas.

Raghubaṃśha—Kālidās.

Rājtarangini—Kalhana (Edited by Dr. Stein).
Rāmāyana—Eng. Trans. by Griffith.
—————— R. C. Dutt.
—————— J. Wheeler.
—————— M. N. Dutt.
Ratnābali—Śrī Harṣha.
Rig-Veda, The—Kaegi (Trans. by Arrowsmith, Boston, 1886).
Rig-Veda, The—Eng. Trans. by H. H. Wilson.
—————— E. B. Cowell.
—————— W. F. Webster.
Sacred Books of Ceylon—Upham.
Śakuntalā—Kālidās.
Sanchi and its remains—Maisley.
Śatapatha—Brāhmana.
Shipbuilding and Commerce in Ancient Bengal—a pamphlet by Tamonāśh Dās Gupta.
Sir Ashu Tosh Mukerji Jubilee Commemoration Volumes, Vols. I. and III.
Social Organisation in North-East India in Buddha's time—Richard Fick (Eng. Trans. by Dr. Śiśir Kumar Maitra).
Studies in Ancient Hindu Polity, Vol. I—Dr. N. N. Law.
Sukranītisāra—Eng. Trans. by Professor B. K. Sarkar (Panini Office Publication).
Suttas, Buddhist—Eng. Trans. in the S. B. E. Series.
Sand-buried Ruins of Khotan—Sir M. A. Stein,
Taittiriya Saṃhitā.

Tamil Studies—Srinivasa Iyengar (1914).

Tamils Eighteen Hundred Years Ago—V. K. Pillay.

Technical History of Commerce—Dr. J. Yeats.

Town-planning of Ancient Deccan—C. P. Venkatarāma Iyer, Madras, 1916.

Travels of Hiuen Tsang—Eng. Trans. by Watters.

Upanishads, Chief—(Eng. Trans. by Rājā Rām Mohan Roy.

Upanishads, Chief—(Eng. Trans. by Professor Max Müller.

Vasistha—Eng. Trans. in the S. B. E. Series.

Vedic Index—Macdonell and Keith.

Vedic India—Ragozin (Story of the Nations Series).

Vinaya Texts—Eng. Trans. in the S. B. E. Series.

Virāmitrodaya—Edited by Jīvānanda Vidyāsāgar.

Vishṇu Saṃhitā—Eng. Trans. by Dr. Jolly.

Vishṇu Purāṇa—Eng. Trans. by Wilson.

Vedische Studien—Geldner.

Vivādratnākar—Biblotheca Indica Series.

Western Origin of Chinese Civilisation—Lacouperie.

Yaska.

Yājnabalkya.

Z. D. M. G.

CONTENTS.

ABBREVIATIONS.

Beal. = Buddhist Records of the Western World, by Beal.

C. V. = Chullavāgga (of Vinaya Pitaka).

E. H. I. = Early History of India by V. A. Smith.

Ep. Ind. = Epigraphia Indica.

Fick. = Die Sociale Gliederung Im Nordöstlichen Indian Zu Buddha's Zeit by Richard Fick, Kiel, 1897.

Ind. Ant. = Indian Antiquary.

Ind. Stud. = Indische Studien.

Ins. = Inscriptions.

Jāt. = Jātaka.

Lud. = Luder's List of Brahmi Inscriptions in Epigraphia Indica, Vol. X, Appendix.

Mbh. = Mahābhārata.

Manu. = Manu Saṃhitā.

Nār. = Narāda Saṃhitā.

Rig. = Rig Veda.

S. B. E. = Sacred Books of the East Series.

Viram. = Virāmitrodaya Edited by Jivānanda Vidyāsāgar.

Vin. = Vinaya Pitaka.

Watters. = Travels of Hiuen Tsang by Watters.

The Economic History

OF

Ancient India.

The Palæolithic Age.

" The pleasant belief of poets that primitive man enjoyed in an earthly paradise a golden age free from sin, sorrow, want and death finds no support from the researches of sober, matter-of-fact science. On the contrary, abundant and conclusive evidence proves that the earliest man whether in India, Europe or elsewhere were rude savages, cowering for shelter under rocks or trees or roughly housed in caves and huts" (Oxford History of India, p. 1). He does not know how to pasture cattle, he does not know agriculture or manufactures. He lives by hunting in the forests or fishing in the rivers or by acquiring fruits etc., which grow wild, and so he has great difficulty in getting a regular supply of food. He knows no private property in land and little division of labour. He was ignorant of any metal and even of pottery. He was dependent for tools or weapons of all kinds on sticks, stones and bones. The sticks of course have perished and the bones have shared the same fate on account of the white ants. The stone implements laboriously shaped by chipping into forms suitable for hammering, cutting, boring and scrapping are found in large numbers in many parts of India, more specially in the districts along the eastern coast. The Madras or Chingleput district presents "the most numerous and important traces of palæolithic man known in southern India."

The Neolithic Age.

In the next stage of human advance, men were for a long time still ignorant of metals except gold and were consequently obliged to continue using stone tools. The stone weapons and utensils which are specially characteristic of this age are found scattered over a much wider area than the more rudimentary palæoliths though mainly in regions where the trap rock, used specially in their manufacture abounds. They exhibit a remarkable variety illustrated by at least a hundred distinct types some of which were ground, grooved and polished and thus converted into highly finished objects adapted to divers purposes. They can be studied to special advantage in the Bellary district where Foote discovered the site of an ancient factory with tools in every stage of manufacture. The Neolithic people used pottery, at first hand-made and later turned on the potter's wheel. They kept domestic animals and cultivated the land. They learnt the use of graves which have been discovered by Cockburn in the Mirzāpur district, U. P. The tombs were surrounded by stone circles. Many pre-historic cemeteries exist in the Tinnevelly district along the coast of the Tāmraparṇi river, the most ancient seat of the pearl and chank or conch-shell industry. This connection between the early settlements on the Tāmraparṇi river and the pearl-fishery is not an isolated fact. Professor Elliot Smith rightly observes "Ancient miners in search of metals or precious stones or in other cases pearl-fishers had in every case established camps to exploit these varied sources of wealth and the megalithic monuments represent their tombs and temples" (Manchester Memoirs. Vol. 60. Part I. 1915. p. 29 of reprint). Gold mining was also known in this age and a neolithic settlement existed at Maski in the Nizām's dominions where the old gold-miner's shafts were the deepest in the world.

The Copper Age.

As the Neolithic age gradually passed away in Northern India, it appears to have given place not to an age of Bronze as it did in most parts of Europe but to one of Copper. In Southern India on the other hand, stone tools were superseded directly by iron without any intermediate step. Copper implements have been discovered in large numbers in the Central Provinces, Chota Nagpur, old beds of the Ganges near Cawnpur and elsewhere. Among them are bare and shouldered celts, harpoons, spearheads both plain and barbed, axe-heads, swords and an object suggestive of the human shape. The last mentioned as well as some of the swords which are remarkable for their excessive weight and the form of their handles may have been used for cult purposes. One hoard of these implements which came from Gungeria in the Central Provinces contained as many as 424 specimens of almost pure metal, weighing in all 829 pounds besides 102 ornamental laminae of silver. Such a collection comprising as it did, a variety of implements intended for domestic and other purposes, affords evidence enough, as Dr. Smith has remarked, that their manufacture was conducted in India on an extensive scale; while the distinctive types that have been evolved and are represented both in this and other finds connote a development that must already have extended over a long period, though at the same time, the barbed spear-heads and harpoons and flat celts manifestly copied from neolithic prototypes bespeak a relatively high antiquity. The presence of silver ornaments in the Gungeria hoard has suggested doubts as to its remote date but there seems little reason for assuming that a race familiar with the difficult metallurgical processes by which copper is extracted from its ores were incapable of smelting silver from the rich argintiferous galenas which occur in various localities.

Having regard to this development of industry, it seems desirable to say a few words with regard to the condition of currency that may have prevailed in this country before the advent of the Aryans. "I can quite imagine some doubt crossing the minds of most my readers" says Professor D. R. Bhāndarkar "as to how I could even surmise the state of currency in pre-vedic India. But what Professor Ridgeway has done in regard to the pre-historic or proto-historic currency of Greece can also be attempted on a modest scale in regard to India, provided we follow his method which is typically the anthropological method." It is possible to study the various kinds of currency in use among the savage tribes of various stages of civilisation and compare them to the similar ones that were prevalent in India. Now the earliest stage of civilisation is taken to be the Hunting stage. No form of currency belonging to this stage, such as skins of hunting animals, is known to us from any composition of the Vedic period or from any other source. As the Hunting stage passess to the Pastoral and animals are domesticated, the animal itself, not its skin, becomes the unit of value. The most common of such animals in India is the cow which is found mentioned in the Rig veda. Thus, there is a hymn in this veda (IV. 24. 10.) where Indra *i. e.*, his image is offerred as a fetish for ten cows and another VIII. 1. 5.) where Indra is considered to be so invaluable that not a hundered, a thousand or even a myriad of cows is thought to be a proper price. As the Pastoral develops into the Agricultural stage, a number of agricultural products come to be used as currency. It is in this agricultural stage that commerce is found to develop itself and a greater number of objects are found capable of being used as measures of value, such as garments, coverlets and goat-skins which were so employed in the time of the Atharva-Veda (IV. 7. 6.). Also mineral products such as cowries come to be used first as ornaments and then as currency. Thus we see that traces of the various circulating media of these various stages of civilisation are clearly found in the Saṃhitā portion of the Vedas and that they must have survived down to the Vedic epoch from previous stages of civilisation.

We may also note here that there are not one or two but many pre-historic symbols to be found on the punch-marked coins (c.f. J. B. O. R. S. 1920, p. 400). Mr. Theobald has observed not less than fourteen symbols engraved on the sculptured stones of Scotland. There was a time when Fergusson and archælogists of his kind relegated the rude stone implements of Great Bretain and Scotland to the Post-Roman period but no archælogist of any repute now disputes its pre-historic character. When therefore we find so many pre-historic symbols occurring on the punch-marked coins, it is difficult to avoid the conclusion that kārshāpana coins must have been handed down to us from pre-historic times. If any further evidence is required, it is furnished by the fact, first brought to our attention by Elliot that these punch-marked coins "have been discovered along the ashes of the men who constructed the primitive tombs known as Pāndukulis of the south and unearthed from the ruins of buried cities in excavating the head-waters of the Ganges Canal" (I N O-c s i. 45) "A large horde of these coins" says he elsewhere "was discovered in September 1807 at the opening of one of the ancient tombs known by the name of Pāndukulis near the village of Chavadi-paleiyam in Coimbatore, thus identifying the employment of this kind of money with the aboriginal race whose places of sepulchure are scattered over every part of Southern India (Madras Journal of Literature and Science, 1858. p. 227).

The recent surprising discoveries by Rāi Bāhādur Dayā Rām Sāhni at Harappa in the Montgomery District of the Punjab and by Babu Rākhāldās Banerji at Mohenzo Daro have proved the existence of a new type of coins or tokens and have established beyond doubt the fact that five thousand years ago the people of Sind and the Punjab were living in well-built cities and were in possession of a relatively mature civilization with a high standard of art and craftmanship and a developed system of writing—a civilization as highly developed and seemingly as widespread as the Sumerian culture of Mesopotamia with conclusive evidence of a close contact between the two. The remains brought to light in these two places include houses and temples massively built of burnt brick and provided with well-constructed water conduits covered by marble slabs. The other antiquities of equally fascinating interest to the student of economic history are a variety of potteries both painted and plain, some fashioned by hand and some turned on the wheel; terracottas; toys; bangles of blue glass paste and shell; knives and cores of chert; curious stone rings; dice and a number of engraved and inscribed seals bearing inscriptions in a hitherto unknown pictographic Script.

The Rig Vedic Age.

The Aryans of the early hymns of the Rig Veda were for the most part pastoral tribes. Pushan was the God of the shepherds to whom hymns were addressed (Rig Veda I. 42. 1-10). "Give us wide pastures" was their cry. Not only are there innumerable references to grazing but the pastoral habits of the tribes are often described. Horses, kine, sheep and ewes are frequently mentioned (Rig X. 91. 14; also ibid. X. 89. 14). Another hymn (X. 19. 4-6) refers to the practice of taking out cattle to the pasturage and bringing them back. The stress laid by the poets on the possession of cows is almost pathetic. The name of the sacrificial fee Dakshiṇā is explained as referring originally to a cow placed on the right hand of the singer for reward. The singers delight to compare their songs to Indra with the lowing of cows to their calves.

Nevertheless, the agricultural stage has already come, for there are also references to agriculture and hence to landownership. The land was divided into Vāstu, Arable land, Pasture and Forests. The Vāstu was in individual ownership as was also the case with the Vāstu of the German Mark. But while the arable land in ancient India was in private ownership throughout, that in the Mark was at first in communal ownership but ultimately in private ownership. In the Rig Veda, a worshipper prays for meadowland to be bestowed on him alone. Again a woman prays that something may grow on her father's head and on his ploughland. A gambler cries that a god has warned him to go and plough the ploughland instead of playing with dice which leads only to regret as he looks on the happy homes of others. In fact "winning of fields" or "conquest of fields" is recognised as the usual aim of battle so much as the conquest of cattle. The booty of such land conquests was distributed by shares. At a Coronation Oath the prayer is "Grant him the kind as share in village, horses and cattle." Again the heads of families casually mentioned as groups round the "active lord of the host" may possibly imply joint family and joint ownership of land (Rig I. 114). In the Rig Veda, we find that when a father grew old, he was ousted from his property and his sons divided it among themselves. But the marriage hymn of the Rig Veda which indicates that the man takes his bride home and expects her to be mistress of the household which includes her father-in-law and brothers-in-law shows that joint family was existing side by side. The pasture here as in the German Mark was in communal ownership while the forest belonged to everybody who cleared it off.

Coming to the law of inheritance which appears from Rig III. 31. 1-2, we find that the father might distribute his wealth among his sons (Rig I. 114). No will is ever alluded to. In joint families, after the father, the elder brother was to feed and protect all. Still there was no primogeniture. All the sons had a share, though the eldest got a little more than the others. In default of a son, the daughter's son was the heir (Rig III. and VII.). The following were excluded from inheritance: eunuchs, outcastes, born deaf or dumb or blind, one losing a limb, mad man and idiots. They must, however, be maintained by the heirs. The sons of such excluded persons were, however, capable of inheriting.

The existence of city-life in this period has been denied by Professor Keith and others. References have been found by some to iron towns which others explain as forts while some have found references to a hundred stone-built towns (Rig IV. 30. 20). According to Keith, however, "the pūr which is often referred to and which in later days denotes a town was probably no more than a mere earthwork fortification. In certain passages, these pūras are called autumnal and by far the most probable explanation of this epithet is, that it refers to the flooding of the plains by the rising of the rivers in the autumn when the cultivators and the herdsmen had to take refuge within the earthworks which at other times served as defences against human foes" (Cambridge History of India, Vol. I).

Agriculture was already a part of the Vedic economy. The very name Ārya by which the Aryan conquerors have distinguished themselves from the aborigines is said to have come from a root (Kṛish) which means to cultivate (R. C. Dutt's History of Civilisation in Ancient India, p. 35). This meaning of Ārya is found in Rig. I. 117. 21 [c. f. also Charṣana (I. 3. 7) and Kṛishti (I. 4. 6)]. We learn of the use of bulls to draw the plough, of the sowing of seeds in the furrows thus made, of the cutting of the corn with the sickle, the laying of it in bundles on the threshing floor and the threshing and final shifting by winnowing.

Coming to the nature of the grain grown, we find that various preparations from Yava (barley) called পুরোডাস, অপূপ etc., were offered to the gods. That Yava was regularly cultivated by the Aryans is evident from "যবং বৃকেন কর্ষথঃ" (Rig 8. 22. 6) "I have cultivated barley by the help of your plough." Fried Yava was called ধান, *e.g.*, "ভৃষ্টযবা পুনর্ধানা ধানাচূর্ণন্তু সক্তব ইতি হেমচন্দ্র।" From ধান we have probably got our ধান্য, rice which is mentioned in Artharva Veda (Vedic Index. I. 398). Yava is hence called ধান্যরাজ। It is also called শীতশূক (grown in a cold climate). That wheat was not produced in this period will be evident from the following "ব্রীহিভির্যত্ত যবৈর্যজেত ইতি শ্রূয়তে যথোক্ত রস্তুসম্পত্তৌ গ্রাহ্য তদনুকারিয়ৎ। যবানামিম গোধূমা ব্রীহীণামিশালয়।" It is said that "sacrifices are to be offered with ব্রীহি। In the absence of things recommended, things like them may be used *e.g.*, গোধূম (wheat) for Yava, শালি for ব্রীহি।" This shows that wheat and শালি were produced long after the cultivation of barley and ব্রীহি। Sugarcane was cultivated in this period. কুশর is the Vedic name for a species of big grass. From this is derived কুশারী, the general name of sugarcane (Bhāratī, Kārtik, 1320 B. S.). The origin of sugarcane is thus described in the Purāṇas :—

> "অমৃতং পিবতোবক্ত্রাৎ সূর্য্যস্যামৃতবিন্দবঃ
> নিপেতুর্যে ততৃথামী শালিমুদ্গেক্ষবঃ স্মৃতাঃ
> শর্করা পরমস্তস্মাদিক্ষুসারোঽমৃতাত্মকঃ
> ইষ্টারবে রতপুণ্যা শর্করা হব্যকব্যয়োঃ ॥"
>
> ইতি শব্দকল্পদ্রুমধৃত মাৎস্যে ৭২ অধ্যায়।

"When the Sun was drinking nectar, a few drops fell from his lips and from these শালি, ধান্য, মুগ and ইক্ষু are born. For this, sugar, the essence of sugar-cane is a very good thing and a favourite of the Sun.

For this, it is regarded as sacred and offered in পৈত্র and দৈব অন্ন।" The fact that sugarcane is related in its origin to the Sun and is his favourite shows that sugarcane was discovered along with the worship of the Sun in Central Asia. The antiquity of sugarcane is well-proved by the evidences of Comparative Philology. Professor Ragozin in his Vedic India (p. 33, foot-note) says "Latin Saccharum, Slavic Sakhar, German Zucher, Italian Zucchero, Spanish Azucor, French Sucre, English Sugar, not to mention of Arabic Sukkar and Persian Shakar". Professor Ragozin believes that Sugarcandy (মিশ্রি) is a slight corruption of Sanskrit শর্করাখণ্ড।

We find innumerable references to Soma plant from which was extracted a kind of juice used as sacrificial drink. "It stands, however, to reason that the extraordinary preeminence which it acquired for religious purposes can hardly have been attained except through its original popular character; and it is difficult to resist the impression that the Soma was at first a popular drink in their homes when the Vedic Aryans entered India and that in India itself they found no plant which precisely coincided with that whence the Soma had been first produced and so were compelled to resort to substitutes or to use the original plant after it had been brought from a great distance and had thus lost its original flavour" (Cambridge History of India, Vol. I).

Besides agriculture, the Aryans of this period had an eye on the preservation and utilisation of forests. They regularly prayed that the plants and trees would be endowed with sweetness so that they might conduce to the benefit of the people—

"ওঁ মধুবাতা ঋতায়তে, মধু ক্ষরন্তি সিন্ধবঃ।
মাধ্বীর্নঃ সন্ত্বোষধীঃ॥
ওঁ মধু নক্তমুতোষসো, মধুমৎ পার্থিবং রজঃ।
মধু দ্যৌরস্তু নঃ পিতা॥
মধুমান্ নো বনস্পতির্মধুমাঁ অস্তু সূর্য্যঃ।
মাধ্বীর্গাবো ভবন্তু নঃ॥
ওঁ মধু ওঁ মধু ওঁ মধু॥"

The various useful plants and trees mentioned in the Vedic hymns are :—(1) অজশৃঙ্গী and অরাটকী (probably বাবলা) (2) অপামার্গ (আপাঙ্গ, a medicinal plant) (3) অমলা (আম্লকী a medicinal tree) (4) অরুন্ধতী (a cow after drinking its juice will give a larger quantity of milk. Lac was also produced from this tree) (5) অলাপু or অলাবু (লাউ) (6) অর্ক (আকন্দ) (7) অবকা or শীপাল (Blyxa Octranda) (8) অশ্বগন্ধা (a medicinal plant) (9) অশ্বত্থ (10) আদার (ginger) (11) আবয়ু (সরিষা) (12) উডুম্বর (ডুমুর) (12) উর্বারু (শশা) (13) ঔক্ষগন্ধি (a perfumed plant) (14) কুষ্ঠ (a plant used as a medicine for all kinds of diseases and is grown on the Himalayas) (15) জঙ্গিড় (Terminatia Arjuneya) (16) কর্কন্ধু (লাল কুল বা লাল কুমড়া) (17) খদির (18) খর্জ্জুর (19) তিল (20) পাটা (used nowadays for purifying sugar) (21) পূতীক (পূই) (22) ন্যগ্রোধ (বট) (23) পীতুদারু (দেবদারু) (24) প্লক্ষ (পাকুড়)

(25) বদর (26) বিল্ব (27) শন (Hemp) (28) শল্মলী (শিমুল) (29) শমী (its juice says ধন্বন্তরী when applied on the body would deprive the skin of its hair) (30) অমূলা (its juice was used for poisoning the heads of arrows) (31) নারাচী (its juice was used for similar purposes c.f. নারাচ) (32) মদুঘ (used for manufacturing intoxicating drinks) (33) উশনা (used for similar purposes in the absence of Soma plant says Śatapatha Brāhmana) (34) অরটু (Colosanthes Indica; it was used in the construction of tyres for carts).

For the improvement of vegetation and agriculture, watercourses were dug out (Rig X. 68. 1). and in fact canals are mentioned in Rig X. 99. 4 while wells for purposes of irrigation are mentioned in Rig X. 25. Water was raised out of wells by means of well-wheels called Ghāti-Chakra or Araghatta and used for fields and drinking (Rig X. 25. 4; X. 93. 13). In the Rig Veda, the plough and the ploughshare are objects of divine worship. One hymn (Rig IV. 57) is addressed to a deity vaguely personified as the lord who presides over the fields, he being prayed to direct the plough straight into the furrow, to keep the land sweet, so that the husbandman may cheerfully drive the oxen with his goad.

Despite this emphasis upon and care for agriculture, famines were not unknown. In Rig III. 8 a prayer is offered to drive away famine. In Rig III. 53 Sasarhari is said to have dispelled a famine. In Rig VIII. 118 a prayer is offered to save the people from the jaws of famine. In Rig VIII. 55 and X. 42 Indra is invited to set the people free from famine.

As regards the arts and crafts of this period, scholars differ. Professor Kaegi in his Introduction to the Rig Veda says "In arts the race still stood on the lowest stage" (p. 40); while Professors Ragozin and Macdonell hold the opposite view. According to Macdonell "already in this period specialisation in industry had begun". The art of weaving was sufficiently well-known in this period. There is a reference to weaving in Rig X. 120. 1 and VI. 9. 2. In Rig I. 105. 8 we find

"মুষো ন শিশ্না ব্যদন্তি মাধ্যঃ
স্তোতরম্ তে শতক্রতো বিত্তম্ মে অস্য রোদসী।"

"Just as a mouse cuts a thread, so oh শতক্রতু, sorrow is cutting me to the quick". Sāyan in his commentory on the verse says that as মাড় was applied on the weaver's thread, it became the delicious food of mice. From Rig I. 140. 1., I. 152. 1., II. 14. 3., IX. 8. 6., IX. 96. 1 etc., it is evident that a large number of coverlets were used for altars. In Rig V. 29. 15 nice dresses are mentioned : "ভদ্রেব বস্ত্রা স্থকৃতা।" In another hymn (Rig X. 11. 4) we find "জায়েব পত্যে উশসী স্থবাসাঃ। In Rig VIII. 46. 33 we hear of a well adorned maid-servant. Garments were generally manufactured from the wool of sheep (Muir's Original Sanskrit

Texts. pp. 462ff.) In Rig X. 26. 6 we find a reference to weaving and bleaching of sheep's wool. Warf was tantu, woof was bemān and loom was called tasara. Linen corselets are mentioned in Rig I. 31. 15 and in V. 101. 8 as also silken cloth which was called তার্প্য। There is no mention of cotton but Professor Muir is of opinion that cotton was known in this period. Professor Ragozin observes. "The Aryan settlers of Northern India had already begun at an amazingly early period to excel in the manufactures of the delicate tissue which has ever been and is today doubtless incomparably great in perfection, one of their industrial glories—a fact which implies cultivation of cotton-plant or tree" (Vedic India, p. 306).

Some historians are of opinion that the Indians upto the invasion of Alexander the Great did not know the use of any other garment save a Dhuti and a Chāddar. (Muir's O. S. T. Vol. V. p. 462). Mr. Watson in his Textile Manufactures and Professor C. V. Vaidya in his History of Mediæval Hindu India pp. 89-90 of Vol. I. hold the same opinion. But it is inconceivable that the richer folk would be content with wearing Dhuti and Chāddar for all times. (Indo-Aryans Vol. I. p. 177). In fact, we find references in the Rig Veda to the art of sewing. (Wilson's Rig Veda Vol. II. p. 280 and IV. p. 60). As a result, we find a large variety of dress worn by the Vedic Aryans. Thus, the inner garment was called নীবি (Atharva Veda VIII. 2.

16. Over it was worn cloth or বাসস্ and above all was worn অধিবাস (Rig I. 140. 9). Other names of this অধিবাস are অৎক and দ্রাপি। When engaged in sacrificial ceremonies a silken under-garment called তার্প্য was worn. ওপশ was used for adorning the head (Rig X. 85. 8). Its exact meaning is not known. Roth thinks that it was a corruption of অবপশ = অব + পশ and hence hair-tape or hair-net (Rig VI. 53. 9 and I. 173. 6.). Professor Bloomfield (Hymn of the Atharva Veda pp. 538-39) takes it to mean the coverlet for women, ওড়না। The existence of these various kinds of garments presupposes the art of tailoring and gives the lie direct to the theory that it was introduced by the Muhammadans in India. We may add that Col. Medoys Taylor has observed that a figure in the Ajantā caves was adorned with nice indigenous garments which were similar to those of Greak style (Edinburg Review. July, 1867). We further find from Amarkosha that the manufacturers of sewn cloths are called সৌচিক and in later times formed a caste by themselves. They were born of a Vaisya father and a Sudra mother. They still exist in Benares as a separate tribe and have been noticed by Mr. Sherring in his Hindu Castes and Tribes of Benares. Female weavers are referred to in Rig II. 3. 6., II. 38. 4 and VI. 9 2; while there is a fling at spinsters who spin out thread in ignorance in Rig X. 71. 9. To women is also ascribed the plaiting of mats from grass or reeds.

The worker in metal smelted ore in the furnace (Rig V. 9. 5; VII. 2. 4), using the wing of a bird in the place of bellows to fan the flame. Kettles, pans and various other domestic utensils were made of the metal (Rig V. 19. 27, 30, 33, 52, 54, 55, and VI. 2. 27, 46, 47, 48). Soma cup made of hammered metal is also mentioned (Vedic Index I. p. 140). Coats of mail for war (Rig VI. 75. 1), golden coloured mail (Rig IV. 53. 2), helmets of gold (Rig II. 34. 3), spears and weapons bright with gold (Rig V. 52. 6), were manufactured besides arrows, quivers, spears and daggers (Rig V. 57. 2). Rig IV. 39. 4. refers to armour for the shoulders or arms, perhaps a shield. A javelin (rispti) is compared to lightning in Rig V. 52. 6, and V. 54. 11. Also sword or battle-axe is so compared. 3000 mailed warriors are referred to in Rig VI. 27. 6. Sharp-edged swords are mentioned in Rig VI. 47 10. Arrows were of two kinds—one is poisoned and has a head of horn, the other is copper, bronze or iron-headed (Vedic Index). Feathered, sharppointed shafts are described in Rig VI. 46. 11. Gold breastplates, anklets and crowns were manufactured (Rig V. 54. 1), as also gold chains and trappings for horses (Rig V. 54. 11; IV. 2. 8; IV. 37. 4). Razors and scissors are referred to in Rig VIII. 4. 16 and X. 142. 4.

Among the ornaments of the period we find কুরীর (Rig X. 85. 8) for the head. According to Zimmer, it means peacock and therefore it must have been an arch-like ornament. নিষ্ক (নিষ্কগ্রীব in Rig V. 19. 3) was an ornament of the neck. রুক্ম (Rig I. 166. 10), was a gold ornament worn on the breast. রুক্ম has been compared to the sun so that it was probably round in shape. It was hung on the breast by means of a chain which was called রুক্মপাশ (Śatapatha Brāhmana VI. 7. 1. 7). Another ornament was খাদি। According to Roth it was of three kinds—(*i*) an ornament for the legs like মল (Rig V. 54. 11) (*ii*) an ornament for the arms or hands like বালা or তাবিজ (Rig I. 66. 9) (*iii*) ring অঙ্গুরী (Rig I. 168. 3). Another ornament was called ন্যোচনী (Rig X. 85. 6). Its nature is not known. মণি was either pearl or diamond (Rig I. 33. 8). It was worn on the neck (মণিগ্রীব in Rig I. 122. 14) by means of a thread (Panchabiṃsha Brāhmana XX. 16. 6). According to commentator দুর্গাচার্য্য (7. 23) মণি=আদিত্যমণি, সূর্য্যকান্ত মণি In Rig IX. 42. 2 and X. 39. 14, we are told that daughters should be married adorned with fine dress and ornaments. Even bride-grooms used ornaments and perfumes. (Rig. 60. 4.)

Thus it is evident that the metal industry was in a highly developed state but "it is however, still uncertain" says Mr. Macdonell what that metal which was called ayas (অয়স্) was." From Atharva Veda X. 3. 17 and even Rig V. 25 the sense of iron for অয়স্ is certain. But from White Yajur Veda (18. 12) we find reference to six different kinds of metals (হিরণ্যং চমে, অয়শ্চমে, শ্যামংচমে, লোহংচমে, সীসংচমে ত্রপুচমে)—Here লোহ (iron) is differentiated from অয়স্ In any case if on the authority of Athava X. 3. 17 and Rig V. 25, the use of iron is certain in that age, copper is conceivable and bronze quite likely (Vedic Index I. p. 32).

The worker in wood constructed carts, chariots for war and the race, boats and ships (Rig III. 53. 19; VI. 2. 14; IV. 16. 20). He was carpenter, joiner and wheel-wright in one and the wood of অরটু (colosanthes Indica) was his great favourite in the construction of wheels. War chariots and war-drums are mentioned in Rig VI. 47. 26 and VI. 47. 29. The fashioning of chariots was a frequent source of metaphor, the poet comparing his own skill to that of the wheel-wright. Out of মুর্ব্বা plant, the sacrificial thread was made as also the ধনুগুর্ণ which was hence called মৌর্ব্বী।

Liquor was manufactured from the Soma plant and in its absence from মহুঘ and উশনা Rig. I. 191. 10. tells of the vinter's house and of the wine-skins kept within. The process of preparing the Soma drink is described in Rig XI. 66. 2-13., IX. 108. 3., IX. 110. 8 and IX. 113. 9. Rig VIII. 58. 11 refers to all the gods as being intoxicated. Probably the Indo-Aryan worship of Indra was a Bacchanalian feast when the Aryans used to drink deep. But the popular drink was evidently the Surā which was probably distilled from grain. It was extremely intoxicating and the priests regarded it with disapproval. In one hymn, mention is made of men made arrogant by the surā, reviling the gods, while another couples it with anger and dicing as the cause of sin.

The leather-worker and the tanner are mentioned (Muir's O. S. T. pp. 462 ff.). Skin vessels for wine (Rig I. 191. 10) and for curds (Rig VI. 48. 18) are mentioned.

Although the Rig Veda contains many allusions to mansions of thousand pillars (Rig II. 41. 5 and V. 62. 6), we have no extant remains of any architectural works of this period. The arts of painting and sculpture were not cultivated in this period, for, there is no allusion to them in the hymns of the Rig Veda.

The question now presents itself as to the extent to which in the period of the Rig Veda the caste system had been developed and stood as a barrier against the mobility of labour. The orthodox Hindu holds that the caste system is of divine appointment and that it had existed for all time. But the sacred books themselves when they are studied historically, supply evidence both of its origin and of its growth. The Mahābhārata Sānti Parba says "At first there was no caste." The distinction between the colour (barṇa) of the Aryan conquerors and that of the conquered aboriginal tribes first formed the basis of caste (Rig I. 100. 18). The question is thus, narrowed down to the consideration of the arguments for and against the view that among the Aryans themselves caste divisions were appearing. Messrs. Muir (O. S. T. Vol. I pp. 239 ff), Zimmer (Altindischen

Leben pp. 185—203) Weber (Indische Studien Vol. X. pp. 1 ff), have denied the existence of caste in any form in this period. Professor Max Muller says "If then with all the documents before us, we ask the question, does caste as we find in Manu and at the present day form part of the most ancient religious teaching of the Vedes? we can answer with a decided 'No.'." (Chips from a German Workshop Vol. II. p. 307, 1867 edition). Weber in his History of Sanskrit Literature also hold the same view and says "there are no castes as yet, the people are still one united whole and bear but one name that of Visas (Eng. Trans. p. 38). But Messrs. Goldner (Vedische Studien Vol. II. p. 146) and Oldenburg (Z. D. M. G. Vol. L1. pp. 267 ff.), hold the opposite view. It has been argued that the warriors of the community were the agricultural and industrial classes and the priesthood was not yet hereditary. Any person who distinguished himself for his genius or virtue or who for some reason was deemed specially receptive of divine inspiration could be a priest. And the growth of the caste system was the result of the complication of life due to the further penetration of the Aryans from the Punjab to the East. To resist the sudden incursion or to crush the attempts at rebellion of the aborigines, the petty tribal princes formed the nucleus of a standing armed force while the industrial and agricultural population relying on the protection of the warrior class, abandoned the use of arms. Together with the growth in the size of kingdoms and the increasing complexity of civilisation, the simple ritual of an earlier period when the King himself could sacrifice for his people, grew to an extent which rendered this impracticable, while at the same time, the idea grew up that upon the faithful and exact performance of the rites depended the result of battle. The result was the growth of a priesthood, a warrior class and of a third the artisan and the cultivator sharply distinguished from one another and strictly hereditary. But the later origin of this development is proved by the fact that it took place not in the Punjab, the home of the Rig Veda but in the Middle country whose geographical isolation favoured the evolution of this peculiar social system. A student of the Rig Veda, without knowledge of historical facts might reasonably presume that the Indus basin where the Aryans first settled in India would be the Holy land of Hinduism. The Rishis never tire of singing the praises of the mighty Indus with its tributary streams (c. f. Nadi-stuti in X. 75). The combined testimony of the Jātakas and the Greek authors proves that in the fourth century B. C. Taxila in the N. W. Punjab was still a centre of Vedic learning. But the strange fact is that orthodox Hindus regard the whole Punjab between the Indus and the Sutlej as impure land unfit for the residence of strict votaries of Dharma. The reason apparently is that the N. W. territories continued to be overrun by successive swarms of foreigners from Central Asia who disregarded the Brahmins with the result that the original inhabitants of the Punjab intermixed with these barbarian conquerors, imbibed their outlandish practices and did not follow the strict caste system.

While there is much truth in this view, it must be admitted that it exaggerated the freedom of the Rig Veda from caste. For the term 'Brāhmaṇa' 'son of a Brahmā' seems to show that the priesthood was normally hereditary. We are told that there is a case of a King exercising the functions of a domestic priest and sacrifying himself for his people but the alleged case, that of Devapi rests only on the assertion of a commentator of a hymn (X. 98) in which Devapi appears that he was originally a King. Even, however, if this was the case, it must be remembered that even after the complete establishment of the caste system it was still the privilege of Kings to exercise some priestly function such as that of the study of the nature of the Absolute, a practice ascribed to them in the Upanishads. The arguments regarding the warrior class rest on a misunderstanding. Even in the latest Vedic epoch, we have no ground to suppose that there was a special class which reserved its energies for war alone and that the industrial population and the agriculturists allowed the fate of their tribe to be decided by contest between warrior-bands but the Rig Veda certainly knows of a ruling class, the

Kshatriya and the Vedic Kingship was normally hereditary, so that we may well believe that even then there existed, though perhaps in embryo, a class of nobles who are aptly named in the term of the Purushasukta hymn (Rig X. 90), Rājayanas, as being 'men of Kingly family.'

But this Purusha-sukta hymn though commonly supposed to be "the only passage in the Rig Veda which enumerates the four castes," has nothing to do with caste. The hymn has for its subject a cosmogony, a theory of creation. It tells of the creation of all things from the sacrifice of a fabulous monster-man or Purusha, his severed limbs giving birth to the world. As pointed out by Mr. Andrew Lang (Myth, Ritual and Religion, Vol. I. p. 243) the same primitive mode of accounting for creation is found in the Norse legend, where the earth, the seas, water, mountains, clouds and firmament are formed by dividing up the body of the Giant Ymir. So also in the Chaldæn story a monster-woman is devided in twain by Bel to form the heavens and earth. The same story runs through the myths of the Iroquois in N. America as well as through those of Egypt and Greece. The Vedic story which runs close to those of other folk differs from them according to some scholars in this that it goes on to add that from Purusha also sprang the four castes or classes of people. But Mr. V. A. Smith has rightly observed "Both the Brahmin and fire come from Purusha's mouth, just as the servile man or Sudra and earth both proceed from his feet. No suggestion of the existence of caste-groups is made. Mankind is simply and roughly classified under four heads according to occupation, the more honourable profession being naturally assigned to the more honourable symbolical origin. It is absurd to treat the symbolical language of the poem as a narrative of supposed facts." (Oxford History of India, p. 36.) "This is an attempt" says Mr. R. W. Frazer (Literary History of India, p. 25), "to force an antiquity for a social system by connecting it with an undeniably ancient legend."

Thus though there were Kings and sacrificial priests though there were warriors and the great body of the people, cultivators, artisans or dealers in merchandise, the people were not tied down to the rigidity of a caste system whence hereditary occupation was allotted to the members. One poet (Rig IX. 112. 3) tells us that although he is the composer of the hymn he sings, yet his father was a physician while his mother ground grain between mill-stones, proving merely that in the economy of this period there was mobility of labour. The existence of this freedom of movement from one occupation to another would lead to dignity of labour. And as a matter of fact we find the Vedic Rishis themselves preparing sacrificial posts and altars. The Rig-Veda also records instances of Sudra Kings. The worker in wood had clearly the place of honour, needed as he was to produce the war chariots, the ships and boats for trade and carts for agricultural purposes. It is interesting to note that the cultivators, artisans and handicrafts-men are in no way regarded as inferior members of the community. Mr. Baden Powell (in his Indian Village Community, 1896 and Village Communities in India, 1899) assumes that the Aryans had their lands cultivated by the conquered aborigines but the Rig Veda unquestionably describes a society which is not dependent on such servile labour and in which the ordinary tasks of life are carried out by the freemen of the tribe.

We have seen that Rig Vedic Society was sufficiently settled to admit of a high development in the various arts and crafts and the products of these industries must have, therefore, led to an immense volume of trade in them. The trade was carried on inside the country along the land and river-routes but scholars are divided in their opinion as to whether this trade was carried on across the seas to foreign lands. Macdonell, Ragozin and Hopkins hold that the Aryans of the Punjab were unacquainted with the sea. Mr. Keith observes in the Cambridge History of India (Vol. I. p. 101). "The Vedic Indian seems to have been very little of a navigator." Mr. Frazer remarks "It is doubtful if the early Aryans ever knew the ocean. The seas of water they mention may have referred to the wide stretching Indus." (Literary History of India, p. 29). Mr. Macdonell also identifies the western Samudra with the Indus. But then what about the Pūrba or eastern Samudra which also we find? Further the Rig Veda speaks of the Four Samudras. We shall now adduce evidences from the Rig Veda which in Bühler's opinion (Origin of the Brāhmi Alphabet, p. 84) "prove the early existence of the complete navigation of the Indian Ocean and of the trading voyages of Indians." One hymn (Rig. I. 25. 7) represents varuṇa having a full knowledge of the ocean-routes along which vessels sail. Another hymn (Rig. 1. 56.2) speaks of merchants who frequent every part of the sea in pursuit of gain. Another hymn (Rig. I. 48.3) mentions merchants sending out ships to foreign countries under the influence of greed. Rig IV. 55.3. refers to a prayer to the sea by people desirous of wealth, before undertaking a voyage.

Mr. Keith has observed "The use of boats or probably dug-outs for crossing rivers was known but the simplicity of their construction is adequately shown by the fact that the paddle alone was used for their propulsion. There is no mention of rudder or anchor, mast or sails, a fact which incidentally negatives the theory that the Vedic Aryans took any part in ocean-shipping." (Cambridge History of India, Vol. I. p. 101). But we can point out that the Rig Veda has no prohibition against sea-voyages; on the contrary it has distinct allusions to them. The Vedic ships were not simple in their construction as there is a reference in Rig I. 116.3 to a ship with one hundred oars. Moreover, the people crossed the main, not only for trade but also for pleasure trips and warlike purposes. We find a reference to a naval expedition to the distant islands sent by Tugra, the Rishi King under his son Bhujya in Rig I. 163.3 and 5. That these ships were started skilfully on the high seas is proved by Rig VII. 88.3 and 4 in which Vasistha who went out for a pleasant trip says "When I and Varuṇa both boarded the ship, she was far out into the sea and made good progress; then the vessel tossed about and we were pleased with the tossings. The great Varuṇa made Vasistha board the ship on an auspicious day. Vasistha also prayed to that mighty mass of waters. Thus passed away day and night." Referring to this passage even Messrs. Macdonell and Keith observe "It is not easy to refuse to recognise here the existence of longer vessels with many oars and for sea-voyages (Vedic Index, I. 462.). Rig I. 56.2 says. "As merchants desirous of weath surround the sea, so do the priests surround Indra." Here the use of the theme by way of a simile seems to show that sea-voyages were not a rare occurrence but fairly well known to the public at large.

This maritime trade was carried on with Babylon. Assyria, Elam, Judæa, Egypt and Arabia. From the accounts of the earliest historiographers we learn that Navigation made its first efforts on the Mediterranean Sea and on the Persian Gulf. These seas lay open the continents of Europe, Asia and Africa and washing the shores of the most fertile and the most early civilised countries, seemed to have been destined by Nature to facilitate their communication with one another. We find accordingly that the first voyages of the Egyptians and the Phœnicians were made in the Mediterranean and the Red Seas. Their trade was, however, not long confined to the countries bordering on these seas. By acquiring early possession of the ports on the Arabian Sea, they extended the sphere of their commerce and are represented to have opened up communications by sea with India. Dr. Day remarks. "The beginnings of these sea-voyages are lost in the obscurity of the past. We know that they were highly developed by 1500 B. C., when Sidon was the leading city and that they did not cease to extend when the primacy of Phœnician cities passed to Tyre." (History of commerce).

It is a well-known fact that the Phœnician trade had three branches *viz.*, Arabian-Indian, Egyptian and the Assyrio—Babylonion. We are here chiefly concerned with the first. This trade began in the 13th century B. C. According to some scholars the Pani of Rig Veda is Latin Pœni= Phœnicians *i. e.*, a trading people. They were a clan of Asuras whose chiefs Vitra and the Vala were defeated in a fight with the Devas and were therefore, ousted from the north. They, therefore, finally settled on the Levant. Their new colony was called Poni—desh, Lat. Finidis = Phœnicia. The Phœnicians are described by the classical writers of Europe as faithless, treacherous and deceitful—a description quite in unision with the Vedic account. (Vide Rig Veda I. 35. 5; III. 51. 14; VII. 6. 3.). These Phœnician traders would come to India by the Red Sea route and also by the caravan route from the shores of the Persian Gulf to the Mediterranean coast of Syria. Several good harbours of the Arabian Sea were seized by the Phœnicions from the Idumeans. But the distance from Tyre to these ports being very great, they afterwords occupied the nearest Mediterranean port called Rhinocolura. Thither were taken overland all the articles to be reshipped to Tyre. (Robertson's Disquisition on Ancient India, 1792. pp. 7—8). Dr. Royle says " Long before the Persians had made themselves masters of Babylon (531 B. C.) the Phœnicions had established themselves for pearl-fishery and the Indian trade on the isles of Tylos and Aradus, the modern Bahrein islands in the Persian Gulf." (Essay on the Antiquity of Hindu Medicine, p. 122.) The 27th chapter of Ezekiel gives a list of the articles of Phœnician commerce brought from various countries. Among these, "ivory and ebony could only have been procured in Dedan from India, for there were no elephants in Arabia"

(Historians History of the world, Vol. II. pp. 336-37). India according to classical scholars was throughout famous for ivory and ebony (c. f. Strabo XV. 37; Theophrastus quoted by McCrindle in his "India As described by Classical authors" p. 46; Virgil Georgics I. 57. "India sends ivory" II. 116—117. "India alone produces black ebony" Horace's Odes I. 31. The author of the Periplus also mentions logs of ebony being exported from Berygaza.) Moreover, Comparative Philology tells us that Karpasos, Carbasus, Hebrew Karpas, Eng. Canvas = Sans. Kārpās (cotton); Piper, Eng. pepper = Sans. pippala. Zingibery = Eng. ginger = Sans. Sringa-wera. Agallachun or legnum agulia = Sans. aguru. Sandalam = Sans. Chandana. Nardus, Eng. Nard = Sans. Nalada. Kassiteros (Homer) = Sans. Kastira (tin). Beryl = Baidūrya. Tamarind = Tamar—i—hend = Sans. tintiry. Aurum = Swarṇum (gold). [Vide Gotz quoted in Encycl. Biblica. Vol. IV. Article on Trade and commerce]. According to Sir George Birdwood (Industrial Arts of India pp. 263—64) the articles like silver vase mentioned by Homer in II. XXIII. lines 865-70 and the costly garment offered by Hecuba to Minerva as a propitiatory gift mentioned in II. VI. lines 358—67 though produced in later times in Sidon itself, came originally from India.

The fortunes of the Phœnicians soon roused in the neighbouring Jews a spirit of emulation. Under David and Solomon they were great friends of the

Phoenicians under Hiram (980-917 B. C.) and this close friendship produced their combined commercial enterprise. This Jewish trade with India is proved by several allusions in the Bible itself. Thus we are told that Solomon founded a sea-port at Ezion-Geber in 992 B. C. (I. Kings IX. 26). From Ezion-Geber the ships of Solomon sailed under the guidance of the mariners of Hiram for distant lands (I. Kings IX. 27). According to Professor Ball (Article on " A Geologist's contribution to the History of Ancient India in I. A. for August, 1884) some of the stones in the breast-plate of the high priest in the Mosaic period (1491-1450 B. C.) may have come from the far East and India was famous for precious stones. In the days of Solomon (1015 B. C.) there could be supplied from India alone ivory, garments, armour, spices and peacocks. In the Book of Ezekiel which dwells on the commerce of Tyre we find ivory a particularly Indian product. The existence of Dravidian words in the Hebrew Text of the Books of Kings and Chronicles of the Old Testament shows that Indians, specially those of the south carried on their commercial relations with the Hebrew people and the words concerned formed the chief articles of trade between them. Thus, the Hebrew word for peacock in the Book of Kings is tuki and in the Chronicles also is Tuki, while the old poetic Tamil Malayalam name of the peacock is tokei (Dr. Caldwell's A Comparative Grammar of the Dravidian

Languages, p. 91). The Bāvera Jātaka also refers to peacocks as Indian exports to Babylon. Again Hebrew ahalim or ahaloth which means fragrant wood and is also called aloes in Proverbs VII. 17 etc. is derived from the Tamil Malayalam form of the word aghil. Again, almug=Tamil Valgu. Ape=Hebrew Koph=Sans. Kapi. From these evidences we find that Rev. T. Foulkes (Ind. Ant. VIII) is right when he says "The fact is now scarcely to be doubted that the rich oriental merchandise of the days of King Hiram and King Solomon had its starting place in the sea-ports of the Dekhan" Dr. Caldwell has reached the same conclusion and says "It seems probable that Aryan merchants from the mouth of the Indus must have accompanied the Phœnicians and Solomon's servants in their voyages down the Malabar coast towards Ophir (wherever Ophir may have been) or at least have taken part in the trade" (A Comparative Grammar of the Dravidian Languages, p. 122.). The Jewish trade with India lasted a little over a century, for when the fleet of Jehoshaphat, fifth in descent from Solomon, which had started on a voyage to Tarshis, was destroyed, the Jewish commercial spirit cooled down.

Again, according to Wilkinson (Ancient Egyptions II. 237) the presence of indigo, tamarind-wood and other Indian products found in the tombs of Egypt shows India's trade-relations with the land of the Pharoahs. This opinion is further supported by another erudite scholar, the Rev. T. Foulkes who in a learned article in the Indian Antiquary Vol. VIII comes to the same conclusion and says "with a very high degree of probability some of the most esteemed of the spices which were carried into Egypt by the Midiantish merchants of Genesis XXXVII. 25, 28 and by the sons of the Pharoah Jacob (Genesis XLIII) had been cultivated in the spice-gardens of the Dekhan." The evidences of Comparative Philology corroborates this view. Thus Egyptian ebu = Italian ebur = Sans. ebhā-danta = Eng. ivory. Eng. Ape = Egyptian Kafu = Sans. Kapi = Hebrew Koph.

Mr. Pococke, however, goes too far and adduces evidences of the colonisation of Africa from N. W. India and the Himalayan provinces. Firstly, from the provinces and rivers deriving their names from the great rivers of India. "For about ten miles below Attock" says a critic, "the Indus has a clean deep and rapid current; but for about a hundred miles further down to Kalabagh it becomes an enormous torrent. The water here has a dark lead colour and hence the name Nilab or Blue river given as well to the Indus as to a town on its bank about twelve miles below Attock." According to another writer "Aboasin (a classical name for the Indus) gave its name to Abyssinia in Africa." Secondly, from the towns and provinces of India or its Northern frontiers; thirdly, from the ruling chiefs named Rāmas (c. f. Ramses of Egypt) etc.; fourthly, similarity in the objects of sculpture; fifthly, architectural skill and its grand and gigantic character; and sixthly, the power of translating words imagined to be Egyptian through the medium of a modified sanskrit (India in Greece, p. 201) Professor Heeren is astonished at the "physical similarity in colour and the conformation of the head" of the ancient Egyptions and the Hindus. He also finds like Sir William Jones, Dr. Royle, Elphinstone and Col. Tod the still more striking similarity between the whole social, religious and political institutions of the two peoples. According to them our Suryyā rika (sun-burnt land) is perhaps the Sahara desert. The first Egyptian Manes (first solar King) sound like Hindu Manu, the first solar king of India. The bull-bannered Isis is Sans. Isa. Osiris = Sans. Iswara. Tripoli = Tripuri. Professor Heeren concludes "whatever weight may be attached to Indian tradition and the express estimony of Esebius confirming the report of the migrations from the banks of the Indus into Egypt, there is certainly nothing improbable in the event itself, as a desire of gain would have formed a sufficient inducement." But to sober minds, it is reasonable only to assume that whatever similarity there might exist between the place-names, the names of gods and Kings and the social, religious and political institutions of ancient India and Egypt, it was the result of early commercial intercourse between the two couutries.

Nor is this all. The labours of Von Bohlen (Da Alte Indien Vol. I. p. 42) confirming those of Heeren and in their turn confirmed by those of

Lassen (Ind. Ant. Vol. II. p. 580) have established the existtence of maritime trade between India and Arabia from the earliest times. (Hist. Anc. del Orient, Eng. ed. Vol. II. pp. 299, 301 quoted in Ind. Ant. Vol. XIII. p. 228). Professor Max Dunker says "Trade existed between the Indians and the Sabæns on the coast of S. Arabia before the tenth century B. C. (History of Antiquity, Vol. IV. p. 156). The chief article of this trade was probably rice as proved by Comparative Philology. Thus, rice = Tamil arisi = Arabic aurz

But the question of the navigation of the Persian Gulf is still shrouded in mystery as well as that of the Alpha and Omega of all early communications between India and the land of Sumer and Akkad. It is inconceivable that the earliest civilisation of Chaldæ had not engaged in navigation on the "sea of the East". Though no direct evidences regarding this are forthcoming, still we may point out that the great prosperity of Elam and its sturdy resistance first to Chaldæ and then to Assyria may be partly explained by the wealth she acquired in trade with the countries on its eastern frontier; for we know that she had a fleet manned with Phœnician crews at the mouth of the Tigris and the Euphrates.

Dr. Sayce in his Hibbert Lectures for 1887 on the origin and growth of religion among the Baby lonians has proved the existence of commerce between India and Babylon as early as 3000 B. C. when Ur Bagas ruled in Ur of the Chaldæans.

In the ruins of Ur, teak has been found which he considers to be Indian and he is supported by Mr. Hewitt who says that this wood must have been sent by sea from some port on the Malabar coast, for, it is only there that teak grew near enough to the sea, to be exported with profit in those early days. (J. R. A. S. 1888, p. 337). Again Dr. Sayce points to the use of the word Sindhu for muslin in an old Babylonian list of clothes as the clearest proof "that there was trade between the Babylonians and the people who spoke an Aryan dialect and lived in the country watered by the Indus." And if in the Persian time under the fuller light of history the Aramic script wandered to India, such an event may equally have happened in the earlier millenia. This fact is expressed less clearly but still distinctly enough, in the recurrence of the Babylonian legend of the flood among the Indians to which many other points in common will some day be added (Vide the recent excavations at Harappa and Mohenzó Daro. The earliest Indian weights and measures (মানা হিরণ্যয় of Rig Veda VIII. 72. 8) may be traced to Babylonian origin. Further the division of the sky into 24 Nakshatras and the naming of seven days in the week after the Sun, Moon and five other planets may be traced to Babylonian origin. But as these are mentioned in later astronomical works, they are thought to be borrowed directly from Alexandria (Rawlinson's India and the Western world, p. 15). Mr. S. Krishna Swami

Iyengar however supports the Babylonian origin (Beginnings of South Indian History, pp. 327, 329). Again the Mahāsuddha Jātaka is an Indian version of the Judgment of Solon. Moreover, the bas-reliefs of the temple of Deir-el-Bahari at Thebes which represents the conquest of the land of Pun under Hatasu contain a picture in which is described the booty which the Pharoah is carrying to Egypt. And in this booty, according to Leormant "appear a great many Indian animals and products not indigenous to the soil of Yemen—elephant's teeth, gold, precious stones, sandal wood and monkeys. (History of Ancient Del Orient Eng. ed. Vol. II. p. 299 quoted in Ind. Ant. Vol. XIII. p. 228).

This foreign trade could be carried along the three routes suggested by M. D' Anville. The first climbs up the precipitous and zigzag passes of the Zagros range which the Greeks called the Ladders, into the treeless regions of Persia. The second traverses the mountains of Armenia to the Caspian Sea and Oxus and descends into India by the passes of the Hindukush. Lastly, there is the sea. Of these, the overland routes were not impracticable; in fact, the desert steppes of Asia formed the merchantile ocean of the ancients—the companies of camels their fleets. But the commerce was from hand to hand and from tribe to tribe, fitful and uncertain and never possessed any importance. Similarly, the normal trade route from the Persian Gulf to India could never have been along the inhospitable deserts of Gedrosia. Doubtless then more than one adventurous vessel reached India by hugging the shores. But the exploring expedition despatched in later times by Darius (512 B. C.) from the mouth of the Indus under Skylax of Karayandra and two centuries later by Alexandar the Great under Nearchos show the difficulties and dangers of this route, the time it occupied and the ignorance of the pilots. The author of the Periplus, it is true, says that small ships made formerly voyages to India, coasting along the shores until Hippalus first ventured to cross the Ocean by observing the monsoon. But we know from other sources that the monsoon was known from the earliest times to all who sailed along the Arabian and African coasts; and direct sea voyages were attempted only at the commencement of the monsoon (Monsoon = Arabic Mauzim). The route for the direct sea-trade ran down the Persian and Arabian coasts to Aden, up the Red Sea to Suez and from Suez to Egypt on the one hand and Tyre and Sidon on the other. Balkh, Aden and Palmyra were the chief halting stations and emporia of this trade.

Now, was there any combination between merchants in this period? The Vedic expression for a merchant is paṇi which occurs several times in the Rig Veda (VI. 45). This has been differently interpreted by different scholars (Vedic Index I. p. 471). The St. Petersburg Dictionary derives it from paṇ, to barter and explains it as merchant. Zimmer (Alt. Leben 1879 p. 257) and Ludwig (Der Rig Veda 3. 213-215) takes it in the sense of merchant. Now the gods are asked to attack the paṇis who are referred to as being defeated with slaughter (Vedic Index I. p. 471). Ludwig thinks that these references to fights with paṇis are to be explained by their having been aboriginal traders who went in caravans as in Arabia and N. Africa, prepared to fight if need be, to protect their goods against attacks which the Aryans would naturally deem quite justified. If we accept this meaning, we presume a Corporation of merchants strong enough to defy their opponents and carry on fight against them.

Another interesting feature of the trade of these days was the haggling over prices. In Rig IV. 24. 9 it is stated that once a seller received less price from a buyer for a commodity, the real price of which was much more than the price given. So he demanded more, saying that the article was not yet sold and did not accept the low price. The poet here observes that persons clever and unclever, thus first dispute and then only receive what is finally settled at the time of actual sale.

This volume of trade would necessarily presuppose the existence of an excellent system of exchange. But the general view hitherto held was that "in the Vedic Age all exchange was by barter" (Mrs. Rhys Davids in J. R. E. S. 1910). But we find that "cattle formed one of the standards of valuation" (Vedic Index, I. p. 234). Besides cattle as a standard of exchange we find references (Rig I. 125; V. 27. 2; VIII. I. 30-33) to Nishkas in the sense of metallic currency. In the first Mandala of the Rig Veda we have a hymn in which the poet-priest kākshīvat praises the munificence of his patron, King Bhāvayavya thus "A hundred Nishkas from the King, beseeching a hunded gift-steeds, I at once accepted" (I. 126. 2). In regard to this passage, the authors of the Vedic Index (I. 454-5) rightly say "As early as the Rig. Veda, traces are to be seen of Nishkas as a sort of currency, for, a singer celebrates the receipt of a hundred Nishkas and a hundred steeds. He could hardly require the Nishkas for purposes of personal adornment." Prof. H. H. Wilson in his note on V. 27. 2 says "It is not improbable, however, that prices of money are intended; for if we may trust Arrian, the Hindus had coined money before Alexander."

But was the Nishka bullion currency? This may be solved as has been pointed out by Professor D. R. Bhandarkar by reference to hymn 33 of Maṇdala II of the Rig Veda. Here the god Rūdra is described as wearing a Nishka or necklace. But be it noted that this Nishka is called Viswa-rūpa. What can Viswa-rūpa mean? Does it signify omniform? If so, what is meant by saying that Rūdra's necklace was omniform? I am afraid this does not convey any good sense and we must try to find out what could be the natural and proper sense of this term. Before, however, we can hope to arrive at a plausible solution, we must consider, how the word Nishka could come to signify both a currency and a necklace. A little reflection tells us that this is possible only if we suppose that Nishka means not simply a currency but a coin, that Nishka denoted necklace because it consisted of Nishkas, the coins. In Mahārāstra, the poorer classes even to-day get a goldsmith to cast gold coins in imitation of certain Byzantine originals which they call Putalyā which are afterwards strung into a necklace called Putalyā. This custom of making necklaces out of coins is not of modern origin but was also prevalent in Ancient India. Thus the Kalpa-Sutra while describing Sri, the goddess of beauty whom Trisāla, the mother of Mahābir saw in her dream, speaks of the former as bearing urattha-dīnāra-mālya, i. e., a string of dīnārs (the Roman denarius) on her breast. Nishka must, therefore, be taken in the sense of a coin and not merely of a metallic currency. If this natural explanation is accepted, then a good sense of the term Viswa-rūpa is possible to fix upon. The rūpa in Viswa-rūpa can at once be recognised to be a word technical to the old Indian Science of Numismatics and denoting the symbol or figure on a coin which for that reason is styled "rūpya." Thus, the necklace worn by the deity Rūdra was composed of Nishka coins; and just because these Nishka coins bore various rūpas or figures on them, the necklace was naturally viswa-rūpa. . The earliest of coins found in India are the punch-marked coins and we know that no less than three hundred different devices or rūpas have been marked on them.

Besides coins, unstamped metallic currency was also known is this period. In Rig VI. 47. 23 mention is made of daśa-hiraṇya-pinda which the Rishi Garga received from King Divodās, son of Srinjaya. As these hiraṇya-pindas have been specially mentioned as ten, it appears that each hiraṇya-pinda conformed to a definite recognised value. And as the word pinda shows, it was bullion beaten into some definite (probably roundish) shape, we need not be surprised at the existence of both stamped and unstamped money circulating in one and the same period. Not many years ago, the Dhābuās which were unstamped copper coins, circulated freely in Bengal along with stamped coinage of various denominations.

Loans and usury were well known in the Rig Vedic Age. Rishis sometimes regretted their state of indebtedness.

Regarding the wealth of this period we have numerous references in the Rig Veda. Rig V. 30 refers to 400 cattle. In Rig VI. 47. 22 we find reference to ten coffers, ten horses, ten treasure-chests, ten garments, ten hiraṇya-pindas, ten cars with extra steed to each and 100 cows. Rig VIII. 1 refers to 1000 cows while Rig. VIII.

4. 21 to 60,000 cows. Rig VIII. 4. 22 refers to a gift of 100 buffaloes and 10,000 kine. Rig VIII. 4. 23 mentions a gift of 100,000 kine from Parsu. Rig VIII. 21 mentions King Chitra as making thousand myriad gifts. We also read of a magnificent gift in Rig VIII. 46 where 60,000 steeds, 10,000 kine and 2000 Camels were given as reward. Besides this, we find clear indications of the wealth of the aboriginal inhabitants, their forts and their castles in Rig VIII. 34. 9.

Brāhmana Period.

(--600 B. C.).

Definitely later than that depicted in the Rig Veda is the civilization presented by the later Saṃhitās, the Brāhmanas, the Āranyaks and the Upanishads. The story of the Rāmayana may have its origin in the later Brāhmana Period (Cambridge History of India, Vol. I. p. 317) and the epic was composed according to Professor Macdonell before 500 B. C. (History of Sanskrit Literature p. 309). In the period of the Rig Veda, the centre of civilization was tending to be localised in the land between the Saraswatī and the Drishadbatī river; but in the Brāhmana period, as the period under review may conveniently be called, the localisation of civilisation in the more eastern part of the country is achieved. In the Aitareya Brāhmana, a geographical passage ascribes the Middle country to the later Madhya-desha, the Kurus and Panchāls with the Vasas and Usinaras, to the south the Satvats and to the north beyond the Himalayas, the Uttar-Kurus and the Uttar-Madras. On the other hand, while the west recedes in importance, the regions east of the Kuru-Panchāl territory come into prominence, specially Kosala, corresponding roughly to modern Oudh, and Videha, the modern Tirhut or N. Bihar and Magadh, the modern South Bihar. Still further east was the country of the Angas, the modern E. Bihar. In the south, we hear of non-Aryan tribes like the Andhras, Pulindas, Pundras, Mutibas, Sabaras and the Naishadas.

In keeping with this wider geographical outtook, the Brāhmana period is marked by the knowledge of towns and of a developed city-life. There are clear references to Āsandīvant the Kuru Capital, Kāmpīlya the Pānchāla Capital, to Kaushami and to Kāsi, the capital of the Kasis on the river Varaṇāvati, whence in later times Benares derived its name.

In this period, individual ownership of land was general. There are two mythical accounts of father Manu (not as Lawgiver but as the Adam of the race) and of the division of his inheritance. One of them says "Manu divided his property for his sons; one of them living elsewhere as a student he excluded from a share." The other account says, "The brothers excluded from a share one of Manu's sons." In both the accounts, the property is divided in the father's life-time (Aitareya Brāhmana). In the mythology of the Brāhmana Period we find that the children of the Father God viz., gods and devils fight for their respective shares and "enter into their inheritance" by dividing it. In another mythology we find a man who has no son, dividing his property between his two wives. We find the gift of a field; of whole villages; of all the king's lands to a priest; and when thus given, the land cannot be alienated. If the King should at another time, give all his land to another, that piece which he has formerly given to the first priest, is not included in the later donation.

Nevertheless, the king was the owner of land. The Aitareya Brāhmana says that a priest's function is to take gifts, while the Vaisya's peculiar function is to be devoured by the priest and nobleman. From this it is apparent that the Vaisya cannot have any secure hold over his landed property. The country was governed by the king through local officers; "the leader of the host" has become the village headman who was the king's revenue-collector. In one of the Upanishads it is said that the vital breath commands the other breaths just as a Samrāj commissions his officers saying "Be thou over these villages or those villages". Prof. Keith, however, observes "There can be no doubt that he (the king) controlled the land of the tribe. It is not, however, necessary to ascribe to this period the conception of the royal ownership of all the land, though it appears in the Greek source from the time of Megasthenes downwords and is evidenced later by the law books of the time. He had, it is true, the right to expel a Brahmin and a Vaisya at will, though we do not know expressly that he could do this in the case of a Kshatriya. But these considerations point to political superiority rather than to ownership proper and we may assume that when he gave grants of land to his retainers, he granted not ownership but privileges such as the right to receive dues and maintenance from the cultivators. There is a clear distinction between this action and the conferring of ownership, and it may be doubted if the actual gift of land was approved in this epoch. The only case of which we hear is one reported in the Satapatha and Aitareya Brāhmanas in which the King Viswakarman Bhauvana gave land to the priests who sacrificed for him but the earth itself rebuked his action. It is more probable that at this time, the allotment of land was determined by the King or by the noble to whom he had granted rights of superiority according to customary law and that gifts not in accordance with this law were disapproved. It is hardly necessary to point out the close similarity between such a state of affairs and that existing at the present day in parts of West Africa, where Kings have introduced for purposes of personal gain the practice of dealing as absolute owners with lands which according to the strict system of tribal law they have no power to allocate save in accordance with the custom of the tribe. Nor is it inconsistent with this view that the King had an arbitrary power of removing a subject from his land. That power flowed from his sovereignty and though disapproved, was acquiesced in, we may presume, just as in West Africa; while the dealing of Kings with lands by way of absolute ownership was regarded as a complete breach of the tribal law, the actual removal from his land, of any individual was recognised as a royal prerogative, even if the power was misused" (Cambridge History of India, Vol. I. pp. 132—33).

In Agriculture, progress was doubtless made (Atharva Veda III. 17). The plough was large and heavy; we hear of as many as twentyfour oxen being harnessed to one; it had a sharp point and a smoothed handle. In addition to irrigation (Atharva Veda III. 13.) the use of manure was referred to several times. Besides barley, wheat, beans, corn, sesamum from which oil was extracted, Panicum miliaceum, frumentaceum and italicum, wrightia antidysenterica, Dolichos uniflorus, Ervum hirsutum, Coix barbata and various other kinds of grain were grown. The Brihadāraṇyaka Upanishad VI. III. 13. mentions ten kinds of seeds *viz.*, rice (brihi) barley (yava) sesamum (tila) bean (masa), millet, and panic seed (anupriyangavas) wheat (godhuma) lentils (masum), pulse (Khalves) vetches (Khalakulas). The white Yajur Veda (XVIII. 12) adds mudga, nibara and Syāmākas. Rice (Vedia Index I, 398) both domesticated and wild was much used. The Taittiriya Saṃhitā briefly sums up the seasons of the different grains thus "Barley sown in winter as at present, ripened in summer. Rice sown in the rains, ripened in autumn. Beans and sesamum planted in the time of the summer rains, ripened in the winter and the cold season". There were two seasons of harvest according to the same authority and another text tells us that the winter crops were ready in March. The winnower was called Dhānyakṛt and the grain was measured in a vessel called ūrdara (Vedic Index, I. p. 182). From the Rāmāyana we learn that agriculture was an important art, for, learning consisted of the Vedas, Agriculture and Commerce. Rāma asks Bharat the question whether agriculturists and cowherds found favour in Bharat's sight. That agriculture was carried on is proved by the fact that Ajodhyā is described as full of cultivators (Ajodhyā Kānda LXVIII), abounding in paddy rice (Bāla V). The King is represented as boasting of his kingdom abounding in corn (Ajodhyā III.14). Villages are described as having ploughed lands on their skirts (Ajodhā XLII).

The farmer had as now constant trouble to contend with: moles destroyed the seeds; birds and other creatures destroyed the young shoots and both drought and excessive rain destroyed the crops. The Atharva Veda provides with a considerable number of spells to avoid blight and secure a good harvest.

Despite these precautions, famines were not unknown. No doubt in the time of Rāma, the people were free from famine (Bāla I). But the fact that the King was to have a clear idea regarding the prevention of famines shows that famines were not unknown even in those days (Ajodhyā C). And as a matter of fact, we find that famines did overtake the kingdom of Ramapada for his sin (Bāla IX).

Dairyfarming was carried on this period. From the Rāmāyana we find that Ghosa-pallis—the villages of milkmen were prosperous and famous for their milk, butter, clarified butter etc. From the Taittiriya Brāhmana I. 4. 9. 2, we find that the cows were driven out to graze thrice a day and were well cared for.

Coming to the forest products, we find references to cucumbers and frequent mention of Aśvatha, the Ficus religiosa and the Nyagrodha, the Ficus Indica and the different forms of Jujube are specially named. In the Atharva Veda we find mention of ভঙ্গ = ভাঙ্গ, an intoxicating plant.

More striking, however, is the great development of industrial life and the consequent subdivision of occupations. The Vedic Index supplies us with the following functional groups as living in this period :—Karmakār (Smith), kulāl (potter), Gaṇaka (Astrologer), Gopāla (Herdsman), Takṣhan or Teshtri (carpenter), Dhaibara (fisherman), Nāpita (barber) Malaga (washerman), Vayitri (weaver), Surakāra (liquor-manufacturer). A large number of professions are enumerated in the White Yajur Veda in Chapters 16 and 30. Thus, we hear of carpenters, arrow-makers, horse and cattle-keepers, gate-keepers, painters, tanners, engravers, hunters, several classes of fishermen, of ploughers, of fire-rangers, of charioteers, of makers of jewels, basket-makers, rope-makers, dyers, chariot-makers, workers in gold, sellers of dried fish, makers of bows, wigmakers, smelters and so forth. Of women's work we learn of the dyer, the embroiderer, the worker in thorns and the basket-maker. In Rāmāyana also we hear of the various classes of artisans who dwelt in Ajodhyā (Bāla V.) and in the forts (Ajodhyā C.). They were the jewellers, expert and agreeable pot-makers, persons skilled in tools and the use of weapons, dentists, extractors of wine, perfume-dealers, renowned goldsmiths, wine-keepers, weavers, painters, makers of ramparts, garland-makers, experts in brick-works, badge-makers, shoe-makers, black-smiths, makers of ironbars and bows, skilful chemists.

The weaving industry was carried to its perfection. We hear of silver and golden robes (Sundara kānda), of excellent yellow cloth made of golden fibres (Sundara) and of coverlets studded with jewels (Sundara). In this age, the Brahmins used to wear Kauseya (Rāmāyana 2. 32. 16.) In Ajodhyā-Kānda

Chapter 3. 7, we find that Rāma and Lakshmaṇa wore the bark of trees leaving aside their white linen garments. In Rāmāyana 2. 52. 82 we find that Sitā gave presents to Brahmins a large number of cloths of variegated colours. From the Ādi-kānda, Chapter 77, we find that after Daśaratha had returned to his kingdom with his four daughters-in-law, Kaikeyi and others went to the temple clad in khauma. From these it becomes apparent that in the age of the Rāmāyana, white and coloured cloths were in use while Khauma was used for ceremonial occasions (*Vide* the term বয়ন in বিশ্বকোষ). It is interesting to note in this connection that in this age, an instrument was invented for winnowing cotton.

Woolen sheets were also used (Ajodhyā LXX). Woolen carpets made of the fleece of deer (Ajodhyā LXX), blankets, (Ajodhyā XXX), spacious and parti-coloured woolen cloth figured in the bed-room of Rāvaṇa (Sundara IX).

Silk cloths are frequently mentioned. On the occasion of Sitā's marriage, King Janaka gave among other presents a large quantity of silk dress (Bāla LXXIV):

> "অথ রাজা বিদেহানাম্ দদৌ ধনম্ বহু।
> গবাম্ শত সহস্রানি বহূনি মিথিলেশ্বরঃ॥
> কম্বলানাঞ্চ মুখ্যানাম্ ক্ষৌম্যান্ কোট্যম্বরাণি চ
> হস্ত্যশ্চ রথপদানাম্ দিব্যরূপম্ স্বলঙ্কৃতম্॥"

After this, when the daughters-in-law approached the City of Ajodhyā, Kausalyā and other ladies in welcoming them found that their silkdress had increased in their beauty thousand-fold (Gorresio's Rāmayana, Part I. p. 297). The queens of Daśaratha were clad in silk, when they welcomed their new daughters-in-law (Bāla LXXVII). We find Rāma and Sitā clad in silk while at home (Ajodhā XXXVII; also LXXIX) and even an ordinary nurse is seen in silk dress (Ajodhyā VII). Sitā when going to Daṇdaka forest wore silk and when in Daṇdaka wore silk (Ajodhyā VI, XX, XXXII, LXV). Bharat was in silk dress when he went to meet Rāma in the forest (Ajodhyā LXXXIX). When Rāvaṇa came to Sitā in the forest, he wore silk and Sitā also was clad in silk dress (Araṇyakānda LXVI). Even in the Aśoka forest, when surrounded by Chedis, we find Sitā clad in silk. We find Rāvaṇa sleeping with a dress of yellowish silk (Sundara X). He was decked with silk before cremation (Sundara CXIII).

The under-wear of the people was called নীবি (Atharva Veda 8. 2. 16.). Over it was worn as in the Rig Vedic period, the বাসস্। Above it was worn অধিবাস। This অধিবাস was also called অৎক and তার্পয।
From Śatapatha Brāhmana we find that নীবি was called চণ্ডাতক। The ends of cloth (পাড়) or of dress (ঝালা) were called ভূষ (Taittiriya Brāhmana, Taittiriya Saṃhita, Pancha-biṃsha Brāhmana). In Śatapatha Brāhmana it is also called দশা। Women in those days wore উষ্ণীষ, head dress (Aitareya 6. 1.) In Śatapatha we find the wife of Indra dressed with head dress.

The advance of civilisation is seen also in the more extended knowledge of metals and the large number of mining industries of this period. From the White Yajur Veda 18. 10., we find that six distinct metals were known *viz.*, হিরণ, অয়স্, শ্যামং, লোহ, সীস and ত্রপু। The Rāmāyana also mentions gold, silver, copper, iron, lead, mercury, tin etc. In the description of the forest areas like Danda -kāranya and Chitrakūta we find passages referring to the existence of mines—

"শ্বেতাভি কৃষ্ণতাম্রাভি শিলাভিরূপশোভিতম্।"৭

"নানাধাতু সমাকীর্ণম্ নদীদূদ্দর সংযুতম্। কি—২৭

"বিরাজন্তেহচলেন্দ্রস্য দেশাধাতুবিভূষিতা: ।৬।২।৯৪

There were mines in the northern parts of Ajodhyā as well. Beautiful articles were made of these metals. In the outer courtyard of Rāma's palace at Ajodhyā we find on the altars golden images. The walls surrounding Lankā, the rooms, the roofs, the pavement, the floor (কুট্টিম) and even the steps were made of gold. The description of the palace of Rāvaṇa ornamented with plastered jewelled pavements, studded with gems, crystals and pearls, with elephants of burnished gold and speckless white silver, girt round by a mighty golden wall, furnished with golden doors, with beautiful golden stairs embellished with ornaments of burnished gold, with lofty edifices having excellent windows made of ivory and silver, covered with golden nets shows the improvement of art and the luxury of the age. Well might Hanuman exclaim at the sight of the bed-chamber of Rāvaṇa with its jewelled staircase illumined with heaps of gems, its terraces of crystal and statues of ivory, pearls, diamonds, corals, silver and gold, adorned with jewelled pillars that this must be Swarga. (Sundara IX). We learn of images of beasts made of metal (Ajodhyā 15), images of gold (Ajodhyā 14), golden thrones decked with pearls and diamonds (Ajodhyā 3), altars made of gold and silver (Ajodhyā 10), Chāmar bedecked with gold (Lankā Kānda 11 and Ajodhyā 6), golden chariots (Bāla 53), ropes made of gold (Lankā 128), golden Kabacha (Araṇya 64), swords with helmets of gold (Araṇya 43), gold crown (Sundara 10), golden bowls (Sundara 1), golden jars and pitchers (Sundara 11), golden lamps (Sundara 11), golden bed (Ajodhyā 91), golden pot for washing the hands (Ajodhyā 91), silver plates for dinner (Bāla 53), seats made of gold (Sundara 1), ভৃঙ্গার (Ajodhyā 14), রৌপ্য পঞ্জর (Lankā 65).

The Rāmāyana treats of royal families generally and as such we do not frequently hear of articles used by ordinary men. Nevertheless, we hear of কাংস্যময় দোহন পাত্র (Bāla 92) and of bell metal vessels (Kiṣkindhā L and Bāla LXXIII). We also hear of iron shafts decked with gold (Kiṣkindhā VIII), feathered shafts plated with gold (Araṇya III, XXI, XL), bows decked with gold (Sundara XLVII), coats of mail (Ajodhyā XL), iron armour for horses and elephants (Lankā 24), gold-hilted scimitars (Araṇya XLIV), golden armours (Araṇya XLIV), vessels made of gold and silver (Kiṣkindhā L and Bāla LXXIII), vessels of burnished gold with silver covers (Bāla XVI) and of cars decked with gold (Araṇya XLIX).

Various ornaments were also made of gold and silver. An ornament of the head was called ওপশ (Atharva Veda 6. 138. 1.). According to Roth it means hair-tape or hair-net but according to Bloomfield it means ওড়না, worn by women. Another ornament of the head was কুম্ব (Atharva 6. 138. 3.). Sāyan says that it is an ornament used by women in hair-culture (কেশপ্রসাধন). Probably it is comb. In Atharava Veda we hear of কুরীয়ন। According to Zimmer it means peacock. If this meaning is accepted, then কুরীয়ন is a tiara-like ornament of the head (চূড়াকৃতি). In Aitareya Brāhmana we hear of the term নিষ্কগ্রীব। From this it is apparent that necklaces of Nishka coins were worn. From Panchabiṃsha Brāhmana (17. 1. 14) we learn that the Brātyas used to wear on their necks silver Nishka. We hear of রুক্মপাশ in Śatapatha Brāhmana (6. 7. 1. 7), a chain by means of which রুক্ম was worn on t e breast. We hear of earrings called প্রবর্ত in Atharva 15. 2. 1., of কর্ণশোভন in Śatapatha and the Taittriya Saṃhitā. We hear of পরিহস্ত (Atharva 6. 81) which was something like bangles or bracelets. Tiaras were also worn called তিরীত (Atharva 8. 6. 7). Amarkoṣha explains it as an ornament of the head

(মুকুটমণি or শিরোভূষণ). স্থাগর (Taittriya Brāhmana 2. 3. 10. 2) was an ornament made from স্থগর (a perfume). Hair was combed by means of শললী and eye-ointment (অঞ্জন) was used (Kaṭhaka Saṃhitā 23. 1; Śatapatha Brāhmana 2. 6. 4. 5; Taittiriya 1. 5. 6. 6). From Taittiriya Saṃhitā we learn that shoes (উপানহ) were worn. Generally, these were made of the skins of boars (Śatapatha Brāhmana). We find frequent mention of প্রাকাশ in Taittiriya, Śatapatha and Panchabiṃsha Brāhmanas. It means looking glass. Geldner thinks that প্রাবেপ (Maitrāyani Saṃhita 4. 4. 8) means the same thing. In Rāmāyana also we hear of bangles studded with gems Aranya LII), of elegant ornaments (Araṇya LIV), garlands of well-melted gold (Ajodhā IX) and pendants of pure gold (Araṇya LI).

We hear of mixed metals (যৌগিক ধাতু) in this age. In Bāla Kānda 7th Sarga we are told that "after the marriage ceremony of his sons was over, Daśaratha on reaching home presented four Brahmins with cows together with calves and কাংস্যদোহন ভাণ্ড।" Pittal is another mixed metal made of copper and Zinc. In Araṇya Kānda, 29th Sarga Khar (নিশাচর খর) angrily speaks to Rāma thus "just as the gold-like pittal is blackened when put to fire, so are you showing only your hollowness by self-laudation."

In Rāmāyana we find mention of mercury but not of sindura manufactured from it. Ladies in those days used tilaks of red-coloured মনঃশিলা by the side of their cheeks. মনঃশিলা was a metal found in the mountains (গিরিজধাতু). Sitā is speaking to Hanuman thus " just remind Rāma of the fact that he used to colour my cheek with the help of মনঃশিলা (Sundara 40).

Whether alchemy was known in this period is not certain. Alchemy is the process by means of which an inferior metal is converted into a superior one. We find reference to this process in Bāla Kānda, 67th Swarga where the origin of metals is discussed. But some scholars look upon this passage as a later addition (প্রক্ষিপ্ত).

In the Rāmāyana, we find various other mineral (আকরিক পদার্থ) products like গৈরিক, জাম্বনদ, সুধা (lime), etc.

The finer arts like painting were also known. Frescoes (Patibhāna or Conversation-pictures, i. e., love scenes) are mentioned in the oldest Pali literature and the very fact that Buddha prohibited these paintings and permitted only the representations of wreaths and creepers show the pre-Buddhist origin of painting.

Architecture and Town-planning were also known. Lankā in the Rāmāyana is likened to a mind-wrought city in the air; and again to a beautiful woman with banners for her earrings and the towers upon the walls for her breasts.

In this period, the caste-system was getting stereotyped. Besides the priesthood and the nobility, there comes into existence a new factor, the introduction of divisions among the ordinary freemen—the

Vaisyas. In this development, there must have been two main influences—the force of occupation and the influence of the aborigines. In the Taittiriya Brāhmana, the chariot-makers appear as a special class along with the Vaisyas and in this special position we can see how the chariot-makers, the type of skilled workers in the Rig Veda, have through their devotion to a mechanical art, lost status as compared with ordinary freemen. Moreover, contact with the aborigines (c. f. the cases of Kavasha and Vatsa) must have raised questions of purity of blood very much like those which at present agitate the southern states of the U. S. A. or the white people in South Africa.

The question how far change of caste and occupation was possible raises difficult problems. The most that can be said is that such change does not seem to have been impossible. The Pancha-Viṃsha Brāhmana speaks of certain persons as royal seers and the later tradition preserved in the Anukramani or index to the composers of the Rig Veda ascribes hymns to such royal seers. Viswāmitra, Devapi and Janaka became Brahmins (Śatatatha Brāh. XI. 6. 2. 1.). Kavasha, son of Illusha, a low caste woman was admitted as a rishi for his purity, learning and wisdom (Ait. Brāh. II. 3. 19). " Perhaps the most notable feature of his life is that he, Śūdra as he was, distinguished himself as the Rishi of some of the hymns of the Rig Veda " viz., Rig. X. 30-34

[Shyāmji Krisnabarṇa in his paper on 'Sanskrit as a living language in India,' read before the International Congress of Orientals held at Berlin on 14th September 1881]. A Brahmin imparts knowledge to a Sudra accepting presents and aking his daughters for his wife (Chhāndogya Upanishad IV. 2.) Viswāmitra, the Purohit of king Sudas mentioned in Rig Veda is described in the Panchaviṃsha and Aitareya Brāhmanas as of royal descent, of the family of the Jahnus. Yaska represents a prince Devapi as sacrificing for his brother Sāntanu, the king. Similarly, king Viswantar sacrifices without the help of priests in Aitareya Brāhmana. The Upanishads tell us of kings like Janaka of Videha, Aśwapati, king of the Kekayas in the Punjab, Ajātsatru of Kāsī and Probahana Jābāla of Pānchāl disputing with and instructing Brahmins in the lore of the Brahmā. Similarly, the Jaiminīya Upanishad speaks of a king becoming a seer. Another case of interest is that of Satyakāma Jābāla who waş accepted as a pupil by a distinguished priest, because he showed promise, although he could not tell of his ancestry—infact, he was the son of a slave-girl (Chh. Up. V. 4.). This shows the elasticity of the caste-system in this age. Jābāla, it may by noted, was the founder of a school of the Yajur Veda. In the Rāmāyana also, we find the king of Mithilā engaged in ploughing (Bāla LXVI). A Brahmin is seen earning his livelihood by ploughing, with no stigma attached to his action. Moreover, who was Vālmiki, the author of the Rāmāyana itself, but a Śūdra?

The question now presents itself whether there existed in this period industrial combinations called craft-guilds. Geldner and Roth find references to them in the Brāhmanas but there are other Vedic scholars who hold the opposite view. No doubt, considered by themselves merely as literary passages, these references seem to be doubtful indications of a formal and well-defined institution but if we combine with the literary evidence, the evidence of history, the evidence furnished by the evolution of Aryan life, the spread of Aryan culture from the Rig Vedic period downwards, much of the uncertainty of the purely literary evidences will disappear. No doubt guild-life belongs to a considerably advanced stage of economic progress in which individual mechanics, artisans and traders have sufficient business instinct developed in them and have achieved sufficient success in their respective businesses to appreciate the necessity of organising themselves into a community for the purpose of promoting their individual and collective interests. But we have already seen the enormous extent to which the differentiation of economic occupations was carried on and the fabulous progress which the arts and crafts achieved in this period. And this will lead any sober and unbiassed historion to the conclusion that those scholars who choose to find in certain passages of the Brāhmanas proofs of the existence of guilds cannot very well be considered as guilty of making any extravagant claim and taking up an untenable position.

Let us now proceed to the passages themselves. All of these contain the use of the words "Śtesthin" and "stresthtya" which from their context would mean headman of a guild and the foremost place that belongs to such a headman. In the Atharva Veda I. 9. 3. there is the expression "bestow on him lordship (শ্রেষ্ঠত্ব) over his follows". In Śatapatha Brāh. XIII. 7. 1. 1. শ্রেষ্ঠত্ব is similarly used. In Aitareya III. 39. 3. there is a reference to the position of the chief of the guild who favours with a draught from his goblet whom he likes. In IV. 25. 8-9 and VII. 18. 8, the position of leadership is indicated by শ্রেষ্ঠত্ব and শ্রেষ্ঠতা। শ্রেষ্টি and শ্রেষ্ঠত্ব are similarly used in Chh. Up. V. 2. 6.; Kausītaki Up. IV. 20; II. 6 and IV. 15. 20. In Brihad. Up. I. 4. 12 we read—"স নৈব ব্যভবত। স বিশমসৃজত যান্যেতানি দেবজাতানি গণশ আখ্যায়ন্তে"। Commentator শঙ্করাচার্য্য says "ক্ষাত্রস্বষ্টোঽপি স নৈব ব্যভবৎ কর্ম্মণে ব্রহ্ম তয়া ন ব্যভবৎ বিত্তোপার্জ্জনয়িতুরভাবাৎ। স বিশমসৃজত কর্ম্মসাধনবিত্তোপার্জ্জনায়। কঃ পুনরসৌ বিট্? যান্যেতানি দেবজাতানি, স্বার্থে নিষ্ঠা য এতে দেবজাতিভেদা ইত্যর্থঃ গণশ গণং গণং আখ্যায়ন্তে কথ্যন্তে গণপ্রায়া হি বিশঃ। প্রায়েন সংহত্য হি বিত্তোপার্জ্জনসমর্থাঃ নৈকৈকশঃ।" Thus the gods of the Vaisya class were called গণশ on the analogy of their human prototype because they could earn money, evidently by trade, industry and commerce, not by their individual efforts but in a corporate body. Metaphorical and indirect allusions to guilds made in order to explain obstruse philosophical subjects show that they are already well-known existences within the range of common observation and the allusions are warranted on the logical principle of arguing from the known to the unknown, of explaining the unfamiliar and the abstract, from the familiar and the concrete. This is further corroborated by the Rāmāyana where we are told that in the procession of citizens who accompanied Bharat in his quest of Rāma figured the gem-cutters, potters, weavers, ivory-workers, well-known goldsmiths, the foremost merchants and citizens of all classes, so that the Rāmāyana recognises the position held by trades and crafts in society (II. 83. 12. 13).

Indeed the artisans enjoyed special privileges and some of the higher craftsmen specially those engaged in the canons of the rituals of the Silpasūtras enjoyed a high social status. Similarly those engaged in irrigation works and in the preparation of public buildings enjoyed high privileges. Ajodhyā was inhabited by all classes of them (Bāla V) and they had to be specially entertained (Bāla XIII). We have seen that originally agriculture was carried on by Aryan tillers but in this period, the position was changing gradually; and for the peasant working on his own fields, was being substituted the land-owner cultivating his estate by means of slaves or the merchant carrying on his trade by means of the same instrumentality, though we cannot with any certainty say how far this process was proceeding. The industrial workers like the chariot-makers, the smiths, the tanners and the carpenters were sinking in estimation and forming distinct castes of their own.

An interesting reference to the position of women with regard to agriculture is to be found in Taittiriya Brāhmana III. 3. 10 and Śatapatha Brāhmana II. 5. 2. 20 where we are told that in a sacrificial ritual "as a rule the wife of the sacrificer was present, with hands joined to her husband". This participation of women in harvest-offerings can be explained by the fact that in primitive times the duties of agriculture lay, for the most part, in the hands of women (Jevon's Introduction to the History of Religion, pp. 240-41). The historical development of this portion of the sacrifice is tersely summed up in the words of Mr. Jevons "It is, therefore, an easy guess that the cultivation of plants was one of women's contributions to civilisation and it is in harmoney with this conjecture that the cereal duties are usually both in the Old world and in the New, female". Agriculture, however, when its benefits became thoroughly understood, was not allowed amongst civilised races to continne to be the exclusive prerogative of women and the Corn goddess, maiden or mother had to admit within the circle of her worshippers, the men as well as the women of the tribe. The gradual transition from the early sacrifice of human beings to the stage in which horses kept in droves and tended by man during the pastoral stage were sacrificed, thence to the substitution of of various animals as they became domesticated, ending with the offering of fruits of the earth, when agriculture became widely known, is set forth as a recognised fact in the Aitareya Brāhmana.

Professor Keith observes "There is still no hint of sea-borne commerce or of more than river navigation, though we need not suppose that the sea was unknown, at least by hearsay, to the end of the period " (Cambridge History of India, p. 136). But as a matter of fact we find distinct references to sea-borne commerce in this period. The Atharva Veda compares the ruin of a kingdom where Brahmins are oppressed to the sinking of a ship which is leaking. The Yajur Veda Adhyāya VI. Mantra 21 says "সমুদ্রঙ্গচ্ছ স্বাহা অন্তরীক্ষঙ্গচ্ছ স্বাহা দেবং সবিতারঙ্গচ্ছ স্বাহা।" In Rāmāyana, Sugriva asks his followers to go to the cities and mountains in the islands of the sea in search of Sitā (Kiṣhkindhā-Kānda 40. 25). In another passage they are asked to go to the land of the Koṣakāras (i. e., the land where grows the worm which yeilds the thread of silken cloth, generally identified with China (Kiṣhkindhā 40. 23). A third passage refers to the Yavana Dwīpa and Subarṇa Dwīpa which are usually identified with the islands of Jāvā and Sumātrā [M. Reinaud in Journal

Asiatique tome IV. IVe serie p. 265]. While the fourth passage alludes to the Red Sea—

"ততো রক্তজলম্ ভীমং লোহিতং নাম সাগরম্।"

In the Ajodhyā-Kānda (84. 78) there is a passage which hints at preparations for a naval fight thus indicating a thorough knowledge and a universal use of the waterway. The passage in question runs thus—

"নাবাং শতানং পঞ্চানাং কৈবর্ত্তানাং শতম্ শতম্।
সন্নদ্ধানাং তথা যূনাস্তিষ্ঠন্ত্বিত্যভ্যচোদয়ৎ॥"

"Let hundreds of Kaibarta young men lie in wait in five hundred ships (to obstruct the enemy passages)."

The chief article of the trade with China hinted in Rāmāyana (Kiṣkindhā 40. 23) was silk. Mr. J. Yeats in his Growth and Vicissitudes of Commerce observes "The manufacture of silk among the Chinese claims a high antiquity, native authorities tracing it as a national industry for a period of 5000 years." This intercourse with China is corroborated by Professor La Couperie in his Western Origin of Chinese Civilisation which refers to the maritime intercourse of India with China as dating from about 680 B. C. when the sea-traders of the Indian Ocean founded a colony called Lang-ga (after the Indian name Lankā or Ceylon) about the present Gulf of Kiao-tchoa.

Professor Kieth says "A sea-borne commerce with Babylon cannot be proved for this epoch"

(Cambridge History of India, p. 140). But ample evidence is forthcoming which proves India's trade with Babylon in this period. Firstly, Dr. Wincler has pointed out that Shalmanesar IV of Assyria (727-722 B. C.) received presents from Bactria and India specially Bactrian camels and Indian elephants. Secondly, Mr. H. Rassam found a beam of Indian cedar in the palace of Nebuchad. rezzor III (C. 580 B. C.) at Birs Nimrud, part of which is now exhibited in the British Museum. Thirdly, the Bāveru Jātaka relates the adventures of certain Indian merchants who took peacocks by sea to Babylon. The Jātaka itself may go back to 400 B. C. but the folk-tale on which it is based must be much older. Professor Minayeff saw in the Bāveru Jātaka the oldest trace in India of Phœnico-Babylonian intercourse. Fourthly, certain Indian commodities were imported into Babylon even in the days of Solomon (900 B. C.) and they were known to the Greeks and others under their Indian names. Rice, for instance, had always been a principal article of export from India (*Vide* the Periplus of the Erythrean Sea) and it was a common article of food in the time of Sopphocles (Gr. Oryza = Tamil arisi = rice). Fifthly, Baudhāyana's condemnation of the Northern Aryans who took part in the sea-trade proves that they were not the chief agents though they had a considerable share in it. These evidences would justify the following conclusion of Mr. Kennedy "Maritime commerce between

India and Babylon flourished in the 7th and 6th but more specially in the 6th century B. C. It was chiefly in the hands of Dravidians, although Aryans had a share in it. And as Indian traders settled afterwards in Arabia and on the coast of Africa and as we find them settling at this very time on the coast of China, we cannot doubt that they had their settlements in Babylon also" (Article on Early commerce between India and Babylon in J. R. A. S. 1898). Mr. Keith, however observes "It is indeed probable enough that even before the time of Darius, Cyrus had relations with the tribes on the right bank of the Indus and Arrian (Indica I. 3. McCrindle p. 179) asserts that the Assakenoi and the Astakenoi were subject to Assyrian Kings" (Cambridge History of India). The Historians' History of the World says "The pictures on the black obelisk of Shalmanesar shows us such beasts as apes and elephants being brought as tribute to the conquerors or confirming in the most unequivocal way the belief based on Ktesias and Strabo that the Assyrians had commercial relations with India...The first article which we may confidently assert the Babylonians to have obtained at least in part from these countries were precious stones, the use of which in seal-rings was very general among them. Ktesias says expressly that these came from India and that onyxes, sardines and the other stones used for seals were obtained in the mountains bordering on the sandy desert............The passage of Ktesias to which we have just referred contains some indications which relatively to onyxes appear to refer to the Ghat Mountains, since he speaks of a hot country, not far from the sea. The circumstance of large quantities of Onyxes coming out of these mountains at the present day, *viz.*, the mountains near Cambay and Broach (the ancient Barygaza) must render this opinion so much the more probable as it was this very part of the Indian coast with which the ancients were most acquainted...............Also the Babylonians imported Indian dogs. The native country of these animals according to Ktesias was that whence the precious stones were obtained. And this account of the regions has been confirmed by Marco Polo who mentions that the large dogs of these regions were even able to overcome lions. A third and a no less certain class of productions which the Persians and the Babylonians obtained from this part of the world were dyes and amongst them the Cochineal or rather Indian lākṣhā. The most ancient though not quite accurate description of this insect is also found in Ktesias." (Vol. I. pp. 484—90). According to Lee Warner (Citizen of India). "The muslins of Dacca were famous in Roman and even Assyrian times."

The Rāmāyana mentions the fact that traders from other lands came to Ajodhyā (Ajodhyā LXVI) which was also inhabited by foreign traders (Bāla V). The traders were an important section of the population and we find them gracing the army of princes when Rāma went to the forest (Ajodhyā XXXVI).

That considerable haggling over prices was prevalent is shown by a passage in Śatapatha Brāhmana (III. 3. 3. 1—4) where the priest on behalf of a sacrificer went to buy Soma from a seller but the price is not settled until he asks the latter for the fifth time.

We have already seen that the Rig Veda speaks of Hiraṇyapinda and Nishka. The former was an un-stamped metallic bullion while the latter was a coin. A different kind of currency was known in this period called Śatamāna. Reference to it occurs in the Taittiriya Saṃhitā. If Satamāna was known when the Saṃhitās were composed, it stands to reason that it was known also when the Brāhmanas were written. Thus, it is referred to not only in the Taittiriya but also in the Śatapatha Brāhmana. In the Kānda dealing with the Rajasūya, we have a a section which treats of the Ratho-bimochanīya oblations. And in connection therewith, we are told that behind the right hind-wheel of the cart-stand, the King fastens two round Śatamānas which he has afterwards to give to the Brahmin priest as his fee for this ceremony (Śatapatha Brāh. V. 4. 3. 24 and 26). Again in another place, the same Brāhmana has the following "Three Śatamānas are the sacrificial fee for this (offering) he presents them to the Brahmin; for, the Brahmin neither performs (like the Adhvaryu) nor chants (like the

Udgātri) nor recites (like the Hotri) and yet he is an object of worship: therefore, he presents to the Brahmin three Śatamānas." (V. 5. 5. 16). Of course Sāyan in this and the preceding passage takes Śatamāna to denote a round plate but the case is not unlike that of Nāgoji-bhatta who commenting on a celebrated passage in the Mahābhāsya has explained the Mauryas as idol-manufactures. But just as no scholar would now explain Mauryas as idol-manufacturers but take them to denote Maurya princes only, so no one can explain the term Śatamāna in the way in which Sāyana has done. Śatamāna may, however, have been 100 Mānas or gunja-berries in weight as explained by Sāyana and accepted by Professor Eggeling but as it is spoken of as britta or round in shape in the first of the two instances just adduced, it must stand for coined money.

Another class of coins has been mentioned in the Śatapatha Brāhmana side by side with the Śatamāna. The first passage is "সুবর্ণং হিরণ্যং ভবতি রূপস্য এব আভরুদ্ধৈ শতমানম্ ভবতি শতায়ু´বৈ পুরুষঃ" (XII. 7.2.13). The second passage is "হিরণ্যং দক্ষিণা, সুবর্ণং শতমানং তস্য ওক্তম্ (XIII. 2.3.2.). It will be seen that here subarṇa is associated with Śatamāna and both are called হিরণ্য or gold. Subarṇa must like Śatamāna, therefore, denote a coin. Two passages of similar import are noticeable in the Taittiriya Brāhmāna (I. 7.62 and I. 2.7.7.). And it is interesting to note that the passage (Taitt. Brāh. I. 7.

6. 2.) occurs also in the Taitt. Saṃ. III. 2. 6. 3 and II. 3. 11. 5 which forms the Saṃhhitā text of the Black Yajur Veda, thus proving that Śātamāna was prevalent not only when the Brāhmanas were written but also in the early period when the Saṃhitās were composed.

Another class of coins called Pāda are mentioned in the concluding Kānda of the Śātapatha Brāhmana where we are told that king Janaka of Videha celebrated a sacrifice in which he bestowed huge largesses upon the Brahmins of the Kuru-Pānchāl country. A curiosity sprang up in his mind as to who was the best read of these Brahmins. He collected a 1000 kine and we are told that to every single horn of each cow were tied ten pādas and it was proclaimed that they should be taken away by him alone who is best cognisant with Brāhman. Now, what were these pādas? It has been suggested by Böhtlingh and Roth and accepted by Professor Rhys Davids (Ancient coins and Measures of Ceylon p. 3, n. 2) that the word pāda here denotes the fourth part of a certain gold weight and not a coin. Are we then to suppose that as the cows were 1000 in number, as each cow had two horns and as each horn carried ten pādas, King Janaka ordered 20,000 pieces of gold to be hammered out, each again weighing just $\frac{1}{4}$th of a certain weight—all this just on the spur of the moment, when the idea of testing the erudition of Brāhmins occurred to him? I am afraid, this idea is too rediculous for any scholar to entertain seriously in his mind. On the other hand, pāda is known to be the name of a coin and has been referred to in Pāṇini's sūtras (V. 1.34). and also in an inscription of the tenth century A. D. (Epigraphia Indica I. 173.23 and 178.11). Only if pāda is taken to stand for a coin, it is easy to understand that Janaka could at any moment get hold of 20,000 such coins from his treasury for being tied to the horns of the cows.

There is another class of coins referred to in the Taittiriya Brāhmana called Kṛishnāla where we are told of a gift of Krishnāla to each racer (I. 3. 6. 7). Kṛishnāla denotes the well-known raktikā or gunja-berry and what Kṛishnāla here means is a coin, possibly of gold weighing one gunja-berṛy. This receives confirmation from the fact that the Kaṭhaka Saṃhitā (XI. 4) makes mention of hiraṇya Kṛishnāla or gold Kṛishnāla. Kṛishnāla continued to be a coin as late as the time of Manu (VIII 215 and 330; IX. 84; XI. 137). Thus in Chapter VIII he ordains that "a hired servant or workman, who without being ill, out of pride fails to perform his work according to agreement, shall be fined eight Kṛishnālas."

The wealth of this period was in gold, silver, and jewels; in other metals like borax, tin, lead, iron, copper, etc., (White Yajur Veda, XVII. 13; Chh. Up. IV. 17. 7); in cars, horses, cows and slaves; in houses and fertile fields (Chh. Up. V. 13.

17 and 19; VII. 24; Śat. Brāh. III. 48; Taitt. Up. I. 5. 12. etc.). An idea of the immense wealth of the period can be gathered from the gifts bestowed by the kings on the Brahmins. We have already seen that Janaka besides ordinary gifts, bestowed 1000 cows with 20,000 pādas (gold coins) to the best read Brahmin. This story of the Sat. Brāh. is repeated in the Brihat. Up. III. 31. 1. and ff. Again, we hear of the liberality of a worshipper who gave 85,000 white horses, 10,000 elephants and 80,000 slave girls adorned with ornaments to the Brahmin who performed the sacrifice (Weber, Ind. Stud. X. p. 54. *See* also Śat. Brāh. II. 6. 3. 9; IV. 1. 11; IV. 3. 4. 6; Taitt. Brāh. III. 12. 5. 11-12).

The Age of Gautama Buddha.

(600 B. C.—321 B. C.)

The chief sources of our knowledge of the economic conditions prevailing in this period are the Jātakas or the Birth stories of Buddha and to a more limited extent the Vinaya and Suttapitakas. It is true that the evidence is drawn very largely from stories. But it is fairly clear that the folk in those tales have given them a parochial setting and local colour. And this is frequently borne out by the coincident testimony of other books not dealing with folk-lore. Of such books which furnish corroborative evidence, the Sūtras and the works of Greek writers like Scylax, Hecateus of Miletus and Herodotus are important. Whatever may be the age of their representative works in their present form, undoubtedly they had their roots in a period at least as early as the rise of Jainism and Buddhism. The purpose of the Sūtras, so called from the Sūtra which means a thread, is to afford a clue through the mazes of Brahminical learning contained in the Brāhmanas and the earliest of them represent a phase which is transitional between the language of the Brāhmanas and Classical Sanskrit as fixed by the grammarians.

The economy of India in this period was mainly rural, based on a system of village communities of peasant proprietors. The Jātakas do not bear testimony to the existence of isolated large estates or to feudal lords. When in the Jātaka legend the King of Videha abandons the world as an anchorite, he is described as renouncing both his capital, the City (Nagara) of Mithilā, seven Yojanas (in circumference) and his realm of 16,000 gāmas (Jāt. III. 365). It may sound incredible that a country owning such a wealth of villages should contain but one town and that so vast in extent as to suggest inclusion not only of parks but also of suburban gāmas (Jāt. IV. 330). There was not, however, any such hard and fast line between gāma and nigama (small town) to warrant the exclusion, in this description of some gāmas which may have amounted to nigamas. A similar vagueness holds between our town and village. A gāma might apparently mean anything from a group of two or three houses (Pali Dictionary s. *v.* by Childers) to an indefinite number. The number of inhabitants in the gāmas of Jātaka tales varied from 30 to 1000 families. Now, family (Kula), it must be remembered, included not only father and mother, children and grand-parents but also wives and children of the sons. Gāma, it is true, might be used to differentiate a class of settlement as in the compound "gāma-nigama" (villages and towns); but it is also used in the wider, looser sense of group as opposed to single house. For instance, when a Bhikkhu leaves park, forest or mountain to seek alms, he 'enters the gāma' (Vin. passim, e. g., Cull. V. Chap. V. 12; 29. c. f. Thīg. Ver. 304; Comm. p. 175) whether it be a neighbouring village or the suburbs of great Savatthi (Jāt. I. 106; Psalms of the Brethern p. 34, c. f. p. 24). [Cambridge History of India, Vol. I].

Instances of collective initiative reveals a relatively advanced sense of citizenship in the village. The villagers had a nominal head in the Bhojaka or headman who was paid by certain dues and fines (Jāt. I. 119). But all the village residents met to confer with him and carried the up-shot of their counsels into effect. In Jāt. I. 119 we find that Bodhisatta and the villagers went about the village with axes and clubs. With the clubs, they would roll out of the way stones that lay on the four highways and other roads of the village. The trees that would strike against the axles of chariots, they cut down; rough places they smoothed down; causeways they built; dug water tanks and built a hall but they wanted to put a pinnacle on it. They found it in the possession of a lady from whom they could not buy for want of money. But the lady gave it to them when they agreed to make her a partner in their work. A further glympse into the sturdy spirit of village life is afforded by the sentiment that for a peasant to leave the tillage and work for impoverished kings was a mark of social decay (Jāt I. 339).

Around the gāma which appears to have been classed as of the country (Janapada), of the border (paccanta) or as suburban, lay its Khetta or pastures and its woodland or uncleared jungle—primeval forests like the Andhavana of Kosala, the Sītavana of Magadha, the Pacīnavaṃsa-dāya of the Sākiya territory, retreats traditionally haunted by wild beasts and by gentler woodland spirits (Psalm of the Early Buddhists I. II passim; c. f. II. p. 151 n. 1). Different from these were such suburban groves as the Baṃboo grove belonging to the King of Magadha, the Anjanabana of Sākota and the Jetabana of Savatthi. Through those other unclean woodlands and moorlands where the folk went to gather their firewood and litter (Jāt. I. 317; V. 103) ran caravan routes.

Adjoining or merged into these wilder tracts were supplimentary grazing pastures (Jāt. I. 388) of herds of cattle (Jāt III. 149) and goats (Jāt III. 401)—herds belonging to King (Jāt I. 240; IV. 326) or commoners (Jāt I. 194, 388; c. f. Rig Veda X. 19). Commoners customarily entrusted their flocks to a communal neatherd as we find in the Pennine Alps to-day (le fromageur). We find him either penning his herds at night in the sheds (Jāt I. 388; III. 149) or more often bringing them back every evening and counting them out to the several owners (A. I. 205; M. Dhp. comm. I. 157).

The arable ground of the gāma lay without the clustered dwellings since these were apparently enclosed by a wall or stockade with gates (gāmadvāra) [Jāt. I. 239; II. 76, 135; III. 7; IV. 370], fences (Jāt I. 215), snares (Jāt. I. 143, 154); and field watchmen (Jāt. II 110; IV. 277) guarded the Khetta from intrusive birds and beasts while the internal boundaries of each householder's plot were apparently made by channels dug for co-operative irrigation (Dhp. ver. 80 = 145 = Therag. 19; Jāt. IV. 167; I. 336; V. 412). These dividing ditches, rectangular and curvilinear, were likened at least in the Magadha Khettas to a patchwork robe, prescribed by the Buddha as a pattern for the uniform of his order [Vin. Texts II. 207-9 (Mah. VIII. 12); c. f. Psalms of the Brethern p. 152] The limits of the whole Khetta might be extended by fresh clearing of forest land (Jāt II. 357; IV. 167). And whereas the majority of the holdings were probably small, manageable single-handed or with sons and perhaps a hired man (Jāt I. 277; III. 162; IV. 167), estates of 1000 karīsas (acres ?) and more occur in the Jātakas, farmed by Brahmins (Jāt. III. 293; IV. 276). In the Suttas again, the Brahmin Kāsibhāradwaja employed 500 ploughs and hired men (bhatikā) to guide plough and oxen (Jāt II. 165, 300). [Cambridge History of India, Vol. I].

Like the Jātakas, the Sūtras also depict the life of the country as mainly rural. Cities are not ignored but despised. Āpasthamba in his Dharma-Sūtra says "Let him avoid going into towns" (I. 32. 21). So says Baudhyāyana "It is impossible for one to obtain salvation who lives in a town covered with dust" (II. 3. 6, 33). Gautama says "one should not recite the holy text at any time in a town". Even in the description of a royal residence, the hall has a thatched roof. The Sūtras do not prescribe any ceremony for urban life. There is a rite for ploughing when sacrifice is made to aśanī (thunderbolt) and to Sītā (the furrow) as well as to Aradā, Anghā, Parjanya, Indra and Bhaga with similar offerings on the occasion of the furrow sacrifice, the threshing floor sacrifice, when one sows, reaps or takes in the harvest, all indicating that the life portrayed is that of the village agriculturist who ever offers a sacrifice at mole-heaps to Ākhurāja (the King of moles) [Gobila Grihya Sutras IV. 4. 28f; Ibid. 30f.]. So the constant injunctions to go out of the village to sacrifice at a place where the four roads meet or on a hill etc., imply life in the villages even for householders and scholars rather than life in the towns (Gobila III. 5. 32-35). And as a matter of fact, only twenty cities are named (Buddhist India pp. 34f.). Six of them only are reckoned by Thera Ānanda as sufficiently important cities (Mahā-nagara) to be the scene of Buddha's final passing away *viz.*, Sāvathi, Champā, Rājgaha, Sāketa, Kosambi and Benares. Kusinara where that event actually took place he depreciates as not a village but a jungle townlet. (Nagaraka) [D. II. 146]. The greatness of Pātaliputra was yet to come. Aristobulus when he was sent on a commission by Alexander to a region left desert by a shifting of the Indus to the east, saw the remains of over a thousand towns and villages, once full of men (Aristobulus, Frag. 29=Strobo XV. C. 693.). It is also interesting to note that eight towns belonged to the eight tribes of the Vrijjis *viz.*, Vaisāli, Kosaria, Janakapur, Novandgarh, Saran, Dwasbhanga, Purneah and Matihari.

In the monarchies, the king had a right to a tithe on raw produce collected as a yearly tax and only to this extent could be considered the ultimate owner of the soil. The tithe on produce was levied in kind, measured out either by the village-syndic or headman (gāma-bhojaka) or by an official (Mahāmatta) at the barndoors (Jat II. 378) or by survey of the crops (Jāt. IV. 169). The amount levied seems to have been $\frac{1}{6}$, $\frac{1}{8}$ or $\frac{1}{10}$th of the produce (Gautama X. 24.) according to the decision of the ruling power (Jāt. III. 9) or other circumstances. And the contributions raised at one or more gāmas rural or suburban could be made over by the king [or his chief queen (Jāt V. 44)] to any one he wished to endow *e.g.*, to a daughter on her marriage (Jāt. II. 237,403), a minister (Jāt. I. 354; VI. 261) a Brahmin (Jāt. III. 229; D. I. 87) and a merchant (Jāt VI. 344). Again the king could remit the tithe to any person (Jāt. IV. 169) or group (Jāt. I. 200).

We have no direct evidence of such a tithe being levied by any of the tribal republics such as the Sākiyas, Koliyas, Lichchhavis, Mallas etc. But that they did so raise the revenue in the case at least of the Sākiyas seems to be attested by Asoka's inscription on the Lumbini or Rummindeī Pillar (J. R. A. S. 1898. p. 546 f.). The tithe thus remitted on the occasion of Asoka's visit to the birthplace of the Buddha must have been imposed by the Sākiyas at a date prior to Maurya hegemony. We hear of the Mallas laying down a rule which imposed a fine of 500 (pieces) on any one who did not go to welcome the Blessed One when he drew near on his tour to their town [Vin. I. 247. (Mah. VI. 36)].

Moreover, the King might dispose of all forest-land (D. I. 87). All property left intestate or ownerless [S. I. 89 (Kindred sayings I. 115); Jāt. III. 302; c. f. IV. 485] reverted to the crown. The King was entitled to a tax paid by the nation when an heir was born to him (milk-money) [Jāt. IV. 323]. He could declare a general indemnity for prisoners on any festal occasion (Jāt. IV. 176; V. 285; VI. 327). Besides these privileges he could impose forced labour (Rājakāriya) on the people but this may have been limited to the confines of his estates. Thus, the peasant-proprietors enclose a deer-reserve for their King that they might not be summoned to leave their tillage to beat up game for him (At Benares Jāt. I. 149; the Arjuna wood at Sāketa Jāt. III. 270). Gautama in his Dharmasūtra says that the King was to force artisans to pay one day's work monthly, to proclaim by crier lost property and if the owner be not found in a year, to keep it, giving $\frac{1}{4}$th to the finder, (but all teasure-trove belongs to the King), to protect the property of infants. An exception in case of the treasure-trove is made when a priest is the finder and some say that any body who finds it gets $\frac{1}{6}$th. In the rules for taxes, if the stock is cattle or gold, the tax according to some is $\frac{1}{50}$th and if it is merchandise $\frac{1}{20}$th, while $\frac{1}{10}$th is the tax on roots, fruits, flowers, herbs, honey, meat, grass and firewood. (Gautama X. 25 f.) In the following section, the author says that the King is the master of all except the priests, that he is to be worshipped by all except the Brahmins who shall honour him (Gautama XI.

1. f.). A learned priest and women are not taxed nor are children before puberty, temporary students or ascetics or slaves who wash feet or blind, dumb, deaf and diseased persons. Vasistha (XIX. 1—24) enjoins the King to exempt from taxation a learned priest, a servant, those without protectors, ascetics, infants, very old men, students, widows who have returned to their families, unmarried girls, wives of servants and প্রদত্তা (probably girls whose marriages have been proposed).

Land at least in the kingdom of Magadha' might be given away and in that of Kosala be sold. In the former case, a Brahmin landowner offers a 1000 Karīsas of his estate as a gift (Jāt. IV. 281); in the latter, a merchant entangles an unwilling noble in the sale of a park (Vin. II. 158 f.; Cull. V. Chap. VI. 4, 9. f.). And in the law books we read that land might be let against a certain share of the produce. [Āpasthamba II. 11, 28(1); I. 6, 18 (20).] Unenclosed land was used by all for grazing cattle, obtaining fire-wood, gathering flowers and getting fruits (Gautama XII. 28). Agrarian laws were strict, yet good and reasonable (Gautama XII. 14-17). The holdings too in the arable land called the Khetta of each village would be subject to redistribution and redivision among a family as one generation succeeded another. It is not clear whether any member of a Village Community could give or sell any of the Khetta to an outsider. It is just possible that the old tradition expressed in the

Brāhmanas when a piece of land was given as a sacrificial fee—"And the earth said: Let no mortal give me away" (Śatapatha Brāhmana XIII. 7, 15) may have survived in the villages as a communal *anti*-alienating feeling concerning any disintegration of the basis of their socio-economic unity.

In proving property, documents, witnesses and possession are admitted as proof of title by the late Sūtra of Vasistha (XVI. 19) and if the documents conflict, the statements made by old men and by guilds and corporations are to be relied upon. (Vas. XVI. 15). Vasistha gives some good provisions on the right of way and evidence in disputes regarding immovable property (XVI. 10-15). Gautama (XII. 37-39) and Vasistha (XVII, 16-18) give the law of acquiring property by usage: The following eight things used by another for ten years continuously, are lost to the owner:—ancestral property, a purchased article, a pledged property given to a wife by her husband's family, a gift property received for performing a sacrifice, the property of re-united co-partners and wages. A pledge, a boundary, property of minors, an open deposit, a sealed deposit, female slaves, the property of a King and the wealth of a Śrotriya are not lost by being enjoyed by others. Animals and females also are not so lost to the owner. Property entirely given up by its owner goes to the King who is also enjoined to administer the property of widows and minors (Vasistha XIV. 8—9).

The rules of inheritance supplied by the Sūtras make Sapiṇdas the heirs after or in default of sons. The Sapiṇda here is one within six degrees and is a male only. The widow is excluded and the daughter according to Āpasthamba inherits only in default of sons, teacher or pupil (II. 6. 14. 4). These, however, are recommended to employ the inheritance for the spiritual good of the deceased. The nuptial presents and ornaments of a wife were inherited by the daughters (Baudhyāyana II. 2. 3. 4; Vasistha XVII. 46). Probably, the general rule anticipates not the death of the owner but a division of property among the sons during his life-time. The King inherits in default of the others named and some say that among the sons, only the eldest inherits. These rules are sufficiently vague but local laws are also provided for in the additional rule: "In some countries gold or black cattle or black produce of the earth (grain or iron ?) is the share of the eldest" (Āpas. II. 14, 7). Then in regard to what the wife receives, the Sūtra leaves it doubtful whether the rule "the share of the wife consists of her ornaments and wealth received from her relations according to some (authorities)" is to be interpretted in such a manner that 'according to some' refers only to the last clause or to the whole. "What is obvious" says Mrs. Rhys Davids "is that the whole matter of inheritance was not yet regulated by any general State-law. Different districts of

India have different laws of inheritance. Baudhāyana treats the subject of inheritance first under the head of impurity where he says that Sapiṇdas inherit in default of nearer relations and Sakulyas (remoter relations) in default of Sapiṇdas; but afterwards he adds that the eldest son in accordance with the quotations cited by Āpasthamba may receive the best chattel or the father may divide equally between the sons. Here also the fact that the same subject is treated in different sections shows that as yet the matter of civil law was not treated systematically but incidentally" (Cambridge History of India, Vol. I).

Nevertheless we can partially reconstruct the law of inheritance as it prevailed in those days. According to Baudhyāyana, of the 14 kinds of sons, Aurasa (legitimate), Putrikāpūtra (son of an appointed daughter), Kshetraja (bastard), Datta (adopted), Kritrima (made), Guḍhaja (secretly born) and the Apabiddha (abandoned by the parents) were entitled to inheritance. The next six, Kanina (son of an unmarried daughter), Punarbhava (son of a remarried female), Swayamdatta (self-given son) and Nishāda (son of a twice-born father in a Śūdra mother) were regarded as members of the family. The last Parāśara was not even regarded as a member of the family. Gautama names 12 kinds of sons of whom the Aurasha, the Kshetraja, Datta, Kritrima, Guḍhaja, Apabiddha can inherit, while Kaṇina, Sahoda (son of a pregnant bride), Punarbhava, Putrikāpūtra, Swayamdatta and Krīta (purchased) cannot inherit, though they are maintained as members of the family. Vasistha regards Aurasha, Kshetraja, Putrikāpūtra, Punarbhava, Kanina and Gudhaja as heirs while Sahoda, Datta, Krīta, Swayamdatta, Apabiddha and Nishāda cannot inherit except when there are no legitimate heirs of the first six classes above mentioned (XVII). Āpasthamba who flourished a few centuries later recognised the Aurasa sons alone as the legitimate heir, for, the recognition of other sons as heirs could not be allowed among sinful men of his age (II. 6. 13; II. 10. 27). Yet the ancient customs did not die out soon.

Gautama, the earliest lawgiver of this age, seems to have favoured partition of an estate, for "in partition there is an increase of spiritual merit" (XXVIII. 4.). According to him, the eldest son should get, as an additional share, a 20th part of the estate, some animals and a carriage; the middlemost son shall get sheep, grain, utensils, a house, a cart and some animals and then the remaining property is equally divided. Or, Gautama also allows the eldest son two shares and the remaining sons one share each. Or, they may take one kind of property by choice according to seniority; or the special shares may be adjusted according to their mothers (XXVIII. 5—17). Vasistha allows the eldest son to have a double share and a little of kine and horses; the middlemost gets utensils and furniture, the youngest takes the goats, sheep and house (XVIII. 42f.). Baudhāyana allows all the children to take equal shares or the eldest son to take one-third in excess. (II. 2. 3. 2 f.).

The property of un-reunited brothers, dying without issue goes to the eldest brother; the property of a reunited co-parcener goes to the co-parcener; what a learned co-parcener has acquired by his own labour may be withheld from his unlearned co-parceners and unlearned co-parceners should divide their acquisitions equally (Gau. XXVIII. 27. 31.).

A Brahmin's son by a Kshatriya wife, if the eldest, shares equally with a younger brother by a Brahmin wife. The sons of a Kshatriya by a Vaisya wife share equally. The sons by a Śūdra wife, if virtuous, is maintained, while even the son of a wife of equal caste does not inherit, if he be living unrighteously (Gau. XXVIII. 35—40). According to Baudhāyana (II. 2. 3. 2—10) the sons of wives of different castes will take four, three, two and one shares according to the order of castes. According to Vasistha (XVIII. 42—50) if a Brahmin has sons by Brahmin, Kshatriya and Vaisya wives, the first gets three shares, the second two and the third one share.

Āpasthamba, however, protests against such unequal division of property and declares that all the virtuous sons should inherit but he who spends money unrighteously shall be disinherited, though he be the eldest son (II. 6. 14. I—15).

Ordinarily, the heirs shall pay the debts of a deceased person. But the money due by a surety, a commercial debt, a fee due to the parents of a bride, immoral debts and fines shall not devolve upon the sons of a debtor (Gau. XII. 40-41).

Coming to the agriculture of the period, we find that according to Greek authorities there were two annual harvests, the winter and the summer one, the sign of an astonishing fertility (Strabo XV. C. 693 = Meg. Frag. 9). They knew that rice and millet were sown in the summer, wheat and barley in the winter (Strabo XV. C. 690) and Aristobulous described the cultivation of rice in enclosed sheets of water (Aristobulous Frag. 29 = Strabo XV. C. 692). Rice was the staple article of food (Jāt. I. 340; II. 43, 135, 378; III. 383; IV. 276), besides which seven other kinds of grain are mentioned (M. I. 57). Barley is also mentioned in Jāt. II. 110. Sugarcane was also cultivated [(Jāt. 1. 339; Vin. (Mah. VI. 35. 6)]. The Greek writers also speak of the sugar-cane, the reeds that make honey without the agency of bees (Nearchos Frag. 8 = Strabo XV. C. 694). Megasthenes seems to have attempted a scientific explanation of its sweet juice. It was due to the water which it absorbed from the soil being so warmed by the sun's heat, that the plant was virtually cooked as it grew (Meg. Frag. 9 = Strabo XV. C. 693).

The cultivation of lands by a whole kinship working in association was noted by Nearchos. Each individual at the in-gathering took as much as was calculated to support him for a year and the remainder of the common stock was destroyed, so as not to encourage idleness (Nearchos Frag. 7 = Strabo XV. C. 716).

The Greeks also saw trees which the generative power of the soil endowed with a strange capacity for self-propagation—the branches curving to the ground to become themselves new trunks, till a single tree became a pillared tent, under whose roof of broad leaves a troop of horsemen could find shade from the noonday heat (Strabo XV. C. 694; Arrian Ind. 11; Pliny XII. Arts. 22 f.). Among the plants, the most important was the cotton plant, yielding vegetable wool "surpassing in beauty and quality the wool of sheep and the Indians wear clothing from these trees" (Mccrindle's Ancient India, III. 106). Some of it, the Macedonians used uncarded as stuffing for saddles and suchlike (Nearchos Frag. 8 = Strabo XV. C. 693). Precious spices were also associated in the Greek mind with India.

Horticulture was in a high state of efficiency. We find frequent mention of parks in the Jātakas where plants and trees were planted. Ælian describes such a park in Pātaliputra :—"There were shady groves and trees set in clumps and branches woven together by some special cunning of horticulture. And the more impressive thing about the beauty of that climate is that trees themselves are of the sort that are always green; they never grow old and never shed their leaves. Some of them are native and some are brought from other lands with great care and these adorned the place and gave it glory – only not the olive; the olive does not grow of itself in India and if it is transported there, it dies... ......there are lovely tanks made by hand of men with fishes in them very large and gentle and nobody may catch them except the sons of the King when they are yet children!" (Ælian, Natural Animals, XIII. 18).

As to the minerals, India was the land of gems and gold. In Pliny's Natural History which deals with precious stones (Bk. XXXVII) a great many are said to be products of India. Among those enumerated, the diamonds (Arts. 55 f.), opals (Arts. 80 f.), and agate (Art. 140) are important. The ultimate source of information would here, of course, be not a literary one but the practical knowledge of merchants. As to gold, Nearchos and Megasthenes confirmed the account given by Herodotus (III. 102f.) of the ants as big as foxes which dug up gold. The facts on which the account was based seem now clear. Gold dust was actually brought as tribute by the tribes of Dardesthan in Kashmere and was called by the Indians pipilika (ant-gold) [Mahābhārat 1860, Cal. edition mentions the gold-digging ants]. When Herodotus says that the ants were of the size of dogs and fiercely attacked any one carrying off the gold, it has been plausively suggested that the account was derived from people who had been chased by the formidable dogs kept by the native miners (McCrindle, Ancient India, p. 44. note 2.). Megasthenes had added the useful information that the country from which gold came was the country of the Derdae (in Sans. Darad or dārada; modern Dardisthan in Kashmere) [Meg. frag. 29 = Strabo XV. C. 706]. Megasthenes says "stones are dug up of the colour of frankincense, more sweet than figs or honey" (Frag. 10 = Strabo XV. C. 703). This is probably sugarcandy which he took to be a kind of crystal.

The wildest statements of Ctesias about the Fauna aud Flora of India have been made to bear a short of resemblance to something real by Professor H. H. Wilson in his Notes on the India of Ctesias (Oxford, 1836), but it seems ingenuity wasted to attempt to establish these connections. The climate of the country, the new laws of weather no doubt struck the Greeks. They had never known anything like the rains which broke upon them in the summer of 326 B.C. Aristobulous (Frag. 29. = Strabo XV. C. 691 Cf. C. 697) recorded that rains began when the European army reached Taxila in the spring of 326 and became continuous with the prevalence of monsoou, all the time they were marching eastword along the foothills of the Himalayas. The rainfall in Sind is scanty and irregular. When the Greeks looked round upon the features of the country itself, India seemed, before anything else, to be the land of rivers (Strabo XV. C. 689). Megasthenes mentions 58 rivers of which 35 names are preserved and are still recognisable to-day. (Frag. 18 = Arrian Indica, 4; Pliny Nat. Hist. VI. Art. 64f.).

Despite this abundant supply of water, rainfall and the fertility of the soil which ensured two harvests in the year, famines were not unknown. The famines were due to draught or to floods and extended even over a whole kingdom (Vin. I. 211, 213ff; Vin. Texts III. 220. n. 1; Jāt. I. 329; II. 135, 149, 367; V. 193; VI. 487). This contradicts the assertion of Megasthenes that famines were unknown in India (McCrindle, Ancient India as described by Megasthenes, 32), unless of course, Megasthenes meant a very general and protracted famine. The times of scarcity in Buddhist records probably refer only to brief periods over restricted areas.

As to industries, it is curious that these European observers should call the Indians backward in the scientific development of the resources of their country. They had, for instance, good mines of gold and silver, yet "the Indians inexperiencod in the arts of mining and smelting do not even know their own resources but set about the business in too primitive a way." (Strabo XV. C. 700). "They do not pursue accurate knowledge in any line except that of medicine; in the case of some arts it is even accounted vicious to carry their study far, the art of war, for instance" (Strabo XV. C. 701). They also used only cast bronze but not hammered, so that their vessels broke like earthernware, if they fell (Strabo XV. C. 716 = Nearchos Frag. 7). On the other hand, Nearchos spoke of the cleverness of the Indian craftsmen. They saw sponges used for the first time by the Macedonians and immediately manufactured imitations of them with fine thread and wool, dying them to look the same (Nearchos quoted by Strabo XV. 67). Other Greek articles such as the scrapers and oilflasks used by athletes they quickly learnt to make. For writing letters, they used some species of fine tissue closely woven. In describing the dress of the people of the Indus region Nearchos tells us that they wore clothes of cotton "and this linen from the trees is of a more shining white than any other linen......... They have a tunic of tree-linen down to the middle of their skins and two other pieces of stuff, one thrown about their shoulders and one twisted round their heads. And the Indians wear earrings of ivory, those that are very well off...........also they dye their beards in different colours, some so as to make them appear as white as white may be and some dying them blue-black; others make them crimson and others purple and others green. In the summer they protect themselves with umbrellas...... ......they wore shoes of white leather very elaborately worked and the soles of the shoes are variegated and high-heeled so as to make the wearer seem taller" (Nearchos Frags. 9 and 10=Arrian Ind. 16). Nearchos described the foot soldiers as carrying a bow as long as the body and using arrows six feet long. In their left hands, they carried long narrow shields of raw hide, nearly co-extensive with the body. Some had javelins instead of bows. All carried long two-handed swords with a broad blade. The horsemen had two javelins and a shield smaller than that of the foot soldier (Nearchos Frag. 7= Arr. Ind. 16; Strabo XV. C. 716). Herodotus also describes the Indian army in the service of the Persian king Xerxes as wearing garments made from trees (cotton) and carrying bows of reeds and arrows of reeds with iron heads (VII. 65). In fact, the metal industries were highly specialised. The word Kammāra was as comprehensive as our "Smith." Vaḍḍhaki again apparently covered all kinds of woodcraft including ship-building, cart-making (Jāt. IV. 207) architecture (Jāt. 1. 201; IV. 323); thapatitacchaka (lit. planner) and bhamakāra (or turner) being occupied with special modes of woodwork. (Dhp. verse 80). A settlement of Vaḍḍhakis is able to make both furniture and sea-going ships (Jāt. IV. 159). A worker in stone (pāsaṇakottaka) builds houses with the ruined materials of a former gāma and also hollows a cavity in a crystal as a cage for a mouse (Jāt. I. 479.) Other important crafts were ivory-work, tanning, weaving, confectionery, pottery, garland-making, head-dressing and jewellery. The Dharmapada describes the great 'creeper-parure' made by 500 goldsmiths in four months and worn by the daughter of a King's treasurer thus—"when this parure was on, it extended from head to foot..........a part of this parure consisted of a peacock and there were 500 feathers of red gold on the right side and 500 on the left. The beak was coral, the eyes were of jewels and likewise the neck and the tail feathers. The mid-ribs of the feathers were of silver and likewise the shanks of the legs." Vasistha in his Dharmasūtra III. 49-63) speaks of objects of gold, silver and copper, of stones and gems and conch-shells, pearls and of things made of bone, wood, leather, cloth etc. Gobhila's Grihya Sūtra treats of dress, kanthā (now rags, formerly meant a kind of quilt) [Pāṇini II. 4. 20 ; IV. 2. 142-43]. Carpet was in use (Pāṇini IV. 2. 12). Patamaṇdapas (tents), Kānda-patas (ladies' tents) and Bitāna were in use. Nearchos ascribes to Indians the art of manufacturing paper from cotton. Strabo XV. 67 states that the Indians wrote on smooth cloth very cleverly woven and hard pressed. Curtius VIII. 9 says that the Indians at the time of Alexander used the tender sides of barks for writing.

Pearl-fishery was carried on in an extensive scale in the south. It was chiefly as the country from which pearls came that the Greeks knew Southern India. Pearls came from the coasts of the Pāndya Kingdom (corresponding roughly to the modern districts of Mādura and Tinnevelly) and Megasthenes also connected the pearl with Pandæa, the daughter of Heracles (Kṛishna) who had become queen of a great Kingdom in the south. Some confused knowledge of how pearls were procured, had come to the Greek writers through traders' stories. They knew that they grew in oysters. Androsthenes of Thasos who had gone in the fleet with Nearchos and the chief usher chares refer to some varieties of pearls and the chief fisheries (Athanaeus (III. 93 A—D). The oysters, Megasthenes understood, were caught in nets; they went in shoals each shoal with a King of its own, like swarms of bees and to capture the King was to capture the shoal. The oysters when caught were put in jars and as their flesh rotted, the pearl was left disengaged at the bottom (Megasthenes Frag. 23 = Arrian Ind. 8; Pliny, Natural History IX. Art. 111).

Painting was well known and the painters were organised in a guild (Jāt. VI. 427). A picture gallery (Chittāgāra) belonging to King Pasenadi of Kosala is mentioned. The Bharut sculptures imply the existence at least of a contemporary school of painting.

Town-planning and Architecture were known. In the Māhabaṃsa we are told that a King of Kandy "raised for himself a monument of glory by building a wall enclosing the great Bo-tree, the Chaitya and the Nāth Devāli that stood in the middle of the city—a wall of stone thick, high, shining with plaster-work, like unto a beautiful string of pearls adorning the neck of the city that was like a fair woman." The Buddist Jātaka stories tell us that the rich in those days lived in seven-storied buildings. Śuddhakarma (white-wash), lepa (plaster and cement), gotambuja [lit. round lotus (cupola) corrupted into modern Gambooj], mangaleṣhtaka (foundation stone) etc. were well-known. Temple of the gods is mentioned in Pāṇini V. 3. 96-100. The Mānava Grihya Sūtra says "Let a daughter be married in a temple" [I. 7. 10; c. f. (Sānkhayana Grihya Sūtra, IV. 12. 15.)]. The Baithak of Jarāsandha and the walls of Rājgriha the ruins of which are still extant were built before the 5th century B. C. (General Cunningham). Many of the Buddhist caves like those of Khandagiri and Udayagiri in Orissa were anterior to the time of Alexander (326 B. C.). Again in 1898 a stupa was discovered on the Nepal frontier at Piprawah about which the Imperial Gazetteer of India (New ed. Vol. II. p. 102) rightly observes "The construction and contents of the Stupa offer valuable testimony concerning the state of civilisation in N. India about 450 B. C. which is quite in accordance with that elicited from early literary sources".

Some of these handicrafts were organised into guilds and the Mūgapakkha Jātaka mentions eighteen guilds (Jāt IV. 411) but it is to be regretted that only four of these eighteen crafts thus organised are specifically mentioned viz., the wood-workers, the smiths, the leather-dressers and the painters. Nevertheless Dr. R. C. Mazumdar has found out the following guilds of artisans on the evidences of the Jātakas and the law-books of this period :—(1) workers in wood including ship-builders (Jāt VI 427) (2) workers in metal including gold and silver (Ibid) (3) garlandmaker and flower sellers (Jāt. No. 415) (4) Painters (Jāt. VI. 427) (5) caravan traders (Jāt. II. 295) (6) money-lenders (Gautama XI. 21) (7) cultivators (Ibid) (8) Traders (Ibid) (9) Herdsmen (Ibid). Jātāka II. 18 mentions the division in one of the large centres of woodcraft of the population of 1000 families into two equal groups each under a Jettaka. Similarly, the groups of mariners (Jāt. IV. 137), garland-makers (Jāt. III. 405), caravan traders (Jāt. I. 368 ; II. 295), the moss-troopers numbering 500 of a little robber village in the hills *e. g.*, near Uttar Pānchāla (Jāt. I. 296, 297 ; II. 388 ; IV. 330) and the forest police who escorted the travellers (Jāt. II. 335) were all organised under a Jettaka. These craft-guilds had three characterities (1) an Alderman at the head (2) heredity of profession and (3) localisation of industry. The position of the foreman of the guild is indicated in Jāt. II. 12. 52 and III. 281 where he is an important minister in attendance upon the King. These heads of guilds were called Pamukka (President) and also Jettaka (elder, alderman) the distinction between these two words being not apparent. Similarly the elder of a village of 1000 smiths in whom were combined the functions of the headman of the village, the village syndic and the president of the local guild is described as a favourite of the King of Benares, rich and of great substance (Jāt III. No. 387). There is one instance of all the guilds having a common chief who was also lord of the treasury of the kingdom of Kāśī. The centralisation in this case was perhaps due to quarrels between the foremen of the subordinate guilds such as those at Sāvathi mentioned in Jāt. II. 12. 52.

There seems to have been also a considerable localisation of crafts. Suburban villages grew up to serve the cities where certain crafts were exclusively localised *e. g.*, smith villages of 1000 families (Jāt. III. 281-6), villages of wood-wrights numbering 500 (Jāt. II. 18. 405; IV. 208), villages of potters (Jāt. III. 376, 508). On the Ganges or further afield there were trapper-gāmas supplying skins, ivory etc. [Jāt. VI. 71, nishādgāma; c. f. (III. 49.); Therig. (comm.) 220, migaluddakagāma.] There were also crafts localised in special quarters of the cities *e. g.*, ivory-workers' bazar in the city of Benares (Jāt. I. 320; II. 197), the localities of dyers, perfurmers and florists (Jāt. IV. 81. 82); the cook's quarters in Sravathi (Jāt. III. 48), the weavers' place (Jāt I. 356). Sometimes, the crafts were associated with special street named after them in the cities *e. g.*, the washerman's street (Jāt. IV. 8), the Vaisya street and quarter (Jāt. VI. 485).

Combined with this widespread corporate regulation of industrial life, there was a very general but by no means cast iron custom for the son to follow the calling of his father. Not only individua. but families are frequently mentioned in terms of their traditional calling. The smith *e. g.*, is Smithson; Sāti the fisherman's son is Sāti the fisherman; Chunda the Smith is called Chunda the Smithson etc. (M. I. 256; D. II. 127f.; Jāt. I. 98, 194, 312; II. 79. c. f. nesādo = Luddoputto = luddo; Jāt III. 330 f.; V. 356-8.). Āpastamba (II. 2-3; 10-11) says "In successive births men of the lower castes are born in the next higher ones, if they have fulfilled their duties." Gautama (XI. 29) says "Men of the several castes and orders who always live according to their duty enjoy after death the rewards of their works." Āpasthamba (II. 11. 11) says "In successive births men of the higher castes are born in the next lower ones, if they neglect their duties." Āpasthamba (II. 10. 12-16) enjoins the king to punish those who have transgressed the caste-laws (c. f. also Āpasthamba II. 27. 18). Gautama XI. 31 authorises the king to punish such transgressors of caste laws.

The functions of these guilds were legislative, judicial and executive. The Vinaya Pitaka enjoins that a thief should not be ordained as a nun without the sanction of the guilds—"ৱাজানম্ বা সঙ্ঘম্ বা গণম্ বা পূগম্ বা শ্রেণিম্ বা অনপলোকেতব্যা।" From Vinaya Pitaka IV. 226 we learn that the guilds had the function of arbitrators to settle differences between members and their wives. And Gautama XI. 21 lays down that they had legislative functions.

The learner or apprentice (antebāsika, lit. the boarder) appears frequently in Buddhist book one of which indicates the relative position of pupil and master woodwright (Jāt. 1. 251; V. 290 f; Attha Sālinī p. 111). Mahābhāgga I. 32. 1. says "The ācharya, O Bhikkhus ought to consider the antebāsika as a son; the antebāsika ought to consider the ācharya as a father. Thus these two, united by mutual reverence, confidence and communion of life will progress, advance and reach a high stage in the doctrine and discipline." "I prescribe, O Bhikkhus, that you live (the first) ten years in dependence upon an Ācharya." The Vinaya also gives elaborate rules regarding the duties of Saddhi-vihārika (pupil) towards his Upajjāya (teacher) and *vice versa* and also rules regulating the relation between teacher and pupil and the conditions determining its admissibility or cessation. But these rules relate to the education in the sacred lore, religion and humanities and not to the training in the crafts with which we are concerned. The apprentice in the industrial sense indeed appears frequently in the Jātakas but no conditions of pupilage are given. Thus in Jātaka

No. 97 we have a publican and his apprentice while in Kusha Jātaka (No. 531) a prince apprentices himself to a potter, basket-maker, florist, etc., in succession. In Jāt. V. 457-9, two princes receive instruction in arts at the hands of the same teacher who had besides 101 pupils. The senior pupil also acts as Assistant Master (piṭṭhiāchariya). The position of a senior pupil to a Mahā-Vaḍḍhaki is indicated by Buddhaghosa (Asl. 111, 112). We have also instances of fees being paid by apprentices to teachers (Jāt. IV. 224, 225; 38, 39) where two merchant-sons paid 2000 pieces each. But the conditions of pupilage, though not given in the Buddhist books, are roughly given in the Sanskrit books of the period. Thus, Gautama II. 43-44 says "The apprentice may forsake his master either of his own motion (in which case he is liable to correction) or under instructions from his kinsmen who consented to his pupilage. In the latter case, the deserted master can sue the pupil's guardians for a breach of contract (Colebrooke's Digest of Hindu Law, Vol. II. p. 8). But a contract can never be one-sided. Hence Kātyāyana [who according to Macdonell (History of Sanskrit Literature, p. 431) flourished in the 3rd Century, B. C.] fixed a penalty upon the master for employing the apprentice in other work. "He who does not instruct the scholar in the art and causes him to perform other work shall incur the first amercement; and the pupil may forsake him and go to another teacher, released from the indenture (Colebrooke's Digest of Hindu Law, Vol. II. p. 7).

Another interesting fact to be noticed is that though normally the crafts were organised on a hereditary basis and technical talent descended from father to son and was confined to a particular family yet the way was still open to exceptions to that rule. Spiritual ministrations were the work of Brahmins and administration that of Brahmins and Kshatriyas though some share of it was being appropriated by the Vaisyas [as in the case of the office of the King's treasurer (Jāt. IV. 43) with which was coupled the judgeship of the merchant-guilds.]. But these distinctions did not hold good in the economic sphere where all castes seemed to have stood together. The choice of occupations was quite free. Thus in Vinaya I. 77 and IV. 128 we find parents discussing the best profession which their son might choose without a reference being made to the fathers' trades. In Chullyvāgga V. 28, the Viskkhus are allowed the use of a loom and of shuttles, strings, tickets and all the apparatus belonging to a loom. We also read of Brahmins as physicians (IV. 361) goatherds (III. 461), merchants, hunters, snake-charmers (IV. 357), archer and the servant of an archer who was formerly a weaver (III. 219; V. 127 and 128; I. 356, 357), low caste trappers (II. 200; VI. 170) and even cartwrights (IV. 207, 208). In Jāt V. 290-3 Kusā, a king's son in his infatuation for Pabhāvatī apprentices himself incognito in succession to the court-potter, basket-maker, florist and cook to his father-in-law, without a word being said as to his social degradation when these vagaries became known. In Jāt. IV. 84 a prince takes to trade while in IV. 169 another resigning his kingdom goes to the frontier where he dwells "with a rich merchant's family, working with his own hands." The Kusa Jātaka (No. 531) mentions a prince who only consents to marry when a princess is found exactly like a golden image which he himself had fashioned and which was far superior to that made by the chief smith employed for the purpose. Instances of other royal craftsmen are furnished by the Mahābaṃsa XXX and XXXIV.) A king is described as a skilful carver and painter who wrought a beautiful image of the Bodhisattva and also a state-room with beautiful work in ivory made for it and who himself taught the arts to his subjects. In Jāt. II. 87 we hear of a monarch as an archer. We also hear of a child of Vaccha Brahmins as the sand-playmate of tha little Siddhārtha afterwards the Buddha (Psalm of the Brethern, 17). Jāt. IV. 15 f. speaks of a Brahmin who takes to trade to be better able to afford charitable gifts. Brahmins engaged personally in trading without such pretext are also mentioned (Jāt. V. 22, 471). Again, we hear of a deer-trapper becoming the protege and then the inseparable friend of a rich young Setthi without a hint of social barriers (Jāt. III. 49ff); a weaver looking on his handicraft as a mere makeshift and changing it offhand for that of an archer (Jāt. II. 87); a pious farmer and his son with equally little ado turning to the low trade of rush-weaving (Jāt. IV. 318); a young man of good family, but penniless, starting on his career by selling a dead mouse for cat's meat at a farthing, turning his capital and hands to every variety of job and finally buying up a ship's cargo with his signet-ring pledged as security and winning both a profit of 200 per cent and the hand of a Setthi's daughter (Jāt. I. 120ff). "This freedom of initiative and mobility in trade and labour finds further exemplification in the enterprise of a settlement of wood-workers (Jāt. IV. 159). Failing to carry out the orders for which pre-payment had been made, they were summoned to fulfil the contract. But they instead of 'abiding in their lot' as General Walker the Economist said of their descendants "with oriental stoicism and fatalism" (The Wages Question, p. 171) made a mighty ship secretly and emigrated with their families, slipping down the Ganges by night and so out to sea till they reached a fertile island. Stories all of these, not history; nevertheless, they serve to show that in these times the division of caste was not quite rigid and was no bar to the mobility of labour, both vertical and horizontal" (Cambridge History of India, Vol. I.). Social divisions and economic occupations were very far from coinciding. Moreover, the fact that Brahmins claimed credit if born of Brahmins on both sides for generations back (D. I. 93; M. II. 156; Theragāthā VV. 889, 1170) betrays the existence of many born from a less pure connubium. In the Kusa Jātaka a Brahmin takes to wife the childless cheif wife of a king without losing caste thereby (Jāt. V. 280). Elsewhere in the Jātakas, princes, brahmins, setthis and even low castes are shown forming friendships, sending their sons to the same teachers and even eating together and intermarrying without any social stigma. (Jāt. II. 319f.; III. 9-11; VI. 422, 348; Jāt. I. 421, 422). Even in Āpasthamba Sūtra (II. 5-10) we find that a Śūdra can become a Brahmin and a Brahmin can become a Śūdra according to their good or bad deeds. Pāṇini mentions a celebrated grammarian Chakravarman (VI. 1. 130) who was a Kshatriya by birth. All these evidences go to show that the dignity of labour was recognised, though there were certain notable exceptions. Thus, there were recognised certain low tribes and castes and low trades and crafts. As instances of low castes are mentioned the Nisādas (hunters or trappers), the Chandālas who are called the lowest race that go upon two feet, meanest men on earth (Jāt. IV. 397), contact with whom was pollution (Jāt. II. 83; III. 233; IV. 376) who lived apart in their own settlements (Jāt. IV. 200) by hunting and were sometimes employed for street sweeping (Jāt. IV. 390) and policing towns by night (Jāt. III. 30) and the Pikkusas (son of a niṣād by a Śūdra female) whose occupation is said to be that of throwing away dead flowers (Jāt. IV. 205). As examples of low crafts are mentioned those of the worker in bamboo, wheel-wrights, rathakāras, basket-makers, potters, weavers, leather-workers and barbers—all called hīna sippa in the list given in the Suttavibhanga (See Vin. IV. 6-10; Jāt. IV. 413 and V. 337). It should, however, be noted that the social stigma resting on these low trades was due sometimes to their very nature (as in the case of butchering, for example) but chiefly to their association with the aboriginal non-Aryan tribes who followed them as their hereditary occupations. Yet other despised callings were the black arts, explanation of signs, omens, auguries, dreams, forecasting weather. foretelling events etc. (Chullavāgga XII. 1. 3; Mahasila Tevijja Sutta ch. II). Jāt VI. 191 refers to the popular belief that even Nāgas do not dance for shame before actors. Jāt. II. 82 refers to "Brethern who used to get a living by being physicians (note the prohibition in the Hindu smriti) or runners, doing errands on foot...........the 21 unlawful callings." It is very interesting to note that there is a substantial agreement between the Pali works and Sanskrit Law Books in this connection. Thus, Vasistha condemns actors (III. 3.); also Baudhāyana (I. 5, 10, 24) who adds to them stage-players and teachers of dancing, singing and acting condemned as Upapātakins (II. 1, 2, 13) [c. f. Āpasthamba I. 6, 14; Gau. XVII. 17; Vasistha XIV. 2. 3.]. It is thus evident that both the Buddhist and Hindu social opinions are practically at one in condemning certain crafts and professions on the basis of an absolute standard, determined on grounds of moral deficiency and in some cases, of uncleanliness of the processes of operation involved in the craft.

It should be noted in this connection that along with the aforesaid crafts or trades, there are certain commodities the trade in which are absolutely forbidden to a Brahmin. Thus, Manu X. 86-94 specifies among others the following articles—condiments, cooked food, cattle, stones, dyed cloth, meat, milk, clarified butter, oil, perfumes, money, indigo, lac, sugar, wines, birds, wild animals, water, weapons etc. Parallel specifications are also contained in Gautama VII. 9—20; Āpasthamba I. 7, 20, 12—13; Baudhyāyana II. 1, 2, 27; Vasistha II. 24—32.

Similar agreement between Hindu and Buddhist books is to be found with regard to mobility of labour already mentioned. Thus all the Hindu Law books authorise the twice-born classes to take to the occupation of an inferior caste in times of distress or failure to obtain a living through lawful labour (Gautama VII. 6; Vasistha II. 22; Baudhāyana II. 4. 16). Gautama in his Dharmasūtra says that a Brahmin can be a farmer and a trader (X. 5).

Baudhāyana also admits the doctrine that a priest who cannot support himself by the usual occupations of a Brahmin may take up and follow the profession of a warrior. Vasistha (II. 40) prohibits Brahmins and Kshatriyas from being usuers but Baudhyāyana (5, 10, 21) says that the Vaisya may practice usury. Even the Brahmin priest who neglects his duties may at the king's pleasure be be forced to do the work of a Śūdra. (Bau. II. 4, 7, 15). Thus with certain restrictions as to what he sells, a priest or warrior may support life by trade and agriculture (Vas. II. 24 f.). But a man reborn who persists in trade cannot be regarded as a Brahmin nor can a priest who lives as an actor or physician (Vas. III. 3.). Again, Brahmins lived not only as gentlemen farmer but also as humble ploughmen (Vas. III. 33) in this period. In fact there were recognised customs, not approved in one part of the country but admitted as good usage because locally approved in other parts. For in discussing usage, Baudhyāyana (Dharmasūtra I. 1. 17 f.) expressly enumerates customs peculier to the south and certain others peculier to the north and adds that to follow these practices except where they are considered right usage is to sin but that for each practice, the local rule is authoritative, though Gautama denies this. (See Bühler, S. B. E., Vol. II. p. XLIX.).

The pursuit of agriculture in this period was associated neither with social prestige nor with social stigma. The stricter Brahmin tradition not only in the law books but also in the Sutta-Nipāta, the Majjhima Nikāya and the Jātakas expressly reserved the two callings of agriculture and trade for the Vaisyas and judges them unfit for the Brahmins or the Kshatriyas. Thus, the Brahmin Esukāri of Sāvathi considers tillage and dairy-farming as not less the property and province of the Vaisya than are bow and arrow, endowed maintenance (by alms) and sickle and yoke, the property and province of noble, brahmin and work-ing classes respectively. [M. II. 180; The Vāsettha-sutta (M. No. 98; S. N. III. 9.) reveals the same exclusive spirit as correct]. And in Jāt. IV. 363 f. brahmins who engage in agriculture, trade and other callings are declared to have fallen from Brahminhood. On the other hand, in both Jātakas and Suttas not only are brahmins frequently found pursuing tillage, cowherding, goat-keeping, trade, hunting, wood-work, weaving, caravan-guarding, archery, carriage-driving and snake-charming (Jāt. II. 165; III. 293; IV. 167, 276; III. 401; IV. 15; V. 22, 471; II. 200; VI. 170; IV. 207, 457; V. 127) but also no reflection is passed upon them for so doing, nay the Brahmin farmer at times, is a pious man and a Bodhisatta to boot (Jāt. III. 162). Dr. Fick is disposed to think that the N. W. (Udicca) Brahmins of the Kurus and Pānchāls inherited a stricter standard (Sociale Gliederang Indien, 138 f.). Nevertheless, it is not claimed for the pious ones just mentioned, living near Benares and in Magadh that they were Udicca immigrants. As for the Kshatriya clansmen of the tribal republics, they were largely cultivators of the soil. For instance, in the Kunāla Jātaka it was the workmen in the fields of the Sākiyan and Koliyan "bhojakas, amaccas and Uparājas who began to quarrel over the prior turn to irrigate" (Jāt. V. 412).

The slave or servant (dāsa, dāsī) was an adjunct in all households able to command domestic service. Slavery might be incurred through capture (Jāt. IV. 220, VI. 135), commuted death-sentence, debt (Jāt. VI. 521; Therig. ver. 444), voluntary self-degradation (Vin. I. 72; Sum. Vil. I. 168) or judicial punishment (Jāt. I. 200). But slaves do not appear to have been kept in large numbers (Vin. I. 72; D. I. 60, 72, 92 f.) either in the house or as in the West, at mining or plantation work. The lot of the slave was far better than that of either the Greek or the Roman slave. Thus we find in the Jātaka, the slave petted. permitted to learn writing and handicrafts besides his ordinary duties as valet and footman (Jāt. I. 451 f.). No doubt in the same Jātaka, we find the slave saying to himself that at the slighest fault he might get beaten, imprisoned, branded and fed on slave's fare but nevertheless, of actual ill-treatment there is scarcely any mention. Two instances of beating occur and in both the victims were maids. One lies abed repeatedly (to test her pious mistress's temper) (M. I. 125), the other of a slavish girl let out to work on hire but returning home without her wage. (Jāt. I. 402 f.). The slaves were not, while still undischarged, admitted to the religious community (Saṃgha) [Vin. I. 76]. Nevertheless, we do not meet with run-away slaves. Vasistha exempts slaves from taxation. They might be manumitted (D. I. 72; Psalms of the Sisters p. 117; Psalms of the Brethern p. 22; Jāt. V. 313) or might free themselves by payment (Jāt. VI. 547). [Cambridge History of India, Vol. I].

The low position of the Śūdra in the eye of law will be evident from Gautama XII. 8 ff. where it is said that if a Brahmin abuses a Kshatriya he pays only 50 Kārshapanas, only 25 if he abuses a Vaisya and nothing if he abuses a Śūdra.

The hireling, wage-earner, daylabourer was no man's chattel yet his life was probably harder sometimes than that of the slave (Jāt. I. 422; III. 444). Similarly in a list of callings given in the Buddhist books he ranks along with the mere hewers of wood and flower-gatherers and below the slave (D. I. 51; c. f. Mil. 331; 147; A. I. 145, 206). He was to a great extent employed in the larger land-holdings (Jāt. III. 406; IV. 43; S. N. p. 12). Jāt. I. 468 gives an instance of a millionaire with his hired labourers. In the Suttas again Kāsibhāradwaja is employing 500 ploughs and hired men (bhatikā) on his estate. (Sutta Nipāta, I. 4.; c. f. S. I. 171; Jāt. III. 293). He was paid either in board and lodging or in money wages (Jāt. II. 139; III.

326, 444; V. 212). [Cambridge History of India, Vol. 1].

There was brisk trade in India at this time both inland and sea-borne. Dr. Fick considers navigation in the Jātaka as not in high seas but this view is long exploded. As a matter of fact, we find even fishermen throwing their nets in high seas (Jāt. No. 402). There was a very flourishing ship-building industry and large merchantile marines were built up. Thus, the Samudda-baṇija Jātaka (Jāt. IV. 159) mentions a ship which accomodated 1000 families of woodwrights who emigrated to an island over-sea. Vālahassa Jātaka (Jāt. II. 128) contained 500 dealers. The Supparaka Jātaka (Jāt. IV. 138-142) mentions the sea-voyage undertaken by 700 merchants in a ship. The ship in which the prince of the Mahājanaka Jātaka (Jāt. VI. 32-35) sailed with other traders, had on board seven caravan with their beasts. The ship in which was rescued from a watery grave the philanthropic Brahmin of the Saṃkha Jātaka (Jāt. VI. 15-17) was 800 cubits in length, 600 cubits in width, 20 fathoms in depth and had three masts. Janaka Jātaka mentions a ship that was wrecked with 700 crews and passengers in addition to Buddha (Bishop Brigandet's Life of Godama, 415). The ship in which Bijoya's Pandion bride was carried to Ceylon was large enough to accomodate 18 officers of state, 75 menial servants and a number of slaves besides the princess herself and 700 other virgins who accompanied her (Turnour's Mahābaṃsa, 51). Acording to Rājaballīya, the ship in which Prince Bijoya and his followers were sent away by King Siṃhabāhu of Bengal was so large as to contain full 700 passengers (Upham's Sacred and Historical Books of Ceylon, II. 28, 168; Turnour's Mahābaṃsa 46, 47). The wives and children of Bijoya's followers making up more than 700 were cast adrift in a similar ship (Turnours Mahābaṃsa, 46). The ship in which Prince Siṃhala sailed from some unknown part of Jambudwīp to Ceylon contained 500 merchants besides himself (Si—yu—ki, II. 241). Again in the Mahāummagga Jātaka (No. 546) the Great Being says "Ānanda Kumār, take 300 wrights, go to the upper Ganges, procure choice timber, build 300 ships, make them cut stores of wood from the town, fill the ships with light wood and come back soon". Thus, "the vessels according to Jātaka tales seems to have been constructed on a fairly large scale, for we read of hundreds, embarking on them, merchants or emigrants. The numbers have, of course, no statistical value, but the current conceptions of shipping capacity are at least interesting". (Mrs. Rhys Davids in the Cambridge History of India, Vol. I. p. 213.)

Brisk trade was carried on in these ships between India on the one hand and Ceylon, Burma, Persia, Babylon, Subarṇabhūmi and Greece on the other. The chief article of trade with Ceylon must have been pearls. The traders, started generally from

Tāmralipti but also sometimes from Siṃhapura [c. f. Bijoya's ship touching at Supara=Bassin, (according to Dr. Burguess)], Sagal (c. f. the ship of Bijoya's nephew) and Morapura on the Ganges (c. f. the ships of a princess and her six brothers who became the consort of Bijoya's nephew).

From Bishop Brigandet's Life of Godama, 101 we learn of two Burmese merchant brothers Tapoosa and Palekat who crossed the Bay of Bengal in a ship that conveyed full five hundred cart-loads of their own goods which they landed at Adzeitta, a port in Kalinga in the northern section of the Eastern coast on their way to Suvama in Magadha. This trade is corroborated by Ctesias who refers to a lake in the land of the Pygmies upon the surface of which oil is produced. This is supposed to mean Upper Burma where there is a tribe answering to their description and where " there are also the only largely productive petroleum deposits which moreover, we know to have been worked since the earliest times (Professor Ball in the I. A. Vol. XIII. p. 230).

In one of the Chinese legends of the lion-prince Siṃhala (Si—yu—ki, II. 246) it is related how the boat in which the daughter of the Lion was cast away was driven by the winds westwards into the Persian Gulf where she landed and founded a colony in the country of the western women". The tradition embodied in the Dīpabaṃsa version of the legend (Si—yu—ki, XIII. 55) makes her land on an island which was afterward called the "Kingdom of women". As the Rev. T. Foulkes (Ind. Ant. 1879) remarks "Underneath the legendary matter we may here trace the existence of a sea-route between India and the Persian coasts in the days of Buddha". And as a matter of fact, we find the Persian King Darius despatching in 516 B. C. an expedition under Skylax with orders to prove the feasability of a sea-passage from the mouths of the Indus to Persia. "Skylax equipped a fleet on the upper waters of the Punjab rivers in the Gāndhāra country, made his way down to the coast and in the 13th month reached the sea. Darius was thus enabled to annex the Indus valley and to send his fleet into the Indian Ocean" (Oxford History of India, p. 45). This political intercourse with Persia must have led to merchantile intercourse as well. The Indian Satrapy paid annually a tribute of £ 1, 290, 000 in gold. This supply of gold she obtained not as did Europe from America by conquest and rapine but by her mining industries and by the more natural and peaceful method of commerce "by the exchange of such of her productions as among the Indians were superfluities but at the same time not only highly prized by the nations of western Asia, Egypt and Europe but were obtainable from no other quarter except India or from the Farther East by means of the Indian trade" (C. Daniell, Industrial Competition of Asia, p. 225).

The Bāveru Jātaka narrates that Indian merchants exported peacocks to Babylon. In the words of Professor Bühler "The story indicates that the Banias of W. India undertook trading voyages to the shores of the Persian Gulf and of its rivers in the 5th perhaps in the 6th century B. C. just as in our days. This trade very probably existed already in much earlier times, for the Jātakas contain several other stories, describing voyages to distant lands and perilous adventure by sea in which the vessels of the very ancient western ports of Supparaka—Supara and Bharukaccha—Broach are occasionally mentioned". Babylon according to Herodotus (I. 192 in McCrindle's Ancient India as described in Classical Literature) obtained precious stones and dogs (probably Tibetan mastiffs) from India.

The Mahājanaka Jātaka (Jāt. VI. 32-35) speaks of a prince who having got together his stock-in-trade (*viz.*, store of pearls, jewels and diamonds) put on board a ship with some merchants bound for Subarṇabhūmi (Subarṇabhūmi is either Burma or the Golden Chersonese or the whole Father Indian coast). The Sussondi-Jātaka (Jāt III. 188) mentions the voyage of certain merchants of Broach for the Golden Land, from which as also from other Jātakas it is evident that Subarṇabhūmi was another commercial objective of Indian traders in these days.

In Ctesias' Indica (400 B. C.) is to be found the existence of a really Dravidian word which Ctesias used for cinnamon (Ctesias translated by McCrindle, p. 29). The word used by Ctesias is Karpion which Dr. Caldwell (A Comparative Grammar of the Dravidian Languages, p. 105) derives from Tamil-Malayalam word Karuppa or Karppu to which is akin the Sanskrit word Karpur—'camphor.' This proves the probable existence of at least an indirect trade in cinnamon and other purfumes between India and Greece. In fact, Baudhyāyana's condemnation of the Northern Aryans who took part in the sea-trade implies that the people of the Punjab had some share in the trade between India and the Western World by the Persian Gulf route.

The trade-routes were innumerable and were both by land and water. According to the Jātakas, it was possible to reach Ceylon direct by water not only from Champā (Bhagalpur) but even from Benares. Thus, the defaulting woodwrights (Jāt. IV. 159) sail along the Ganges from Benares to a distant island on the sea. Prince Mahājanaka (Jāt VI. 34 f.) set out for Subarṇabhūmi from Champā. And Mahindra travels by water from Patna to Tāmralipti and on to Ceylon (Vin. III. 338). Again, in the Sītānisaṃsa Jātaka (II. 112) a sea-fairy as helmsman brings passengers for India by ships from off the sea to Benares. Other traders are found coasting round India from Broach to Subarṇabhūmi (Jāt. III. 188). Other water routes already mentioned are:—(1) from Siṃhapūra *via* Supara to Ceylon (2) from Sagal to Ceylon (3) from Morapura on the Ganges to Ceylon (4) from Tāmralipti to Ceylon (5) from Burma to Adzeitta, a port in Kalinga in the northern section of the East Coast (6) from Broach to Babylon (7) from Pāndya territorry to Ceylon (8) from Srāvasti to Ceylon (Tibetan Legend of the Siṃhalese princess Ratnābalī).

As to inland routes, we find Punna, a merchant of Supparaka trading with Northern Kośala; Anāthpiṇdaka's caravans travelling S. E. from Srāvasthi to Rājgriha and back (Jāt. I. 92, 348) and and also to the borders (Jāt. I. 377 f.). Another route from Sāvathi to Patittana with six halting places is given in the Sutta Nipāta, verses 1011—13. From east to west traffic was by river, boats going up the Ganges up to Sahājāti (Vin. Texts III. 401) and up the Jumna to Kausāmbi (Vin. Texts, p. 382). Further westward the journey would again be by land to Sind whence come large imports in horses and asses. (Jāt. I. 124, 178, 181; II. 31, 257) and to Sovira [Vimāna-vattu (comm.) 336] and its ports. Northward lay the great route connecting India with central and western Asia by way of Taxila near Rawalpindi and probably also by way of Sagala in the Punjab. That this route was safe is evident from the fact that students went unarmed (Jāt. II. 277) to be educated at Taxila. Besides these inland routes, we find that Benares has trade relations with (1) Kamboja (Jāt. VI. 110) (2) Kampilya (Jāt. III. 52, 230;

V. 11, 18, 54; VI. 198, 224) (3) Kapilābastu (Jāt. I. 85; II. 63; IV. 4, 32, 92, 96, 179, 199; V. 219, 221; VI. 246) (4) Kośala (I. 50, 77, 91, 105, 118, 164, 172, 183, 184; III. 21, 191, 291; IV. 83; V. 116, 226, 231) (5) Kosambi (Jāt. I. 47., 206; II. 43, 139, 233, 289; III. 43, 139, 233, 289; IV. 17, 36, 246; VI. 120) (6) Kurukshetra (Jāt. VI. 141) (7) Kuru (Jāt. II. 150, 251; III. 241; IV. 227, 275, 276; V. 31, 246) (8) Kuśinara (Jāt. IV. 93). (9) Kuśabati (Jāt. I. 231; V. 141, 146, 147) (10) Mithilā (Jāt. 31, 32; II. 230; VI. 54, 68) (11) Madhurā (Jāt. IV. 99). (11) N. W. Country (Jāt. I. 178, 216). (12) Pānchāla (Jāt. IV. 248, 268) (13) Sindh (Jāt. I. 61, 63; II. 166, 233; III. 5; V. 132) (14) Ujjain (Jāt. II. 172; IV. 244) (15) Videha (Jāt. I. 31; II. 27, 231; III. 222, 230; IV. 201, 202; V. 50, 86; VI. 19, 28, 34).

The nature of the articles of foreign trade is not specified. Nevertheless, as Professor Rhys Davids says (Buddhist India p. 98) "silk, muslins, the finer sorts of cloth, cutlery, armour, brocades, embroideries and rugs, perfumes (like cinnamon) and drugs, ivory and ivory work, jewellery and gold—these were the main articles in which the merchants dealt."

The importance of foreign trade is shown by the fact that in the halls of the great merchants, places were set apart "for foreign merchants to store their goods" (Jāt. No. 546). And to facilitate this trade, there was the system of having "Correspondents" (Jāt. No. 90).

Of the chief ports, the most important were Champā and Tāmralipti on the Eastern Coast and Supara and Broach on the West. Besides these there was Adzeitta in Kalinga.

As to inland trade, foodstuffs for the towns were apparently brought only to the gates, while workshop and bazaar occupied their special streets within (V. p. 208; Bud. Ind. p. 76). Thus, there was a fish-monger's village at a gate of Sāvathi (Psalms of the Brethern, 166; c. f. Jāt. I. 361). Greengrocery is sold at the four gates of Uttar-Pānchāl (Jāt. IV. 445) and venison at the cross-roads outside Benares (Jāt. III. 49; c. f. M. I. 58; III. 91). The slaughter-houses (Sūnā) mentioned in the Vinaya (Mah. VI. 10; Cull. V. X. 10. 4) were presumably outside also unless by singhātaka we understand street-corners. Arrows and carriages and other articles for sale were displayed in the āpaṇa (Jāt. II. 267; IV. 488; VI. :9. Vin. IV. 248; c. f. Cull. V. X. 10. 4) or fixed shop or it might be, stored within the Antarāpaṇa (Jāt. I. 55, 350; III. 406). The portable stock-in-trade of the hawkers is mentioned in Jāt I. 111 f. and connexion of the successful shopkeeper is discussed in the Nikāyas (A. I. 115 f.); and among trades five are ethically proscribed for lay believers—daggers, slaves, flesh, strong drink and poisons (A. III. 208). Textile fabrics (Vin. IV. 250 f.) groceries and oil (Vin. IV. 248-49), green-groceries (Jāt. I. 411), grain (Jāt. II. 267), perfumes and flowers (Jāt. I. 290 f.; IV. 82

VI. 336; Vin. Texts III 343), articles of gold and jewellery (Jāt. IV. 223) are among the articles of trade in the bazaars; and for the sale of liquors there were the taverns (Jāt. I. 251 f., 268 f.; VI. 328; c. f. Dhp. Com. III. 66). [Cambridge History of India, Vol I].

The trade of the traders may well have been largely hereditary (Jāt. II. 287; III. 198). Traditional goodwill handed down from father to sire would prove specially effective in commanding confidence and thus be a stronger incentive to hereditary trade than the force of caste-rule. But the merchant-guilds do not seem to have attained the same development as the craft-guild. The reason seems to have been that the merchant was necessarily a wanderer while industrial organisation in these older times depended largely upon settled relations and ties of neighbourhood. A Hansa League for instance, can only grow in highly developed markets and seaports. Nevertheless there is some significant evidence of corporate concerted action among the merchants. The Chullaka-Seṭhi Jātaka mentions a hundred or so merchants offering to buy up a newly arrived ship's cargo (Jāt. I. 122). 500 traders were fellow-passengers on board the ill-fated ships mentioned in Jāt. II. 128 and V. 75; 700 others were lucky enough to secure Supparaka as their pilot (Jāt. IV. 138—142), thus showing co-operative chartering of the same vessel. Again caravan traders had a common chief who was to give directions as to halts, watering, precautions against robbers and in many cases as to routes, fords etc. (Jāt. I. 98, 99, 107, 174; II. 295, 335; III. 200).

Further, several partnerships are mentioned *e. g.*, in the deal in birds exported from India to Babylon (Jāt. III. 126, 127), in horses imported from the north to Benares (Jāt. II. 31); partnerships of traders of Sāvathi who carried on joint business and set out with 500 cartloads of merchandise (Jāt. IV. 350-4), of two other traders of Sāvathi who joined partnership and loaded 500 waggons full of wares (Jāt. II. 181); partnership business in pots and pans (Jāt. I. 111); partnership business of two merchants of Benares who took 500 waggons of merchandise from Benares to the country districts with an equal interest of both in the stock-in-trade and in the oxen and waggons (Jāt. I 404).

A concerted commercial enterprise on a more extensive scale appears in Jāt. II. 294-96 where some traders of Sāvathi carried on a joint business and came upon rich finds of minerals of all sorts from iron to lapislazuli which they stowed away to a common treasure-house, giving food to the brotherhood on joint account.

The existence of a merchant-guild ruling the trade of the city of Sopara is mentioned in the legend of Pūrṇa translated by Burnouf from Nepalese and Tibetan sources apparently of the third or fourth century B. C. (Bombay Gazetteer, old ed. Vol. XIII. p. 406).

It is very interesting to note in this connection that as if to facilitate the business relations of the country there was a nice system of Commercial Education. Thus, in the Mahābhāgga (S. B. E. XIII. p. 201 f.) we are told of three professions—Lekha, Gaṇanā and Rūpa. Lekha signifies the art of writing which includes nor only the niceties of style and diction but also the different forms of correspondence (c. f. "correspondents" in Jāt. No. 96. already mentioned) as will be seen from chapter X of the Adhayaksha-prachāra of Kautilya's Arthaśāstra which in its concluding verse tells us that there were not one but many verses on the subject. The word gaṇanā for similar reasons cannot mean arithmatic, but 'accounts' corresponding to Gaṇanākhya of Kautilya. Even in later times, this word had this meaning and we thus find the term Gaṇanāpati used by Kalhana in his Rājtarangini (V. 26) and understood correctly by Stein to denote "Head of Account Office." The third word rūpa is taken by Professor Rhys Davids to mean money-changing and by Bühler commercial and agricultural arithmetic. But as Professor D. R. Bhāndārkar has pointed out that in chapter XII. of Adhyaksha-prachāra of Kautilya's Arthaśāstra, Kautilya speaks of Rūpya-rūpa and tāmrarūpa which cannot but signify silver and copper coins, respectively. He also signifies an officer Rūpa-darśaka, the examiner of coins so that rūpa must be the science of coinage, a study of which is essentially necessary for a stable home and foreign trade.

The act of exchange between producer and consumer or between either and a middlman was a free bargain, a transaction unregulated with one notable exception by any system of fixed prices. It was left free for the producer and dealer to prevail by competition (c. f. Jāt. III. 282 f.) and also by adulteration (c. f. Jāt I. 220). Instances of price-haggling are not rare (Jāt. I. 111 f, 195; II. 222, 289, 424 f.) and we notice the dealer's sense of the wear and tear of articles (Jāt. I. 99) and a case of that more developed competition called " dealing in futures " (Jāt. I. 121 f.). In Jāt. I. 99 two traders about to convey commodities to some distant city agree who shall start first. The one thinks that if he arrive first, he will get a better, because a non-competitive price; the other also holding 'competition is killing work' (lit. price-fixing is liking robbing men of life) prefers to sell at the price fixed by his predecessor and yields him a start. We also notice local 'cornering in hay' in Jāt. I. 121. [Cambridge History of India, Vol. I].

Though free competition was the rule, nevertheless, custom may very well have fixed price to a great extent. " My wife is sometimes as meek as a 100 piece slave girl " (Jāt I. 299)—reveals a customary price. For the royal household, prices were fixed by the Court-valuer without appeal (Jāt. I. 124 f; II. 31 ; Psalms of Brethern 25, 212). It may also have been the duty of this official to assess the duty of $\frac{1}{20}$th on each consignment of native wares imported into a city and of $\frac{1}{10}$th plus a sample of each foreign import as stated by Gautama (X. 26) and Baudhyāyana (I. X. 18.; VV. 14, 15). Such octrois are alluded to in one Jātaka where the King remits to a subject the duty collected at the gates of his capital (Jāt. VI. 347). Finally, it may have been his duty to assess merchants for their specific commutation of the rāja-kariya *viz.*, one article sold per month to the King at a discount (Gau. X. 35). [Cambridge History of India, Vol. I].

Barter was not uncommon in this period. It emerges in certain contingencies *e.g.*, when a wanderer obtains a meal from a woodlander for a gold pin (Jāt. VI. 519) or when among humble folk a dog is bought for a Kahapana plus a cloak (Jāt. II. 247). Barter was also permitted in special commodities by Gautama (VII. 16 f.) and Vasistha (II. 37 f.) and was prescribed for Saṃgha in certain cases (Vin. II. 174) to whom the use of money was forbidden (Vin. III. 237; II. 294 ff.). Rice was still a standard of value when the Jātakas were compiled (Jāt. I. 124 f.). From Pānini (V. I. 27) we find that objects could sometimes be purchased with Vasana, pieces of cloth of definite value—a practice which is still followed in some parts of

Rajputna. Similarly from Pāninī (V. I. 19) we find that 'go-puchchha' or bovine tale acted as a circulating medium just as in Nepal of to-day the tale of a yak, a species of ox is prevalent as a medium of exchange.

But for the ordinary mechanism of exchange, the value of every marketable commodity was stated in figures of a certain coin or its fractions. We find from the evidences of the Jātakas that the following kinds of coins were used : (1) Kahapana (Jāt. Nos. 257, 284, 541) (2) Nikkha (Jāt. Nos. 276, 340, 546 where golden Nikkhas are mentioned) (3) Māsaka (Jāt. No. 288) (4) Addha-māsaka (Jāt. No. 546) (5) Kakanika (Jāt. No. 4) (6) Kālakahapana (Jāt. No. 536) (7) Suvanna (Jāt. No. 546) (8) Suvanna-māsaka. It is interesting that Pāninī (550 B. C. according to Professor D. R. Bhāndārkar) refers to at least seven kinds of coins. Not only does he speak of the Kārshāpanas but also of Nikkhas, Śatamānas, and so forth. The Nidānakathā prefixed to the Jātakas speaks of the sisakahapana or lead Kārshāpanas. The Vinaya (III. 45) refers to pādas as coins.

Unfortunately, there was no stability in the relative value of standard coins. Thus, Vinaya says " At that time (of Bimbisāra or Ajātśatru at Rājgriha,) five māsakas were equal to one pāda. (Vin. III. 45). Again, the Nikkha was valued now at five (Childers, Pali Dictionary s. v. Nikkho), now at four suvannas (Manu VIII. 137). Similarly, there was falsification of weights and measures and the King was asked by Vasistha (XIX) to guard against such falsifications.

Besides the regular currency, there was a very large number of instruments of credit, *e.g.*, signet rings used as deposit or security (Jāt. I 121), (2) wife or children pledged or sold for debt (Jāt. VI. 521; Therig. 444), (3) debt-sheets called inna-pannani. In Jāt. IV. 256, a bankrupt asks his creditors to bring with them debt-sheets. (I owe you) for settlement. (Also Jāt. I. 230; c. f. 227.).

Wealth no doubt was hoarded either under the ground (Jāt. I. 225, 375 f. 424; II. 308; III. 24, 116) in brazen jars under the river bank (Jāt. I. 227, 323) or deposited with a friend (Jat. VI. 521). The nature and amount of the wealth thus hoarded was registered on gold or copper-plates (Jāt. IV. 7, 488; VI. 29; c. f. IV. 237).

Nevertheless, money was lent on interest. There is a tolerant tone concerning the money-lender in Jāt. IV. 222 where money-lending together with tillage, trade and harvesting are called four honest callings. Gautama is equally tolerant (X. 6; XI. 21) though Vasistha (II. 41, 42) and Baudhyā-yana (I. 5. 10) condemn it. Hypocritical ascetics are accused of practising it (Jāt. IV. 184). Vasistha (II. 51), and Gautama (XII. 31-35) name six different kinds of interest, *viz.*, compound, periodical, stipulated, corporal, daily and the use of pledge. The legal rate of interest is set at 15% per annum (Five māshas a month for 20 kārshāpanas). [Baudhyāyana I. 5. 10. 22; Gautama XII. 29]. But according to Vasistha (II. 48) "two, three, four, five in the 100 is declared in the Smṛiti to be the monthly interest according to caste. Again articles such as gold, grain, flavouring substances, flowers, roots, fruits, wool, beasts of burden without security could be lent at an enormous rate of interest which could be increased six or eight-fold.

The national wealth of India in this period was immense. Nowhere do we find mention of any merchant who was worth less than 80 crores which even if copper would amount to £ 2,750,000 as Mrs. Rhys. Davids says. Anāthpiṇḍaka lavished 54 crores on Buddhism, lent 18 crores to merchants which he never called in (Jāt. No. 40). His nephew squandered 40 crores gold (Bhadra-ghāt Jātaka). Suchiparivara had 80 crores. A Brahmin merchant gave daily in alms 600,000 pieces of money (Jāt. III. 442). Another Brahmin gave to his wife a fortune amounting to 80 crores (Jāt. No. 443). Another merchant had 80 crores (Jāt. No. 842). A merchant of Benares had 80 crores while another of Magadha had 80 crores (Jāt. No. 131). In Jāt. No. 23 a King is taking his food in golden dishes worth 100,000 crores. Another spent 100,000 crores in one dish (Jāt. No. 260). In Jāt. No. 546 we find Bodhisatta wearing a Kāśī robe worth 1000 pieces of gold. A pair of shoes presented to Buddha cost

1000 pieces while the jewelled trappings of an elephant of a King of Benares cost 20 lakhs pieces.

Nevertheless, living was very cheap. An Addhamāsaka worth of meat was sufficient for one man; a small copper coin was enough for ghee or oil for one man; eight kahapanas could purchase a decent ass (Jāt. No. 546). A pair of oxen would cost 24 pieces (Jāt. No. 257). A slave would cost 100 pieces (Jāt. No. 39). Two half-māsakas could buy a garland, perfume and strong drink to enable a man and a woman to enjoy themselves.

The Maurya Period.

(321-186 B. C.)

It is a well known fact that the socio-economic structure of ancient India was based upon the village. In Kautilya's time, villages were classified not only as of first, middle and lowest rank but also as those that were free from taxes in grains, cattle, gold, forest produce etc., and those that supplied free labour and dairy-produce in lieu of taxes [Arthaśāstra (R. Śham Śāstri's Eng. Trans.) p. 178.]; so that this classification was of much help to Government by supplying information as to which villages formed the most convenient ground for the levy of troops and taxes. In some respects the villages were all similar. The head of the village was the headman who was helped by the village Syndic consisting of village elders (Artha. p. 53). There was no feudal system and no landlord. The houses were all together in a group separated by lanes. Immediately adjoining was the wide expanse of cultivated field, usually rice-field. And each village had a grazing ground for the cattle for which provision had to be made by the King (Artha. p. 54). The cattle belonged severally to the householders but no one had separate pasture. The pasture must have included both large spaces (Vivīta) occupied by the nomad, tent-dwelling (Meg. I. 47) ranchers who were the direct descendants of the old Vedic tribes (Hopkins J. A. O. S. XIII. pp. 79-80, 82-83) and also more restricted areas in the neighbourhood of the villages. The villages had their definite boundaries, their village halls and their independent internal economy. Less organised were the stations (Ghosas) [Hopkins, J. A. O. S. XIII. p. 77] or hamlets which formed the head-quarters of the ranching class. In Chandragupta's time we find a special department to provide for pastures and grazing grounds, for proper supply of fodder and for the welfare of live-stock in general. There were no less than six chief officers for running this department, the most important of whom were the Superintendent of cows (Artha. p. 159), the Superintendent of pastures and grazing grounds (Artha. p. 177). The former had to take care not only of cows, buffaloes, sheep, goats and asses but also of pigs, mules and dogs. One of his for embarkation. If the wind called Hippalus happens to be blowing, it is possible to arrive in 40 days at the nearest mart in India called Muziris (Modern Mangalore). This, however, is not a desirable place for disembarkation, on account of the pirates who frequent its vicinity, nor in fact is it very rich in articles of merchandise. Besides, the roadstead for shipping is at a considerable distance from the shore, and the cargoes have to be conveyed in boats, either for loading or discharging." "At the moment I am writing these pages" continues Pliny "the name of the king of the place is Cœlobotras. Another port and a much more convenient one is that which lies in the territory of the people called Nelcyndi Barace by name. Here King Pandion used to reign dwelling at a considerable distance from the mart in the interior, at a city known as Modeira. Travellers set sail from India on their return to Egypt, at the beginning of the Egyptian month Tybus which is our December; if they do this, they can go and return in the same year".

The places on the Indian coast which the Egyptian merchant vessels then reached, are verified from the coins found there. A hoard of Roman gold coins has been dug up quite recently near Calicut under the roots of a banyan tree. It had been buried by an Alexandrian merchant on his arrival from a voyage and left safe under the cover of the sacred tree to await his return from a second journey. But he died before his return and his secret died with him.

To Pliny's survey we may add the valuable geographical knowledge given by the author of the Periplus of the Erythrean Sea wherein he mentions the several sea-ports and their distances, with the tribes and cities near the coast. The trade of Egypt to India and Arabia was then most valuable but as the merchandise in each case was carried only for short distances from city to city, the merchants could gain but little knowledge of where it come from or of where it was going. Even under Justinian part of the Egyptian trade to the East was carried on through the islands of Ceylon and Socotra, but it was chiefly in the hands of the uneducated Arabs who were little able to communicate to the world much knowledge of the countries from which they brought their highly-valued goods. At Ceylon they meet with traders from beyond the Ganges and China, from whom they bought the silk which the Europeans had formerly thought a product of Arabia. According to the author of the Periplus "the port of Muza was crowded with Arab shipmasters and sailors and perhaps with bales of merchandise ; for these Arabs carry on trade with Barygaza, sending their own ships there (Art. 29).

But the principal carriers of the trade between India and Egypt under the Ptolemies were the Egyptian Greeks ; and as usual this commercial intercourse has left some marks on their language. Thus the Greek names for rice (oryza), ginger (zingiber) and cinnamon (karpion) have a close correspondence with their Tamil equivalents *viz.*, arisi, inchiver and karava respectively. Again the name Yavana which in old Sanskrit poetry is invariably used to denote the Greeks (Weber's Indian Literature, p. 220) is derived from the Greek word Iaones, the name of the Greeks in their own language. Even the Tamil poets use the word to denote the Greeks and the Romans. Thus "the poet Nakkirar addresses the Pandion prince Nan-Maran in the following words" O Mara, whose sword is ever victorious, spend thou thy days in peace and joy, drinking daily out of golden cups, presented by the handmaids, the cool and fragrant wine brought by the Yavanas in the good ships" (Mr. Pillay, The Tamils 1800 years Ago, Ch. III.). The Yavanas alluded to by these poets were undoubtedly the Egyptian Greeks because as stated in the Periplus it was Greek merchants from Egypt who brought wine, brass, lead, glass etc., for sale to Muziris and Bakare and who purchased from these ports pepper, betel, ivory, pearls and fine muslins (*Ibid.*).

Now one of the most curious relics of the trade between Egypt and India during this period has been recently unearthed at Oxyrrhyncus. It is a papyrus containing a Greek farce of the second century A. D. which deals with the story of a Greek lady named Charition, who had been shipwrecked on the Canarese coast. The locality is identified by the fact that the king of the country addresses his retinue as *indon promoi*. Dr. Hultzsch is of opinion that the barbarous jargon in which they addressed one another is actually Canarese. Again Dio Chrysostom, who lived in the reign of Trajan, mentions Indians among the cosmopolitan crowds to be found in the bazaars of Alexandria and he says that they came "by way of trade."

During this period we know Rome was absorbing the remains of the Empire of Alexander. Syria had already fallen and Egypt became a Roman province in 30 B. C. The dissensions of civil war ended at Actium, after which Angustus settled down to organise and regulate his vast possessions. The effect of the Pax Romana upon trade was thus very marked. Piracy was put down, trade routes were secured and the fashionable world of Rome, undistracted by conflict began to demand on an unprecedented scale oriental luxuries of every kind. At about the same time, the Kushans were establishing themselves among the ruins of the Bactrian and other semi-Greek principalities of N. W. India aud thus when the Kushan Empire marched with that of the Roman "Roman arts and ideas travelled with the stream of Roman gold which flowed into the treasuries of the Rājas in payment for the silks, gems and spices of the Orient" (J. R. A. S. 1903 p. 56).

The news of the accession of Augustus quickly reached India and many Indian States sent embassies to congratulate him. Strabo mentions that an embassy was sent to Augustus in 20 B. C. by the Indian King Pandion. Strabo relates that Nicolaus Damascenus met at Antioch, Epidaphne, the surviver of this embassy to Augustus bearing a letter in Greek from the Indian Prince. With them was Zarmanochegus (Sramanāchāryya) of Barygaza, who was evidently a Buddhist monk. Allusions to this embassy are made by Horace in Odes. Florus (Epitome of Roman History IV. 12), Dion Cassius (History of Rome IX. 73), Orosius (History VI. 12) and Suetonius refer to it. It is also mentioned by Hicronymus in his translation of the Canon Chronicon of Eusebius but is placed by him in the 3rd year of the 188th Olympiad, *i. e.*, 26 B. C. (*vide* Reinaud " Relations politiques et commerciales del Empire Romain avec l' Asie Orientale). Dion Cassius (History of Rome IX. 58) also speaks of Trajan receiving many embassies from Indians. Pliny refers to another embassy sent from Ceylon in 41 A. D. to Emperor Claudius. Another embassy was sent to Antoninus Pius about 138 A. D. Eusebius (De vita Constant IV. 50) speaks of Indian ambassadors bringing presents to Constantine the Great; and Ammianus Marcellinus (XXII. VII. 10) of embassies sent by Indians to the Emperor Julian in 361 A.D.

The explanation of this intercourse of India with Rome is to be found in the fact that " from the time of Mark Antony to the time of Justinian, *i. e.*, from 30 B. C. to A. D. 550 their political importance as allies against the Parthians and Sassanians and their commercial importance as controllers of one of the main trade routes between the East and the West made the friendship of the Kushans or the Sakas who held the Indus Valley and Bactria, a matter of the highest importance to Rome." (Bombay Gazetteer, Vol. I. Part I. p. 490). How close was the friendship is shown in 60 A. D. by the Roman General Corbulo escorting the Hyrcanian ambassadors up the Indus and through the territories of the Kushans on their return from their embassy to Rome (Rawlinson's Parthia, 271).

Mr. Sewell has briefly sketched the history of this Indian trade with Rome after an elaborate study of the Roman coins found in India. According to him this trade was most active during the period of 80 years from Augutus to Nero (68 A. D.) for the largest number of coins discovered in southern India refers to this period. The locale of these discoveries points also to the conclusion that the things which India exported comprised mostly spices and precious stones. This is corroborated by the fact that Nero burnt at the funeral of Poppoea fully a year's produce of cinnamon and cassia. In the interval between Nero and Caracalla (217 A. D.) there must have been a decline of this trade, considering the very small number of coins discovered which belong to this period. The coin-finds have been mostly in cotton-growing districts, so that the conclusion is irresistible that the articles of trade consisted of such necessaries as cotton fabrics etc. This is corroborated by the rise of a new era in social manners in Rome at this period under Vespasian, when to use the words of Merivale "the simpler habits of the Plebians and the Provincials prevailed over the reckless luxury and dissipation in which the highest classes had so long indulged." The trade with Rome was at low ebb from the days of Caracalla when Rome was a prey to confusion both internal and external and accordingly there have been few finds of coins belonging to this period. The occidental trade revived again though slightly under the Byzantine emperors. The locale of the coins suggest a brisk trade only in pepper and spices and accordingly when Alaric spared Rome in 408 A. D. he demanded and obtained as part of the ransom 3,000 pounds of pepper (Gibbon Ch. XXXI).

Let us now consider the articles of trade in detail. It is too well known that aromatics were consumed on religious and funeral celebrations in Rome. Incense was burnt at every worship. At the funeral of Sylla 210 loads of spices were strewn upon the pile. Pliny in his Natural History (XII. 7 (14) refers to the pepper and ginger of India and the great demand for them in Rome where they were bought by weight like gold and silver. The auther of the Periplus names Tyndis, Muziris,

Nelkynda and Bacare as the ports from which pepper was exported. Mommsen (Prov. of the Roman Empire Vol. II. p. 301) remarks—"In the Flavian period in which the monsoon voyages had already become regular, the whole west coast of India was opened up to the Roman merchants as far down as the coast of Malabar, the home of the highly esteemed and dear-priced pepper for the sake of which they visited the ports of Muziris and Nelkynda. Somewhat farther to the south, at Kananor numerous Roman gold coins of the Julian-Claudian epoch has been found, formerly exchanged against the spices destined for the Roman kitchens." Then there was the demand on India in Rome for silk, muslin and cotton-fabrics. Indian silk so allured the Roman ladies that it sold for its weight in gold. (Encyclopædia Britannica, Vol. XI. p. 459). Tiberius Caesar had to pass a law forbidding transparent silk as an indecent dress. In fact the demand for these luxuries was so great that it shocked the sober-minded citizens of Rome. Thus Petronius complains that fashionable Roman ladies exposed their charms rather too immodestly by clothing themselves in the "webs of woven wind" as he called the Indian muslins imported from India. Pliny says in the same strain "In no year does India drain our Empire of less than 550 millions of sestereces (about 80 lakhs of rupees) giving back her own wares in exchange which are sold among us as fully one hundred times their cost price." "So yearly do we pay for our luxuries and our women." Other articles in demand at Roman markets were precious stones, pearls and minerals which have been carefully noticed and described by Pliny (Natural History XXXII. C. I.). The most highly prized of these stones was the beryl found in the ancient world only in the mines of Podiyur in the Coimbatore District and it is curious to note that in its neighbourhood the largest number of Roman coins has been found. Besides, the pearl-fishery of the southern seas attracted from untold ages a large crowd of foreign merchants. "We are assured on undisputed authority that the Romans remitted annually to India a sum equivalent to £ 4,000,000 to pay for their investments and that in the reign of the Ptolemies 125 sails of Indian shipping were at one time lying in the ports whence Egypt, Syria and Rome itself were supplied with the products of India." [Life in Western India (Guthric) from Tod's Western India, p. 221].

The fact of this trade with Rome is further very satisfactorily established by the various references we find in the native literature of India. The references has been dealt with in the J. A. S. B. for 1906, New series Vol II. by Dr. Satish Ch. Vidyābhūson. Thus the Mahābhārata speaks of the Romaka or Romans coming to the Emperor Yudhisthir with precious presents on the occasion of the Rajsūya Yajna at Indraprostha or Delhi. (Sabhāparva Ch. 51). In the famous astronomical works named Paitāmaha, Vāsishtha, Sūryya,

Paulisa and Romaka Siddhantas, some of which were compiled in the third or second century A. D. Romaka is often mentioned as a Mahāpuri, Pattana or Visaya i. e., a great city, state or dominion. Lastly the Romaka-Jātaka describes a sham priest killing a pigeon to eat it contrary to Buddhist practices, evidently to show the contrast of a Buddhist ascetic with a Roman ascetic.

This trade is further corroborated by evidences from foreign works. We have already referred to the description of mineral products which India sent abroad by Pliny. Even as far back as 177 B. C. Agatharchides describes Sabaea (Yemen) as being the centre of commerce betweenAsia and Europe and very wealthy because of the monopoly of the Indian trade. He also saw large ships coming from the Indus and Patala. The evidences of the Periplus are more interesting and detailed.

Trade was also carried on with China in this period. The name China first appears in the Manu Samhitā X. 43-44 ; Mahābhārata, Anuśāsana Parba, Ch. 33, sloka 21 and Ch. 36, sloka 18. Manu mentions the Chinese as denationalised Kshatriyas. In the Mahābhārata the Chinese are spoken of as allies of Bhagadatta of Assam. These Chinese even faught in the Kurukshetra against the Pāndavas. The same Epic gives a list of presents sent by the Chinese to Yudhisthira.

The Chinese records tell us that foreign trade in China had for a long time been covered by the

name of tribute for, the Chinese would refuse to trade unless it was done under their own conditions viz., the appearance of the offering of gifts as a sign of submission and admiration on the part of the distant monarch. In each case, the full equivalent was paid for these offerings in the shape of countergifts presented to the so-called ambassadors by the Chinese court. Such tributory countries were Arabia, Persia and India. Now T'iendu or T'ien-chu is the name by which India was known to the Chinese since the 1st century B. C. when Buddhism was introduced from India to China. But a more ancient Chinese name for India is "Shin-du". This name evidently rendering the Sanskrit Sindhu (river) which was taken for India, appears in the Chinese annals about 120 B. C., after the expedition of General Chong-kien to western Asia, who reported on the country of Shin-du from hearsay" (Dr. Bretschneider, Mediæval Researches). Mr. G. Hirth in his "China and the Roman Orient" gives the following evidences from Chinese texts regarding transmarine commerce between India and China in this period:—
(1) The inhabitants of Tats'in (Syria) traffic by sea with Au-hsi (Parthia) and T'ienchu (India) the profit of which trade is ten-fold—"Hon-hen-shu." (2) The inhabitants of Au-hsi (Parthia) and T'ienchu have traded with China, its profit is hundredfold—"Chin-shu" (written 265 A. D.) (3) The merchants of this country frequently visit

Funam (Siam), T'ienchu (India), Jih-nan (Annam), Chiao-chih (Tongking) – "Liang-shu" (date uncertain). (4) The country of Tats'in (Syria), also called Likan, is on the west of the great sea, west of Au-hsi (Parthia). They always wish to send embassies to China but the Parthians wanted to make profit out of this trade and would not allow us to pass their country. Further they are always anxious to get Chinese silk—" Win-lio" (composed 220-24 A.D.). (5) It also appears from " Wu-shih-woi-kuo-chuan" i. e., foreign accounts of Wu (222 A. D.) that " ships were provided with seven sails, they sailed from Kang-tiao-chou and with favourable winds could enter Tats'in (Syria) within a month." Dr. Bretschneider presumed that the city of Kang-tiao-chau was on or near the Indian west coast (See his article in the China Review).

The Milindāpaṇha informs us (pp. 127, 327,) that under Rudradaman (A.D. 143-158) the Kshatrapa dynasty of Kathiawar was at the height of its power and Indians of the Tientes (Sindu) brought presents by sea to China.

It may be noted in this connection that India in this period maintained a sort of politico-religious intercourse with China. Kushana Kadphises II was defeated and compelled to pay tribute to China. And the Chinese annals note that in the reign of the Emperor Ho-ti (89 A. D.—105 A. D.) the Indians often sent missions to China. Kanishka on the other hand succeeded in accomplishing the supremely difficult feat of conveying an effective army across the Pamirs and subduing the chiefs or petty Kings in the Khotan, Yarkand and Kashgar regions which had been tributory to China. Besides these political relations we find from an unauthenticated accouut that Indian missionaries had entered China as early as 227 B. C. and in 122 B. C. a Chinese expedition is said to have advanced beyond Yarkand and to have brought back a golden image of Buddha. Communion between India and China becomes very frequent from this date. Knowledge of foreign doctine entered the country and in 61 A.D. Emperor Mingti sent messengers to India to bring back Buddhist books and priests. The priests were brought and one of them Kashiapmadanga (Kāsyapa Mātanga) translated a Sutta in Layong. He is followed in the same year by Fa-lan like the other, a Śraman of central India.

India's trade with Eastern Turkisthan may be suggested by the expeditions of Kanishka. The recent researches of Dr. Sven Hedin and Sir M. A. Stein have conclusively proved this fact, the chief centres of trade being Samarkand, Kashgar and Khotan all situated in the oases supplied by Nature where the caravans stopped and settled. This is further corroborated by the accounts of a Macedonian merchant Maes or Titianus in the 1st century A. D. How Khotan received her culture and religion (Buddhism) from

India is narrated by Stein in his book "The Sandburied Ruins of Khotan." Dr. Sylvan Levi in his paper on the Hindu Civilisation in Central Asia notes how the Kucha Kingdom adopted Buddhism and Sanskrit literature, how before long Sanskrit works on Astronomy and Medicine were translated into the Kuchian tongue some of which are at Petrograd while others at Tokio.

That India traded with and even colonised Further India has been proved by Col. Gerini. Ptolemy informs us that in his time the coastline of Further India was inhabited throughout its length by the Sindoi (Hindus). This colonisation must have been of transmarine orgin. On the one hand the Hindus did not advance along the land route long hidden and leading through the Ganges delta and Assam, until the second half of the present millenium. On the other hand the proof of the fact that the Hindus made their way to Further India by sea is the predominance of the Hindus along the coast as remarked by Ptolemy. This colonisation cannot have started from southern India for the reason that Brahminism at this period had taken but little hold on the south and the transmission of civilisation from these shores is therefore extremely improbable. It was not until a much later period that the communication between southern India and Further India began, the results of which are apparent in the later temple-buildings of the latter. Further evidences of the northern origin of this colonisation are the names of more important towns of Further India which are almost entirely borrowed from Sanskrit names of the towns of the Ganges valley and also the desire of the rulers of Further India to retrace their origin to the mythical Solar and Lunar dynasties of Madhyadeśha.

The maritime route led straight to Burma but the Indian civilisation at the moment found that province less favourable to its development than that of the great and more hospitable Champā Kingdom in the central south. The Gulf of Ligor and the banks of the great rivers of Cambodia seem to have been the central points of Brahminical influence. According to M. E. Aymonier, most of the traditional names of the Kings of Cambodia are to be read in inscriptions in Sanskrit from the 3rd century A.D. to 1108 A.D. Inscribed memorials, carvings and buildings make it quite clear that immigrants brought with them gods of the Hindu Pantheon (Śiva, Goneśha, etc.) and the beautiful legend of the Rāmāyana. Professor Lacouperie in his Western Origin of Chinese Civilisation also maintains that Cambodia was colonised by the Hindus in the first century A.D.

India's trade with the Malaya archipelago has been proved by Mr. John Crawford but unfortunately the beginning of this commercial intercourse can be proved only by indirect evidence. John Crawford in this connection relies on the fact that the two articles of trade peculiar to the to the Malaya archipelago and in earlier times procurable from no other source were the cloves and the nutmegs. The first appearance of these products must accordingly give an indication of the latest date at which the intercourse of Nearer India with the Malaya Archipelago can have been systematically developed. Both these spices were named among the spices imported to Alexandria for the first time in the Age of Marcus Aurelius, *i.e.*, 180 A. D. while a century earlier the author of the Periplus does not mention them. If then we reflect that a certain time would have been required to familiarise the natives of India with these spices before there was any idea of shipping them further and that perhaps on the first trading voyages which must necessarily have been directed towards the Straits of Malacca, products of that region first and then the spices which grow in the more distant parts of the Archipelago had been exchanged, we are justified in placing the Indian-Malaya trade in the first century of the Christian era. Chinese accounts lead us to suppose that at this time Indian merchants had even reached the south-eastern coast of China. And even before cloves and nutmegs appeared in the trade-lists of Alexandria, Ptolemy the Geographer had already inserted on his Map of the World the names of Malaya and 'Jawa'. And within a short time, following the tracks of the merchants, Indian priests went to the islands and spread their influence.

abacus and over it, the figure of a beast. In the body of some abacus, are executed birds or beasts in relief; in some creepers and flowers. Of these that at village Loria Nandangarh (District Champaran, Bihar) stands almost entire. On it, a flock of swans is very finely represented in the abacus; on the top is carved out an excellent lion facing east and resting on its two hind legs. The lion of the pillar at the village Rampurna (District Champaran) which is now placed at the entrance of the Calcutta Museum is not life-like, yet its limbs appear lively and spirited. The pillar of Sanchi has similar four lions. Their heads are now broken. Yet "their muscles and paws are quite natuaral" says General Cunningham "and may be compared with the samples of the Greecian Sculpture" (Arch. Rep. 1904-5, p. 36.) The capital of the Sarnath Pillar is, however, the best. In the body of the abacus are shown figures of elephants, bulls, horses and lions. Four large lions leaning against one another, stand on the top. The lions are natural and lively and exhibit a thorough lordly mien. Sir John Marshall praises the capital on the Sarnath Pillar in the following terms:—"Both bell and lions are in an excellent state of preservation and masterpieces in point of both style and technique—the finest carvings, indeed, that India has yet produced and unsurpassed I venture to think by anything of their kind in the ancient world." The Aśokan Sculpture was no doubt affected by

Persian and Hellenistic influences but nevertheless is mainly Indian both in spirit and execution. As for instance, the design of the Sarnath capital was suggested by Persia; but even the lions are wholly different from and far superior to their Persian prototypes in pose and style while the the bas-reliefs of the guardian animals of the four quarters on the sides of the abacus are purely Indian. But exclusive of the capital, the monolithic columns of fine-grained sandstone (*e. g.*, the Lauriya Nandangaṛh pillar) some of which exceed forty-feet in height are marvels of technical execution. The sides of the Barāvar caves excavated in most refractory gniess rock are polished like glass mirrors. Hence the remark of Mr. V. A. Smith "The skill of the stone-cutter may be said to have attained perfection and to have accomplished tasks which would perhaps be found beyond the powers of the twentieth century. Gigantic shafts of hard sand-stone, thirty or forty feet in length were dressed and proportioned with the utmost nicety, receiving a polish which no modern mason knows how to impart to the material. Enormous surfaces of the hardest gniess were burnished like mirrors, bricks of huge dimensions were successfully fired and the joints of masonry were fitted with extreme accuracy." The stonework of Aśoka's time is equally well-finished in all other respects. Most of the inscriptions are incised with extreme accuracy in beautifully cut letters. The relief sculptures at Bharut and Sanchi some of which may be regarded as pictures executed in stone exhibit most vividly the details of the life of the age. The artists delighted in representing it with frank realism and in decorating their panels with ornaments of charming design executed with good taste.

We have no specimen of Maurya painting. But it is natural to assume that the art of painting also flourished in this period which is so famous for the sister arts of architecture and sculpture. In fact Vātsyāyana who flourished towards the close of the 4th Century B. C. gives among other things the six canons of Painting in his Kāma-Śāstra, a work on Fine Arts.

The Engineering ability displayed in the handling and transport of huge monolithic coloumns conveyed over immense distances is remarkable. When the excavations in progress at Taxila and Pātaliputra shall be more advanced, additional evidence of the skill of the Maurya engineers may be expected.

Among the less important crafts we might mention the leather industry. Megasthenes refers to white leather shoes. Arrian quoting Nearchos says " They wear shoes of white leather very eleborately worked; and the soles of the shoes are variegated and high-heeled so as to make the wearer seem taller " (Nearchos Frags. 9 and 10=Arr. Ind. 16).

The dying industry was in a highly developed condition in this period. Nearchos (Frags. 9 and 10) refers to the dying of beards in different colours—white, blue-black, crimson, purple and green. Ktesias also refers to the Cochinal plant, the worm and the dyes made from it.

The potters made utensils for domestic use (Artha. p. 123). Besides, the bamboo-workers made utensils of cane and bark (Artha. p. 123) and manufactured straps from cane and bamboo-bark (*Ibid* p. 142).

The fishermen fished in the sea in search of conch-shells and pearls (*Ibid* pp. 156-7). We find a reference to dried fish (*Ibid* pp. 114, 139) and also to dried meat (*Ibid* p. 139).

We also hear of manufacture of flour, extracting oil from oilseeds and manufacture of sugar from the sugarcane (*Ibid* p. 113).

Some of these crafts were organised into guilds. The Superintendent of Accounts had to regularly enter in prescribed registers the history of customs, professions and transactions of the corporations (Artha. p. 69). We find referenee to corporations that subsisted by agriculture (Artha. p. 455). In the ideal scheme of a city places are reserved for the residence of guilds and corporations of workmen (Artha. p. 61) and the taxes paid by them are included among the most important sources of revenue. (Artha. p. 66). It is laid down that "Guilds of workmen as well as those who carry on Co-operative work shall divide their earnings either equally or as agreed upon among themselves (Artha. p. 235)." "There were also temporary combinations of workmen and others engaged under corporate responsibility for the execution of contracts." (Dr. Thomas in the Cambridge History of India p. 478). [Artha. p. 236.]

There was also a considerable localisation of trades and crafts. Kautilya refers to the artificial creation by the King of villages of agriculturists belonging to the Śūdra caste, of Brahmin villages with forests for their undisturbed pursuit of learning and religion, of mines and factories and markets (Artha. Bk. II. Ch. I). Within the city the various trades and crafts were localised in special quarters and their distribution followed a definite plan. Thus every caste and craft had a locality of its own. (See Bk. II. Ch. IV. for the details of distribution.)

In the Punjab, the actual cultivator would still be a man of the three upper classes while in the east he is generally a Śūdra. And Kautilya also refers to the creation by the King of villages of agricultural people of the Śūdra caste (Artha. p. 51). It is to this period, no doubt, that we must ascribe the great complexity of the caste system and the beginning of the association of caste with craft. But even in this period, according to Manu (X. 65) a Śūdra can become a Brahmin and a Brahmin a Śūdra according to their good or bad deeds. Manu (II. 158) says "As liberality to a fool is fruitless, so is a Brahmin useless if he read not the Holy Texts or again he is no better than an elephant made of wood or an antelope made of leather." Megasthenes says that a Hindu of any caste may become a Sophist (Brahmin ?).

Though agricultural labour was not held in high esteem, nevertheless the status of the artisans was very high. They were regarded as being devoted in a special manner to the royal service and capital punishment was inflicted on any person who impaired the efficiency of a craftsman by causing the loss of a hand or an eye (Strabo XV. 54). Kautilya also lays down "Those who conspire to lower the quality of the works of artisans, to hinder their income or to obstruct their sale and purchase shall be fined 1000 paṇas (Artha. p. 259).

The assertion of the Greek travellers that slavery was unknown or according to Onesicritus was unknown in the kingdom of the Musicanus (Upper Sind) [Meg. Frag. 26, 27; Onesic. Frag. 20=Arr. Ind. 10; Strabo XV. C. 710]. That slavery was a regular institution in this period also is proved by Kautilya's Arthaśāstra (Bk. III. Ch. XIII.). The position of the slave was, however, not so bad as that of the helots of Sparta or that of the villeins of the Middle Ages. This is evident from the following humane rules regarding them preserved by Kautilya :—(1) Employing a slave to carry the dead or to sweep ordure, urine or the leaving of food; keeping a slave naked; or hurting or abusing him..........shall cause the forfeiture of the value paid for him. (2) A slave shall be entitled to enjoy not only what he has earned without prejudice to to his master's work but also the inheritance he has received from his father. (3) On paying the value (for which one is enslaved) a slave shall regain his Āryahood. (4) Failure to set a slave to liberty on receipt of the required amount of ransom shall be punished with a fine of 12 paṇas. (5) Putting a slave to confinement for no reason shall likewise be punished. (6) If a slave who is less than 8 years old is employed in mean avocations against his will or is sold or mortgaged in a foreign land or if a pregnant female slave is sold or pledged without any provision for her confinment, his or her master shall be punished with the first amercement. The purchasers and the abetters shall likewise be punished. (7) The property of a slave shall pass into the hands of his kinsmen and in their absence, his master shall take it. (8) When a child is begotten on a female slave by her master, both the child and its mother shall at once be recognised as free (Artha. pp. 231-33). The condition of the labourer in the mines was, however, not satisfactory. For, in Artha. p. 219, labour in the mines is recommended as the alternative for banishment—the highest punishment that could be meted out to a Brahmin.

A large number of rules regarding labourers and their wages are given by Kautilya. Thus, it is laid down that "wages being previously unsettled, a cultivator shall get $\frac{1}{10}$th of the crops grown, a herdsman $\frac{1}{10}$th of the butter clarified, a trader $\frac{1}{10}$th of the sale proceeds (Artha. p. 233). Artisans, musicians, physicians, buffons, cooks and other workmen shall obtain as much wages as similar persons engaged elsewhere usually get or as much as experts shall fix (Artha. p. 233). Disputes regarding wages shall be decided on the strength of evidences furnished by witnesses. In the absence of witnesses, the master who has provided work shall be examined (Artha. p. 233). Failure to pay wages shall be punished with a fine of ten times the amount of wages or 6 paṇas (Artha. p. 233). If the labourers giving up work in the middle supply substitutes, they shall be paid their their wages in full (Artha. p. 235).

But a servant neglecting or unreasonably putting off work for which he has received wages shall be fined 12 paṇas (Artha. p. 234). If an employer having caused his labourer to do a part of a work, will not cause him do the rest for which the latter is ready, then also the unfinished portion of the work shall be regarded as finished. But owing to considerations of changes that have occurred in time or place or owing to bad workmanship of the labourer, the employer may not be pleased with what has been already turned out by the labourer. Also the workman may if unrestrained, do more than agreed upon and thereby cause loss to the employer. In these cases, wages will not be paid for work that is not done or is overdone (Artha. p. 235). It is also laid down that if a healthy person who deserts his company after work has begun shall be fined 12 paṇas (Artha. p. 236).

It will be evident from the various kinds of ships already mentioned that maritime trade was carried on in this period between India and the outside world. The kind and degree of this maritime activity will be ascertained from the various kinds of port-taxes that were levied by the Superintendent of Ships (Artha. pp. 156-59). The latter was also entrusted with the duty of enforcing many humane harbour regulations. Thus, whenever any weather-beaten, tempest-tossed ship arrived at his port, his duty was to lend her the helping hand of a father (Artha. p. 157). Vessels carrying on merchandise spoiled by water may be exempted by him from toll or they may have their toll reduced to half. Again, whenever a ship foundered owing to want of hands or on account of ill-repair it was his duty to make good the loss in part or full as the case might be. He had also to see that pirate ships, vessels which were bound for an enemy country as well as those which had violated the customs and rules in force in port towns were destroyed (Ibid). "The existence of these elaborate regulations" rightly obserses Mr. V. A. Smith (E. H. I. p. 125) "is conclusive proof that the Maurya Empire in the 3rd century B. C. was in constant intercourse with foreign states and that large numbers of strangers visited the capital on business" Reference to foreign maritime commerce in Aśoka's time is also to be found in Bodhisattābadāna Kalpalatā where in chapter 13 we are told how Emperor Aśoka was one day approached by some Indian merchants who traded to the distant islands. They informed him of their losses and complete ruin brought about by the depredations of sea-faring pirates called Nāgas. They said that if the emperor disposed to be indifferent towards them, they would no doubt be forced to take to other means of livelihood but in that case there would be a slackening of the sea-borne trade and a consequent falling off of the import and export duties. Indeed in the days of Aśoka with her systematic intercourse with Ceylon, Syria, Greece, Macedon and Epirus (Rock Edicts II. and XIII.) India become through the efforts of merchants and missionaries "at once the Commercial and Spiritual centre—the very heart of the Old World."

From Arrian we know that the northern part of Ceylon was in a very highly civilised state and that it was a seat of extensive commerce with the countries from the farthest China in the East to Italy in the West (Historical Researches, Vol. II. p. 432). In the days of Alexander when his general Nearchos was entering the Persian Gulf, Muscat was pointed out to him as the principal mart for Indian products which were transmitted thence to

Assyria. Again the Pentingerian Tables show that in India Muziris was a Roman settlement and there was a garrison of 1200 men there for the protection of trade. Trade was also carried on with Egypt in this period. Ptolemy I. who had visited India with Alexander got Egypt as his share and immediately directed his attention to a commercial intercourse with India. For this purpose he built up the famous light-house at Pharos on the mouth of the bay at Alexandria which was dangerous of navigation. Unluckily he died soon. His son and successor Ptolemy Philadelphos gave great impetus to Indian commerce. He sent an embassy headed by Dionysius to Aśoka. He maintained a well-furnished navy in the Red Sea and founded the sea-ports of Berenice and Myos Hormos on the Egyptian coasts. For easy transport of goods he began the construction of a canal joining the Nile with the Red Sea but it was never completed. Ships trading with India arrived at Myos Hormos from where all goods were taken on camels on the 12th day to Coptos, a city on a canal of the Nile and thence to Alexandria by water in another 12 days. Owing to great heat the caravans crossed the desert in the night. There were resting places on the road (Pliny, Natural History VI. 23). The sea-borne trade continued to be conveyed along the coast from Berenice, round the south coast of Arabia and Persia to the mouth of the Indus.

Besides the Red-sea route, there were at least three overland routes by which Indian goods were carried to foreign countries. The first ran across Central Asia along the Oxus, the Caspian and the Black Seas. The second lay through the heart of Persia over to the neck of Asia Minor, while the third was through the Persian Gulf and the Euphrates to Damascus and Tadmore and thence to the ports of the Levant. Professor Heeren thinks that the Persian Gulf was closed to the Indian trade in the time of the Parthan Empire, the articles being then conveyed along the Red Sea to Myos Hormos and then overland to Palmyra (Historical Researches, Vol. II. p. 409). The route was reopened in the days of the Roman Empire (Appian, V. 9; Horace Ep. I. 45).

Within the Empire, the river-routes, the canals and the roads were the high ways of internal trade. From the internal evidence of Kautilya's Artha-śāstra we find that Magadha had internal trade relations with Pāndya, Kerala, Konkan, Māhisa, Kausāmbi, Banga, Kalinga, Kāmrūpa, countries bordering on the Himalayas, Vidarva, Kośala and Benares. Kautilya shows his preference for land-routes on account of lesser risks involved in them (Artha. p. 361). Of water-routes, one along the shore and another in mid-ocean, the route along and close to the shore is better, as it touches many trading port-towns (Artha. p. 367). Kautilya regards the land-routes leading to the south as more important than those leading to the Himalayas for, while the latter facilitated the supply of blankets, skins and horses, the former brought to market the supply of such valuable commodities as diamonds and other precious stones, pearls, gold and conch-shells of which southern India was the home for ages. There were also other routes leading to the east and west. One of these routes was undoubtedly what has been mentioned by Megasthenes as the Royal Road connecting Pātaliputra with the delta of the Indus; another route connected Patāliputra with the Kabul valley. These routes were the continuations of others which passed through Iran to the west. In the routes at intervals of ten stades [1 stade = $\frac{1}{10}$th of a yojana (Rhys David's Bud. Ind. p. 265)] there were signboards noting turnings and distances (Meg. XXXIV. 3.). Besides these, there were certain trade-routes proper (বণিকপথ) mentioned by Kautilya. These were চক্রপথ, স্বরোষ্ট্রপথ, পাদপথ etc. The চক্রপথ was a cart track which admitted of a larger volume of traffic than the পাদপথ while the স্বরোষ্ট্রপথ was so made that it could be used whatever the season and nature of the soil through which it passed. In this connection it may be noted that trees were planted along the roads and water-storages were set up ministering to the comforts of the passers-by. There was provision made by hotelkeepers for the supply of food and resting places for travellers and traders (Artha. p.

277). These facilities anticipated those of Aśoka as set forth in his Rock Edict II.

The articles of trade included (1) precious things like diamonds, precious stones, conchshells, pearls and necklaces which had to pay a certain amount of toll fixed by experts acquainted with the time, cost and finish of the production of such articles (2) fibrous garments (Kshauma), cotton cloth (Dukula), silk, mail armour, sulphuret of arsenic (haritāl), red arsenic (Manaśśilā) vermillion (hingulaka), metals and colouring ingredients (Varṇadhātu), sandals, brown sandal (aguru), pungents (Katuka), ferments (Kinva), dress (āvarana) and the like; wine, ivory, skins, raw materials used in making cloth or fibrous garments, carpets, curtains (Prāvarana) and products yielded by worms (Krimi-jāta) wool and other products yielded by goats and sheep and and these had to pay $\frac{1}{10}$th or $\frac{1}{15}$th as toll (Artha. p. 139) (3) cloths (Bastra), quadrupeds, bipeds, threads, cotton, scents, medicines, wood, bamboo, fibres (Balkala), skins and clay-pots; grain, oils, sugar (Kshāra), salt, liquor (madya), cooked rice and the like and these had to pay $\frac{1}{10}$th or $\frac{1}{15}$th as their toll (Artha. p. 139) (4) flowers, fruits, vegetables, roots, bulbous roots (Kānda), seeds, dried fish and dried meat and these had to pay $\frac{1}{6}$th as toll (Artha. p. 139). Imported salt had to pay $\frac{1}{6}$th portion to the King (Artha. p. 99). But commodities intended for marriages or taken by a bride from her parent's house to her husband's house or taken for the purpose of sacrificial performances, confinement of women, worship of gods, investiture of the sacred thread, gift of cows, any religious rite, consecration ceremony and other special ceremonials shall be let off free of toll (Artha. p. 137).

It is also interesting to note that skins were imported into the country from China and Central Asia, silk from China [(China-patta) Artha. p. 94], pearls and precious stones from Ceylon and the best horses from the Indus countries and beyond. We learn that the best elephants came from the eastern Provinces—Anga (Bhagalpur and Mungher), Kalinga (Orissa) and Karusa (Sāhābād). The import of weapons, mail armour, metals, chariots, precious stones, grains and cattle was forbidden under severe penalties (Artha. p. 137). The imported articles had to pay $\frac{1}{5}$th of their value as toll (Artha. p. 139). The officer in charge of boundaries shall receive a paṇa and a quarter as road-cess (bartanī) on each load of merchandise. He shall levy a paṇa on a single-hoofed animal, half-a-paṇa on each head of cattle and a quarter on a minor quadruped. He shall also receive a masha on a headload of merchandise. After carefully examining foreign commodities as to their superior and inferior quality and stamping them with his seal, he shall send the same to the Superintendent of Tolls (Artha p. 138). One of the rules guiding the import of commodities is significant. " Whatever causes harm or is useless to the country shall be shut out; and whatever is of immense good as well as seeds not easily available shall be let in free of toll" (Artha p. 138).

It is no less interesting to note that the officer in charge of boundaries (antapāla) should make good whatever had been lost by merchants within his jurisdiction like the Superintendent of Ships (Artha p. 138). To encourage foreign merchants, the Superintendent of Commerce was required to show favour to those who import foreign merchandise. Mariners and merchants who import foreign merchandise should be favoured with the remission of trade taxes so that they may derive some profit (Artha p. 119). Similarly, foreigners importing merchandise shall be exempted from being sued for debts unless they are (local) associations and partners (Artha p. 119).

The law required that all articles for sale should be brought to the toll house, there precisely weighed, measured or numbered and then offerred for sale and if sold taxed (Artha p. 136). Toll was paid only when actual sale took place. All goods brought for sale had to be marked with a seal mark (অভিজ্ঞানমুদ্রা) [*Ibid*]. The Greek accounts also refer to the practice of stamping commodities. "The ordinary practice in later times and probably also in the Maurya age was to do the stamping with red-lead (সিন্দুর)" (Ep. Ind. VII. p. 230). Those who smuggle a part of the merchandise on which toll has not been paid with that on which toll has been paid as well as those who put a second portion of the merchandise with the stamped merchandise with a view to smuggle shall pay as much fine as is equal to the quantity smuggled (Artha. p. 137). When merchants with their merchandise arrive at the toll-gate, four or five collectors shall take down who the merchants are, whence they come and what amount of merchandise they have brought and where for the first time the seal-mark had been made (Artha. p. 135-36). Those whose merchandise has not been stamped with seal mark shall pay twice the amonnt of toll (Artha. p. 136). For counterfeit seals, they shall pay 8 times the toll (*Ibid*). If the seal mark is effaced or torn, the merchants in question shall be detained either in the room where persons are locked up for untimely walking in streets (घटिकास्थान) or in the toll-house for one day (*Ibid*). When one kind of seal is used for another, or when one kind of merchandise has been otherwise named, the merchants shall pay a fine of $1\frac{1}{4}$ paṇas for each load (Artha. p. 136). The amount and price of all goods were declared and the sale was by auction, any enhancement accruing to the Treasury (Artha. p. 136).

As a precaution against evasion of toll-dues, it was laid down that "Commerce in commodities manufactured from mineral products shall be centralised and punishments for manufacturers, sellers and purchasers of such commodities outside the prescribed locality were laid down" (Artha. p. 97). The Superintendent of Ocean-mines regulated the commerce in conch shells, salt, diamonds, precious stones, pearls and corals which he collected (Artha. p. 99). When minerals and other commodities are purchased from mines, a fine of 600 paṇas shall be imposed (Artha. p. 139). When flowers and fruits are purchased from flower or fruit gardens a fine of 54 paṇas shall be imposed (*Ibid*). When any kind of grass and grain is purchased from fields a fine of 53 paṇas shall be imposed. When vegetables, roots, bulbous roots are purchased from vegetable gardens, a fine of 51$\frac{3}{4}$ paṇas shall be imposed (Artha. p. 139).

The following rules were laid down regarding the sale of the King's merchandise in foreign countries. Having ascertained the value of local produce as compared with that of foreign produce that can be obtained in barter, the Superintendent of Commerce would find out by calculation whether there is any margin left for profit after meeting the payments to the foreign king such as the toll (śulka), road-cess (bartanī), conveyances (আতিবাহিক), tax payable at military stations (গুল্মদেয়), ferry charges (তরদেয়), subsistence to the merchant and his followers and the portion of merchandise payable to the foreign king (bhāga). If no profit can be raised by selling the local produce in foreign countries, he has to consider whether any local produce can be bartered for any foreign produce (Artha. pp. 119-120).

Some regulations regarding industry and trade have modern features. Thus, the Superintendent of Commerce exercised roughly speaking the functions of a modern controller of prices. Thus we are told that " The Superintendent of Commerce shall fix a profit of 5 per cent over and above the fixed price of local commodities and ten per cent over foreign produce. Merchants who enhance the price even to the extent of half a paṇa more than the above in the sale or purchase of commodities shall be punished with a fine of from five paṇas in case of realising 100 paṇas upto 200 paṇas. Fines for greater enhancement shall be proportionally increased " (Artha. p. 260). Death was the penalty for non-payment of tithe on sales says Megasthenes. Again with regard to the profits of the middleman who is a well-known agent in enhancing the price of articles, we are told that " It is the duty of the trader to calculate the daily earnings of middlemen and to fix that amount on which they are authorised to live; for whatever amount falls between sellers and purchasers (*i.e.*, brokerage) is different from profit " (Artha. p. 260). In case of failure to sell collected merchandise wholesale at a fixed price, the rate shall be altered (Artha. p. 260). The Superintendent shall on consideration of the outlay, the quantity manufactured, the amount of toll, the interest on outlay, hire and other kinds of accessory expenditure, fix the price of such merchandise with due regard to its having been manufactured long ago or imported from a distant country (Artha. p. 261).

The extent of control exercised by the state over trade and industry will be apparent from other rules as well. Thus it was laid down that whenever there is an excessive supply of merchandise, the Superintentent shall centralise its sale and prohibit the sale of similar merchandise elsewhere before the centralised supply is disposed of (Artha. p. 261). The manufacture of salt was a Government monopoly and any one manufacturing salt without license except hermits shall be punished with the highest ammercement (Artha. p. 99). With a view to prevent deception the Superintendent of Commerce shall supervise weights and measures (Artha. p. 258). Those who trade in clarified butter shall give to the purchaser $\frac{1}{32}$nd part more as taptavyāji (i. e.. compensation for decrease in the quantity of ghee owing to its liquid condition) [Artha. p. 130]. Those who trade in oil shall give $\frac{1}{64}$th part more as taptavyāji (Artha p. 130). While selling liquid traders shall give $\frac{1}{50}$th part more as Mānasrāva (i. e., compensation for diminution in the quantity owing to its over-flow or adhesion to the measuring can) [Artha. p. 131]. When a trader sells or mortgages inferior as superior articles, articles of some other locality as the produce of a particular locality he shall not only be punished with a fine of 54 paṇas but also be compelled to make good the loss (Artha. p. 259). The sale or mortgage of articles such as timber, iron, brilliant stones, ropes, skins, earthenware, threads, fibrous garments and woollen clothes as superior though they are inferior shall be punished with a fine of 8 times the value of the articles thus sold (Artha. p. 259). Merchants who conspire either to prevent the sale of merchandise or to sell or purchase commodities at higher prices shall be fined 1,000 paṇas (Artha. p. 260). Those who conspire to obstruct the sale or purchase of the works of artisans shall be fined 1,000 paṇas (Artha. p. 259).

Further, adulteration of merchandise and deceitful mixtures were punished (Artha. p. 259). Thus, it is laid down that "adulteration of salt shall be punished with the highest amercement" (Artha. p. 99). Similarly, adulteration of grains, oils, alkalis, scents and medicinal articles with similar things of no quality shall be punished with a fine of 12 paṇas (Artha. p. 260).

Coming to the trade organisations of the time, we find that the trade-guilds were already an important factor in the economic life of the people. The reputed wealth of the guilds and the way in which they were sometimes exploited by unscrupulous kings may be gathered from Kautilya's Arthaśāstra Bk. V. Ch. 2, (pp. 305 ff). Three commissioners enjoying the confidence of the guilds were appointed to receive the deposits which could be taken back in times of distress (Artha. p. 253). Special privileges were accorded to a merchant belonging to a trade-guild. Thus in p. 228 we are told that "such merchants as belong to a trade-guild need not restore even the value of that merchandise that is lost or destroyed owing to its inherent defects or to some unforeseen accidents". Similarly special concessions were made regarding law-suits between trade-guilds (Artha. p. 190). The power and influence of the guilds at this period also appears indirectly from pp. 403-4 where the point is seriously discussed whether the troubles caused by a guild or its leaders are more serious. Kautilya in opposition to his predecessors declares in favour of the latter.

Besides trade-guilds, we find Joint Stock Companies flourishing side by side. References to them are to be found in the Arthśāstra where in p. 235 we are told that "guilds of workmen (or workmen employed by companies) as well as those who carry on co-operative work shall divide their earnings equally or as agreed among themselves."

Then we come to the organisation of the Traders' League. But both Mrs. Rhys Davids and Richard Fick deny the existence of any such definite organisation which could make the word league applicable to it. These scholars, however, lose sight of the fact that in a legal code of India belonging to the 6th century B. C. the organisation of traders is distinctly referred to as having the authority to lay down rules for themselves and as such a definite place in the constitution of the state (Gautama XI. 21, 22). In fact these organisations soon had a rapid growth and in the next two centuries displayed activities which have a surprisingly modern appearance. Thus Kautilya in his Arthaśāstra (p. 403) refers to "traders who unite in causing rise and fall in the value of articles and live by making profits cent per cent in paṇas and kumbhas (measures of grain)". This activity, seems to be, very much like the modern 'corner' or 'trust system' [Corporate Life in Ancient India, pp. 84-86].

In this period there was a system of currency of standard and token coins issued and regulated by the Government. In Kautilya's Arthaśāstra (p. 98) we find that the examiner of coins regulated currency both as a medium of exchange (ব্যবহারিকম্) and as legal tender admissible into the treasury (কোষপ্রবেশম্)। The State Goldsmith employed artisans for the manufacture of gold coins (Artha. p. 106) while both the State Goldsmith and the Superintendent of Mint carried on the manufacture of silver coins (Artha. pp. 98, 106) which were of various kinds *viz.*, a paṇa, half-a-paṇa, quarter and one-eigth paṇa (Artha. p. 98). The Superintendent of Mint carried on the manufacture of copper coins which were divided into a māshaka, half a māshaka, kākaṇi and half a kākaṇi (Artha. p. 98).

Besides the coins, there was a very considerable use of instruments of credit. The merchants no doubt gave letters of credit on one another. Again we find that in Kautilya's time there was a system called Ādesha—somewhat akin to a modern bill of exchange in its simplest form. An Ādesha is literally an order to a third person to pay up a sum of money on behalf of the sender of the order (Artha. p. 227).

The day is not yet come when the guilds would perform roughly speaking the functions of modern banks. Whether they had begun to receive deposits is not known but we have a reference in Artha. page 305 to their lending out money. Thus, we are told that when a king finds himself in financial trouble and needs money, he may employ a spy in the garb of a rich merchant or a real rich merchant famous for his vast commerce who would borrow from corporations bar-gold and then allow himself to be robbed of it the same night.

We shall now touch on the rules regulating loans which are justly recognised to be of great importance, for on them depends to a large extent the economic welfare of the country রাজন্যযোগক্ষেম as Kautilya puts it (Artha. p. 221). The legal rate of interest for money lent is $1\frac{1}{4}$ per cent per month, that is, 15 per cent per year. But the rate is allowed to increase in view of the risks to which the investment of the money lent and consequently its realisation are exposed. Accordingly money borrowed by persons going to forest for trade is allowed to return an interest of 10 per cent per month, while on the same principle the interest payable by merchants who trade by sea is allowed to mount up to the maximum rate of 20 per cent per annum (Artha. p. 221). A disregard of the maximum limits is punished with fines to be paid not only by the moneylender but also by the witnesses to the transaction (Artha. p. 221). Interest in grains in seasons of good harvest should not exceed more than half when valued in money (Artha. p. 221). Interest on stocks (প্রক্ষেপ) shall be one-half of the profit and be regularly paid as each year expires. If it is allowed to accumulate owing either to the intention or to the absence abroad (of the receiver or payer) the amount payable shall be equal to twice the share or principal (Artha. p. 221). Sons of deceased debtor shall pay the principal with interest. (In the absence of sons) kinsmen claiming the share of the dead man or sureties such as joint partners of the debt shall pay the same (Artha. p. 222). Cultivators or government servants shall not be caught hold of for debts while they are engaged in their duties (Artha p. 223).

An idea of the wealth of the period can be gathered from Bk. II. chap. XI. of Kautilya's Arthaśāstra (pp. 86. ff.). In the towns lived a large number of rich merchants and middlemen, while the royal Court at Pātaliputra was maintained and served with great pomp and splendeur. Gold vessels measuring six feet across are said to have been used. The king when he appeared, was either carried in a golden palanquin or mounted on an elephant with gorgeous trappings. He was clothed in fine muslin embroidered with gold. The luxuries of all parts of Asia including China were at his disposal. In the towns inns, liquorshops and gaming houses are numerous. The liquor shops were made attractive as we have already seen by the provision of seats, couches, scents, garlands, water and other comforts suitable to the varying seasons (Artha. p. 148). The crafts have their public dinner which provided livelihood for various classes of dancers, singers and actors. Even the villagers are visited by them adds the author of the Artha-śāstra who is inclined to discourage the existence of a common hall used for their shows as too great a distraction from the life of the home and the fields (Artha. p. 54). The king provided in amphitheatres constructed for public entertainments, dramatic, boxing and other contests of men and animals.

Though the villagers were not what would now be called rich, nevertheless, there was a sufficiency for their simple needs. According to Megasthenes the society was marked with simplicity of manners and the people were known for their temperate habits. Though finery and ornaments were in use, the usual dress was simple. A cotton dhuti and chaddar, white leather shoes and an umbrella generally made up a man's attire. There were a few paupers and even these were taken care of by the

Government. Kautilya has laid down (Artha. p. 53) that "the king shall provide the aged, the infirm, the afflicted and the helpless with maintenance." "He shall also provide subsistence to helpless women when they are carrying and also to the children they give birth to" (Artha. p. 53).

The only serious inroad upon the comfort and happiness of the people seems to have been famine Megasthenes says that owing to irrigation famines. were unknown. All that we can say having regard to the too many references to times of scarcity in previous periods is that things in this respect have improved in the time of Megasthenes. In fact, elaborate measures were taken by Chandragupta's Government for protecting the people from the ravages of famine. As general preventive, it was laid down that in the Government storehouse, only half of the garnered articles should be used, the other half shall be kept in reserve to ward off the calamities of the people (Artha. p. 115). During famine, the king was advised to provide seeds to secure a good harvest in future. He had to start relief works—(1) by giving work to the famine-stricken for wage-earning (2) by free distribution of alms from the storehouse referred to above (3) by making those in better circumstances to contribute to the famine-fund and (4) by taking the help of allies. These measures failing, the king should according to Kautilya save his people by (i) temporary emigration with his subjects to a different kingdom with abundance of crops (ii) by emigrating to the sea-shores or banks of rivers or lakes where he would found a new settlement and employ his subjects in growing grains and vegetables as well as in hunting and fishing on a large scale and (iii) by the abandonment of his country to some other king (Artha. pp. 262-63).

It is evident from this economic survey of Maurya India that the ancient Indians were not an exclusively religious people that in fact, they did devote their time and energy to the pursuits of the material world. And what is more, we find Kautilya holding "wealth and wealth only are important, in as much as charity and desire depend upon wealth for their realisation" (Artha. p. 14).

Andhra-Kushana period.

(200 B. C.—300 A. D.)

The Age of the Mauryas was followed by the age of the Andhras of the South and Kushanas of the North which witnessed an equal, if not a greater economic development of the country. This is apparent from the remarkable finds of Roman coins, more numerous in the south than in the north, which were poured into all parts of India in payment for her silks, spices, gems and dye-stuffs. These evidences are corroborated by the Sanskrit, Pali and Tamil works and are further strengthened by definite evidences from forign works. The chief of these are Pliny's Natural History, the Periplus of the Erythrean Sea and Ptolemy's Geography, besides the incidental allusions to Indian industry and shipping thrown out by writers like Agatharchides and Strabo.

The people were settled in villages. A little larger than the villages was the Karbata, a still larger was the nagara. Villages were divided into ghoshas or pallis, some of them marches (prantas, on the border). The village headman who was appointed by the king administered justice and levied taxes. The king did not interfere so long as the villagers paid the revenue assessed by the king's officer. Thus the villages were practically autonomous. "Authority rests with the village according to law" (Pār., Grihya Sūtra I. 813) and the Epic seems to uphold even family custom as legally sufficient. Thus one man demands a price for his daughter because that is his family custom (Mbh. 1. 113. 9 f.). So another defends his occupation of killing animals on the same ground.

In this period joint family was existing side by side with single families. An elder brother in the Epic who has all to gain and nothing to lose by keeping up the joint family reproves his younger brother who demands a partition of the family estate thus "Many through folly desire partition but such devilled heirs are weakened before their foes." Again in plaintive retrospect of the good old days it is said "In that age sons did not divide with their father". The ideal family is that of the Epic heroes. But even here we find that in order to give away property belonging to his junior, the head of the family asks the latter's permission and when this is refused the younger retains his possession undisturbed.

The Epic has many passages showing that while the priests claimed a divine right to possess everything in theory, he has abrogated this in practice and in consequence everything belongs to the king to give. Land may be taken possession of by the king says the Epic. And what is more, although we hear much about the various acts of oppression which a king is asked not to commit, he is never asked to refrain from robbing a subject of his land. It is in the 5th century A. D. that the king is admonished "not to upset the two fundamentals of the peasant's life—his house and field" (Nārada). In fact, we find kings giving and gambling away fields and villages at pleasure. That the grantee is made absolute owner of the granted land is evident from the extant copper plate grants of the first centuries of the Christian era. In the Epic also we find constant references to অগ্রহার land grants. The Epic says "When kings conquer earth, they speak of the land just as sons do of their father's property and say 'This land belongs to me'."

The early Tamils divided arts into six groups: ploughing (agriculture) handicrafts, painting, commerce, the learned arts and fine arts. Of these ploughing and commerce they regarded as of first importance. Agriculture was no doubt in a flourishing condition; but it was not looked upon favourably for "the iron-faced block of wood smites the earth and also the animals dwelling in the earth (Manu X. 84). Mr. Hopkins observes "Long before Manu's law-book had arisen the famous Ahiṃsā doctrine of non-injury to living creatures; and the objection to agriculture on the part of the priest is based expressly on this ground in the law-books" (India Old and New, p. 212). But a Vaisya was to pursue agriculture as also tending cattle, giving of alms, study, trade and usury (Manu I. 90). The Vaisya was required to know the manner of sowing seeds and the good and bad qualities of fields (Manu IX. 330). The six distresses (īti) are mentioned (Mbh. III. 279, 35) but are not defined. The Purāṇas define them and it is probable that they already include those classified later as too much rain, drought, grasshoppers, mice, birds and neighbouring kings (invasion). Advance of seed-grain was made by the state which would take only a fourth part of the produce (Mahābhārata, Śāntiparba Ch. 88. 26-30; Ch. 89, 23-24). The state provided irrigation works at public cost and gave takavi advances (Mahābhārata, Savhāparba Ch. 5. 76-79).

The weaving industry reached its highest development in this period. Articles were woven from cotton, silk and wool, Among the woolens we find manufactures from the wool of rats which were particularly warm. There were thirty varieties of indigenous silk besides Chinese silk. The character of cotton goods may be inferred from the comparisons instituted by Tamil poets between them and the "slough of serpents" or "vapour from milk" and the general description of these as "those fine textures, the thread of which could not be followed even by the eye."

An equal development was reached in the sphere of fine arts. The art of Amarābati railings of the second century A. D. is a logical development of the earlier style of Bharut and Sanchi and so good that it is held to mark "the culmination of the art of sculpture in India" (Ferguesson). "The most varied and difficult movements of the human figure are drawn and modelled with great freedom and skill" (Havell).

The railings of Bharut (between Allahabad and Jubbalpur, C. P.) are the only monument in India having inscribed legends etc. Representations of elephants, deer, monkeys, trees, human figures all truthful to nature, is unsurpassed in the world. "For an honest purpose-like pre-Raphaelite kind of art, there is probably nothing much better to be found anywhere." The railing round Sanchi tope in Bhopal has eloborate scrolls, disks and figures. "The sculptures of the four gateways or torans form a perfect picture-Bible of Buddhism as it existed in India in the 1st century A. D."

There is also a group of caves excavated out of rocks 16 miles to the north of Gaya. The Lomaśa Rishi cave (3rd century B. C.) is most interesting. The hall is 33 ft. × 19 ft. The Bedsor caves of the first half of the 2nd century A. D. show great skill. The Nasik cave of the latter half of the 2nd century A. D. has perpendicular pillars and the facade is improved in design. The Karli cave of the first century B. C. is the largest and most perfect yet found in India. "It shows perfect architecture. Its style is chaste and pure." The Hasti cave of Kharavela and the Nasik cave of Nahapana also belongs to this period.

In Ceylon the tope at Abhayagiri is very large being 1100 feet in circumference and 244 ft. in height. The Jetabana tope is dated 275 A. D.

It may be noted in this connection that Dr. R. G. Bhāndārkar has dug out of the town of Bes (Gwalior state) two bits of genuine steel from beneath the Tham Baba pillar, erected in 140 B. C. and a very old brick-wall, the mortar of which according to Dr. Mann was "far superior to any ever used by the Phœnicians and the Greeks."

Actual remains of the paintings of the second and first centuries B. C. exist in caves at Ramgaṛh in Orissa. At Ajantā there exist a far more important series of paintings executed on the walls of excavated Bihārs, ranging from the first to the middle of the 7th century A. D. "The paintings of Ajantā" remarks Dr. Coomarswāmī (Indian Art, p. 82) "though much damaged still forms the greatest extant monument of ancient painting. One does not know whether to wonder most at their advanced technique or at the emotional intensity that informs these works as if with a life very near our own for, they are as modern in their draughtmanship as in sentiment."

As regards jewellery, the Pattinappālai mentions golden carts of the children as toys. The Pattinappālai says "The heavy ear-rings thrown by the ladies of shining brow, shy glances and fair wrought jewels at the fowls that peck at the drying grain in the spacious courts of the famous sea-port at the mouth of the Kāvery obstruct the passage of the three-wheeled toy carts drawn without horses by children whose anklets are of gold." Of northern workmanship a charming illustration is afforded by some fragmentary ceramic wares from the neighbourhood of Peshwar the designs on which are singularly human and singularly Greek in sentiment. On one of them are defected little Amorini at play, on another a child reaching for a bunch of grapes in the hand of its mother, on a third a scene from the Antigone where Haemon is supplicating his father Creon for the life of his affianced bride. Equally Hellenistic in character and equally devoid of any Indian feeling is an iron pendant adorned with two bearded heads from Taxila and the vine-wreathed head of Dionysius in silver repousse from the same site. Then a little later about the beginning of the Christian era we find Indian forms appearing among the Hellenistic. Witness, for instance, the relic casket of gold encrusted with balas, rubies, which was found in a tope at Bimarān. A large number of engraved gems are to be found throughout the whole of north-western India and are proved by the presence of legends in early Brahmi or Kharosthi as well as Greek characters to be the work of resident artists. And an inscription of about 200 to 150 B. C. at Sanchi states that one of the piers of the southern gateway was executed and dedicated by the ivory carvers of Bhilsā. These engraved gems are remarkable for their technique, composition and relief.

Pliny the Elder (1st century A. D.) in his Natural History speaks of Indian minerals and precious stones as being the best in the world. According to him India was the great producer of the most costly gems and of these diamonds and pearls, beryl and opal, onyx and jasper, ametheyst and carbuncle were in great demand in Rome (Nat. Hist. VI. 17, VII. 2; VIII. 31; IX. 3; XII. 4; XXXV. 6; XII. 7; XXXVII. 1, 6). Pliny further speaks of an embassy from a King of Ceylon to Emperor Claudius (41-54 A. D.) under the guidance of a Roman freedman who was driven to a port in Ceylon by a storm from near Arabia. From this source the Romans learnt that the island was rich in gold, silver, pearls, and precious stones. Its Sanskrit name Ratnadwīpa (the island of gems) justifies this account.

Most of these arts and crafts were organised into guilds of which the following are mentioned :—(1) weavers (Nasik Inscription of Ushavadāta (Ludwig 1133) (2) Potters (kularika) [Nasik Inscription, Ludwig 1137] (3) Oil-millers (tilapishaka) [Nasik Inscription, Ludwig p. 37] (4) Bamboo workers (banskāra) [Junnar Ins. 1165 of Ludwig] (5) Braziers [*Ibid*] (6) Workers fabricating hydraulic engines (odayantrika) [Nasik Ins. Ludwig 1137] Nos. 1, 202, 1,203 and 1,204 of Luders' List (Ep. Ind. Vol. X App.) record gift of five entrance pillars to the great Chaitya of Velagiri by the foreman of a guild of artisans named Sidhatta. No. 1,298, an Amarābati inscription mentions another foreman Nadabhuti. The Sanchi Stupa Inscription No. 200 (Bühler, Ep. Ind. Vol II. p. 378) mentions that the carving (Vapa-kamma) was done by the workers in ivory of Vidisha who had organised themselves into a guild and made that collective gift as suggested by Bühler (Ibid. p. 92).

The importance of these guilds is recognised by the great Epic. The guilds are described as one of the principal supports of royal power (আশ্রমবাসিক পর্ব্ব, Art. 7, Verses 7-9). Sowing dissensions among the heads of guilds or inciting them to treason is looked upon as a recognised means of injuring the enemy (Śāntiparba, Art. 59, Verse 49. Also Art. 191, Verse 64). Duryodhone after his defeat by the Gondharbas refuses to go back to his capital for he dares not face the headmen of guilds. He says—

"ব্রাহ্মণাঃ শ্রেণিমুখ্যাশ্চ তথোদাসীনবৃত্তয় !
কিং মাং বক্ষ্যন্তি কিং চাপি প্রতিবক্ষ্যামি তানহম্ ।"

(Banaparba, Art. 248, Verse 16.)

Moreover Manu refers to the usages of the guilds as having the force of law—

"জাতিজানপদান্ ধর্ম্মান্ শ্রেণীধর্ম্মাংশ্চ ধর্ম্মবিৎ ।
সমীক্ষ কুলধর্ম্মাংশ্চ স্বধর্ম্মং প্রতিপাদয়েৎ ।"

He further lays down that if a man belonging to a corporation inhabiting a village or a district after swearing to an agreement breaks it through avarice the King shall banish him from his realm (VIII. 219). Mahābhārata (Śāntiparba, Art. 36. Verse 19) says "No amount of expiation can remove the sins of those who forsake their duties to the guild to which they belong"—

"জাতিশ্রেণ্যাধিবাসানাং কুলধর্ম্মাশ্চ সর্ব্বতঃ ।
বজ্জয়ন্তি চযে ধর্ম্মং তেষাং ধর্ম্মো ন বিদ্যতে ।"

As a result of this organisation of arts and crafts into guilds, a considerable proficiency and specialisation of industry had been reached. A list of callings in the Milindāpanha reveals three separate industries in the manufacture of bows and arrows, apart from any ornamental work on the same (Mil. 331). In the same work, the allusion to a professional winnower of grain indicates a similar division of labour to our own threshing machinists and steam-plough owners who tour in rural districts (Mil 201).

Combined with this corporate regulation of industrial life, there was a very general but by no means cast iron custom for the son to follow the calling of the father. Mahābhārata (V. 132, 30) says "The duty of the priest is to beg for sustenance, of the warrior to defend the people; of the people caste to make money, of the slave to work (manually)" and lays down that "no amount of expiation can remove the sin of those who neglect their duties to their castes." (Śāntiparba Art 36. verse 19.) Manu says in the same strain "The King should carefully compel Vaisyas and and Śūdras to perform the work prescribed for them for if these two castes swerved from their duties they would throw the world in confusion (VIII. 418). And again "A Brahmin, a Kshatriya, a Vaisya and a Śūdra become respectively, for neglecting the duties of their castes an উল্কামুখ্য প্রেত who feed on what has been vomitted, a কটপূতম্ প্রেত who eats impure substances and corpses, a মৈত্রাক্ষ্যজ্যোতিক প্রেত who feeds on pus and a কৈলাসক প্রেত who feeds on moths" (XII. 71-72). In fact we find King Gautamipūtra Balasri taking pride in having "stopped the contamination of he four varnas" (Nasik Cave Inscription).

Nevertheless Manu lays down that a Brahmin unable be subsist by the occupation of his caste can live as a warrior, this failing as a trader and agriculturist (Manu X. 81, 82). Still he could not sell fruits, linen, soma, slaves, wheat, cake, etc. Manu (III. 151 ff.) tells us that Brahmins follow even such occupations as maintaining shops, selling meat, lending money, lending cattle and acting in a theatre and still retained their castes (c. f. Manu III. 152; X. 98-99). Manu VII. 43 lays down that the King must learn from the people the trades and professions, thus showing that in those days, the practice of a craft was not considered derogatory to the dignity of a prince.

Nevertheless there are recognised certain low trades or crafts. Thus Manu condemns a paid servant, temple priests (III. 152, 153) and domestic priests of Kings (XII. 46). Similarly condemned are astrologers (Manu III. 162) those who execute great mechanical works (মহাযন্ত্রপ্রবর্ত্তন) (Manu XI. 64) messengers (III. 163) basketmakers (IV. 215) and the paid priests who sacrifice for a multitude (III. 151). It should of course be borne in mind that the above list of disapproved occupations and low trades is meant only for the guidance of the highest caste in Hindu society whose special religious duties, social status, privileges and obligations alone have determined the list without any reference to the other castes and it is therefore devoid of much economic significance. Thus the aforesaid professions have been disapproved with reference and in relation to two main purposes affecting the Brahmins *viz.*, (1) entertainment at a Śrāddha and funeral dinner (2) receipt of presents or gifts (including food) and in respect of these two purposes the majority of the aforesaid crafts have been declared to be not eligible. The principle of the declaration is therefore strictly relative to the religious necessities of a particular caste and does not point to any absolute standard by which the economic functions of society could be regulated. But the principle is meant to be absolute so far as the Brahmin caste is concerned for which it certainly defines the sphere of legitimate economic activity. Thus along with the aforesaid crafts there are certain articles the trade in which is absolutely forbidden to a Brahmin. Manu X. 86-94 specifies among others the following commodities :—condiments, cooked food, stones, cattle, dyed cloth, cloth of hemp, flax or wool, meat, poison, milk, ghee, oil, perfumes, honey, indigo, lac, sugar, birds, wines, wild animals, weapons, water, etc. Though however, in the majority of the instances mentioned the principle of disapproval is merely religious and relative to a particular caste, there are some in regard to which the disapproval was perhaps determined by an absolute and universal standard expressing the social opinion of the whole community. I mean those crafts or professions which are condemned as ineligible for the supply of witnesses for suits before law-courts. Thus according to Manu, the following are declared incompetent witnesses:—mechanics, actors and dasyus, which are explained by Medhātithi to mean (servants for wages) or hard-hearted men and may have meant as Bühler suggests the aboriginal robber tribes (VIII. 66). The contempt for quackery and black arts irrespective of the caste of the person practising them, is indeed remarkable. Thus, Manu condemns Kusilavas explained by Medhātithi as bards, jugglers, dancers, singers and the like as being unworthy of invitation to a Śrādha (III. 155 and 158); the food given by a musician (IV. 210) and by an actor (IV. 214) is also not acceptable. Manu mentions among the lowest classes the jhallas, mallas *i. e.* fencers with sticks or wrestlers and jesters and natas *i.e.*, stage-players (III. 3).

It is also a significant fact that social stigma is attached to the hireling working with another man's capital and for his profits, for in a list of callings given in the Buddhist books he ranks along with the mere hewers of wood and flowergatherers and below the slave. (D. I. 51; Mil. 331). Again a hired servant or workman who without being ill and out of pride failed to perfrom his work according to the agreement, was to be fined in addition to his losing wages. If he was ill but after recovery he performed the works, he was to receive the same. But the work had to be done according to the agreement (Manu VIII. 215-18). There were rigid rules with respect to agreements made by men belonging to a corporation. There was a similar law regarding those who violated agreements in villages and castes (Manu VIII 220-21).

The slave posessed nothing; his tax was paid in manual labour for he had no money or other possessions (Mbh. XII. 60, 37). The Śūdra comes from the foot of God and hence is born to servitude. Though the Śūdras are told to be faithful to priest and warrior they are said in particular to serve the people-caste (Mbh. I. 100, 1). The military character of the Mahābhārata precludes much attention to the slaves who as a fighting host are naturally not of importance, though they may be referred to under the designation the 'black mass' for the great hosts led in to the fields comprised many of the slaves as campfollwers and helpers. Though the commentator confines the slave to the Śūdra caste yet slaves of war are known in the Epics. The captured warrior becomes the slave of his captor for a year; if the captor allows him to go free, the captor becomes the captured one's Guru or father. What is very important is that the body of farmers is on the verge of mingling with the slave-caste. No priest may become a slave, however distressed for sustenance he may become; but a slave may become a herdsman or trader if he cannot support himself by service and in fact the farmer population was largely composed of slaves. Manu forbids a Śūdra under severest penalties from learning but in the ethical parts of the Mahābhārata where caste-distinctions are theoretically abolished in favour of the rule that there is no distinction of caste (religiously) the slave is even allowed to study and may get a reward for practising religious exercises (Mbh. XII. 328, 49, XIII. 132, 14) and a learned slave* gives moral instruction but this does not seem to correspond to real conditions where the slave is reckoned next to the beast (XIII. 118, 24). The position of slaves will be evident from the rules regulating punishments. Thus in cases of defamation, if a warrior defame a priest, he is fined 100 paṇas; if a man of the people-caste do so, 150; if a slave he shall be corporally punished; but if a priest defame a warrior, 50; if he defame a Vaisya, 25; if he defame a slave, 12; and this last fine is that imposed upon equals defaming equals within the Aryan castes. But if a slave insult an Aryan, his tongue is to be cut out. Again a slave who has intercourse with a guarded high-caste woman may be slain; a Vaisya shall lose his property, a warrior be fined a 1000 and be shaved with wine (Manu VIII. 384-6).

That labour was mobile in this period is proved by evidences from Tamil literature as well. Thus Manimēkhalāe canto IX. tells us that in the building of the royal palace at Puhar, skilled artisans from Magadha, mechanics from Marādam (Mahārāṣtra), smiths from Avanti (Malwa), carpenters from Yavan country worked with the Tamil artisans. Canto XVIII. of the same book refers to a beautiful temple in Puhar built by the Gurjaras. Similarly, the Sanchi Stupa Inscription No. 200 (Bühler's Ep. Ind. Vol. II. p. 378) refers to carving done by the ivory workers of Vidisha.

Coming to the wages of labourers we find that the cowboys should receive according to the Mahābhārata the milk of one cow for the care of six cows and if he tend a 100 heads he should at the end of the year receive a pair. If he acts as overseer of his master's flocks or in agricultural labour he should have $\frac{1}{7}$th of the proceeds or increase, but in the case of small cattle, a small part [($\frac{1}{16}$th) Mbh. XII. 60, 24 f)]. The pay of a rathin (or carman) is 1000 copper coins a month and the King pensions the widows of fallen solders (Mbh. II. 5, 54; c. f. *Ibid.* 61, 20).

That trade had attained a high stage of development is evident from the fact that traders were enjoined to make themselves acquainted with the products and requirements of other countries, with their various dialects and with whatever had a direct or indirect reference to purchase or sale. The nature and degree of the commercial activity of the period may be ascertained from the large number of trade rules and regulations. Thus the King was enjoined to fix the rates of purchase and sale of all marketable goods, having duly considered whence they come, whither they went, how long they had been kept and the probable profit and probable outlay. The King was further enjoined to settle publicly once in five nights or at the close of each fortnight the prices for the merchants (Manu VIII. 402). Further all weights and measures were to be duly marked and once in six months he is to reexamine them (Manu VIII. 399-403). In fact, frequent allusions to merchants using false weights in the Epic (Mbh. I. 64. 21 f.) show that a careful supervision of the market place was necessary. A commodity for sale should be pure (Manu VIII. 222 ff.). One commodity mixed with another was not to be sold as pure, not a bad one as good, nor less than the proper quantity or weight, nor anything that is not at hand or that is concealed (Manu VIII. 203). Adulteration was forbidden (Manu IX. 286) and cheating was punished (Manu IX. 287 ; c. f. IX. 257). It was however laid down that a man repenting of his bargain could return or take back the chattel within 10 days but after this it could be taken only by mutual consent (Manu VIII. 222-223).

In levying taxes on merchandise it was laid down that "the King was to take $\frac{1}{20}$th of that amount which men well acquainted with the settlement of tolls and duties and skilful in all kinds of merchandise may fix as the value for each saleable commodity (Manu VIII. 398). The King could confiscate the whole property of a trader who out of greed exported goods of which the King had a monopoly or the export of which was forbidden (Manu VIII. 399). A trader avoiding a customs house or toll, who bought and sold at an improbable time or who made a false statement in enumerating his goods was fined 8 times the amount of duty he tried to evade (Manu VIII. 405).

As regards the toll at a ferry it was laid down that "for a long passage, the hire must be proportioned to the places and times; know that this rule refers to passages along banks of rivers; at sea there is no settled freight" (Manu VIII. 406). Again "The toll at a ferry is one paṇa for an empty cart, half a paṇa for a man with a load, quarter for beast used in agriculture......waggons filled with goods shall be made to pay toll at a ferry according to the value of goods; empty vessels and men without luggage some trifle (Manu VIII. 404).

These customs rules are partly corroborated by evidences from Tamil literature. From Paṭṭinappālai 134-6) we learn that there was a regular Customs Establishment, the officials of which piled up the grains and stored up the things which could not be immediately measured, leaving them in the dockyards arefully sealed with the tiger-signet of the King.

The existence of maritime trade in the period is evident from the Māhābhārata (Śāntiparba Ch. 169) where we are told that Gautama left home and made for the coast; on the way he met a body of merchants going to the sea; with them he proceeded towards the shore. Again Dayamanti joined trading caravan going to the sea (Mahābhārata: episode of Nala and Dayamanti). With regard to the objective of Indian sea-going commerce in this period R. Sewell remarks "There was trade, both overland and by sea, with Western Asia, Greece, Rome and Egypt as well as with China and the East." This is corroborated by the author of Milindāpanha who says "as a shipowner who has become wealthy by constantly levying freight in some sea-port towns will be able to traverse the high seas and go to Banga, Takkola or China or Sovira or Surat or Alexandria or the Coromondol Coast or Further India or any other place where ships do congregate" (Mil. 359 or S. B. E. XXXVI. II. 269).

The maritime intercourse of Egypt with India in the epoch which immediately preceded the Roman rule, was not great and was carried on mainly by the Arabians. From Strabo we gather that although a considerable amount of Indian merchandise had flowed into Europe by way of the Red Sea and Alexandria when the Ptolemies ruled in Egypt, very few Greek ships had gone further than south Arabia. Goods were carried from India to south Arabia in Indian or Arabian bottoms.

Agatharchides, tutor of Ptolemy Soter II (116 B. C.) says that the merchandise brought by Indian merchants from Potana (Pātala, according to Bunbury, Ancient Geography III. 59) made Arabia wealthy. By the time, however, when Strabo was in Egypt (25 B. C.) a direct trade between Egypt and India had come into existence. "Not 20 Egyptian vessels in the year says a contemporary of Augustus ventured forth under the Ptolemies from the Arabian Gulf; now 120 merchantmen annually sail to India from the port of Myos Hormos alone" (Strabo II. C. 118). During this period, the Red sea route was the most popular. The anarchy reigning in Syria, the growth of hostile Empire in Parthia, the Scythian irruption into Bactria from beyond the Oxus, the sack by Alexander of the important trading centre of Tyre diverted Indian commerce from the northerly route and made Alexandria the centre of trade.

But it was not till the reign of Claudius (41 A.D.) that the route through Egypt to India became really known to the Europeans. The historian Pliny who died in 79 A. D. has left us a contemporary account of these early voyages. "It will not be amiss" says Pliny in his Natural History "to set forth the whole of the route from Egypt which has been stated to us of late, upon information on which reliance may be placed and is here published for the first time . . . . . To those who are bound for India Ocelis is the best place for embarkation. If the wind called Hippalus happens to be blowing, it is possible to arrive in 40 days at the nearest mart in India called Muziris (Modern Mangalore). This, however, is not a desirable place for disembarkation, on account of the pirates who frequent its vicinity, nor in fact is it very rich in articles of merchandise. Besides, the roadstead for shipping is at a considerable distance from the shore, and the cargoes have to be conveyed in boats, either for loading or discharging." "At the moment I am writing these pages" continues Pliny "the name of the king of the place is Cœlobotras. Another port and a much more convenient one is that which lies in the territory of the people called Nelcyndi Barace by name. Here King Pandion used to reign dwelling at a considerable distance from the mart in the interior, at a city known as Modeira. Travellers set sail from India on their return to Egypt, at the beginning of the Egyptian month Tybus which is our December; if they do this, they can go and return in the same year".

The places on the Indian coast which the Egyptian merchant vessels then reached, are verified from the coins found there. A hoard of Roman gold coins has been dug up quite recently near Calicut under the roots of a banyan tree. It had been buried by an Alexandrian merchant on his arrival from a voyage and left safe under the cover of the sacred tree to await his return from a second journey. But he died before his return and his secret died with him.

To Pliny's survey we may add the valuable geographical knowledge given by the author of the Periplus of the Erythrean Sea wherein he mentions the several sea-ports and their distances, with the tribes and cities near the coast. The trade of Egypt to India and Arabia was then most valuable but as the merchandise in each case was carried only for short distances from city to city, the merchants could gain but little knowledge of where it come from or of where it was going. Even under Justinian part of the Egyptian trade to the East was carried on through the islands of Ceylon and Socotra, but it was chiefly in the hands of the uneducated Arabs who were little able to communicate to the world much knowledge of the countries from which they brought their highly-valued goods. At Ceylon they meet with traders from beyond the Ganges and China, from whom they bought the silk which the Europeans had formerly thought a product of Arabia. According to the author of the Periplus " the port of Muza was crowded with Arab shipmasters and sailors and perhaps with bales of merchandise ; for these Arabs carry on trade with Barygaza, sending their own ships there (Art. 29).

But the principal carriers of the trade between India and Egypt under the Ptolemies were the Egyptian Greeks ; and as usual this commercial intercourse has left some marks on their language. Thus the Greek names for rice (oryza), ginger (zingiber) and cinnamon (karpion) have a close correspondence with their Tamil equivalents *viz.*, arisi, inchiver and karava respectively. Again the name Yavana which in old Sanskrit poetry is invariably used to denote the Greeks (Weber's Indian Literature, p. 220) is derived from the Greek word Iaones, the name of the Greeks in their own language. Even the Tamil poets use the word to denote the Greeks and the Romans. Thus "the poet Nakkirar addresses the Pandion prince Nan-Maran in the following words" O Mara, whose sword is ever victorious, spend thou thy days in peace and joy, drinking daily out of golden cups, presented by the handmaids, the cool and fragrant wine brought by the Yavanas in the good ships" (Mr. Pillay, The Tamils 1800 years Ago, Ch. III.). The Yavanas alluded to by these poets were undoubtedly the Egyptian Greeks because as stated in the Periplus it was Greek merchants from Egypt who brought wine, brass, lead, glass etc., for sale to Muziris and Bakare and who purchased from these ports pepper, betel, ivory, pearls and fine muslins (*Ibid.*).

Now one of the most curious relics of the trade between Egypt and India during this period has been recently unearthed at Oxyrrhyncus. It is a papyrus containing a Greek farce of the second century A. D. which deals with the story of a Greek lady named Charition, who had been shipwrecked on the Canarese coast. The locality is identified by the fact that the king of the country addresses his retinue as *indon promoi*. Dr. Hultzsch is of opinion that the barbarous jargon in which they addressed one another is actually Canarese. Again Dio Chrysostom, who lived in the reign of Trajan, mentions Indians among the cosmopolitan crowds to be found in the bazaars of Alexandria and he says that they came "by way of trade."

During this period we know Rome was absorbing the remains of the Empire of Alexander. Syria had already fallen and Egypt became a Roman province in 30 B. C. The dissensions of civil war ended at Actium, after which Angustus settled down to organise and regulate his vast possessions. The effect of the Pax Romana upon trade was thus very marked. Piracy was put down, trade routes were secured and the fashionable world of Rome, undistracted by conflict began to demand on an unprecedented scale oriental luxuries of every kind. At about the same time, the Kushans were establishing themselves among the ruins of the Bactrian and other semi-Greek principalities of N. W. India aud thus when the Kushan Empire marched with that of the Roman "Roman arts and ideas travelled with the stream of Roman gold which flowed into the tre[a]suries of the Rājas in payment for the silks, gems and spices of the Orient" (J. R. A. S. 1903 p. 56).

The news of the accession of Augustus quickly reached India and many Indian States sent embassies to congratulate him. Strabo mentions that an embassy was sent to Augustus in 20 B. C. by the Indian King Pandion. Strabo relates that Nicolaus Damascenus met at Antioch, Epidaphne, the surviver of this embassy to Augustus bearing a letter in Greek from the Indian Prince. With them was Zarmanochegus (Sramanāchāryya) of Barygaza, who was evidently a Buddhist monk. Allusions to this embassy are made by Horace in Odes. Florus (Epitome of Roman History IV. 12), Dion Cassius (History of Rome IX. 73), Orosius (History VI. 12) and Suetonius refer to it. It is also mentioned by Hieronymus in his translation of the Canon Chronicon of Eusebius but is placed by him in the 3rd year of the 188th Olympiad, *i. e.*, 26 B. C. (*vide* Reinaud "Relations politiques et commerciales del Empire Romain avec l' Asie Orientale). Dion Cassius (History of Rome IX. 58) also speaks of Trajan receiving many embassies from Indians. Pliny refers to another embassy sent from Ceylon in 41 A. D. to Emperor Claudius. Another embassy was sent to Antoninus Pius about 138 A. D. Eusebius (De vita Constant IV. 50) speaks of Indian ambassadors bringing presents to Constantine the Great; and Ammianus Marcellinus (XXII. VII. 10) of embassies sent by Indians to the Emperor Julian in 361 A.D.

The explanation of this intercourse of India with Rome is to be found in the fact that "from the time of Mark Antony to the time of Justinian, *i. e.*, from 30 B. C. to A. D. 550 their political importance as allies against the Parthians and Sassanians and their commercial importance as controllers of one of the main trade routes between the East and the West made the friendship of the Kushans or the Sakas who held the Indus Valley and Bactria, a matter of the highest importance to Rome." (Bombay Gazetteer, Vol. I. Part I. p. 490). How close was the friendship is shown in 60 A. D. by the Roman General Corbulo escorting the Hyrcanian ambassadors up the Indus and through the territories of the Kushans on their return from their embassy to Rome (Rawlinson's Parthia, 271).

Mr. Sewell has briefly sketched the history of this Indian trade with Rome after an elaborate study of the Roman coins found in India. According to him this trade was most active during the period of 80 years from Augutus to Nero (68 A. D.) for the largest number of coins discovered in southern India refers to this period. The locale of these discoveries points also to the conclusion that the things which India exported comprised mostly spices and precious stones. This is corroborated by the fact that Nero burnt at the funeral of Poppoea fully a year's produce of cinnamon and cassia. In the interval between Nero and Caracalla (217 A. D.) there must have been a decline of this trade, considering the very small number of coins discovered which belong to this period. The coin-finds have been mostly in cotton-growing districts, so that the conclusion is irresistible that the articles of trade consisted of such necessaries as cotton fabrics etc. This is corroborated by the rise of a new era in social manners in Rome at this period under Vespasian, when to use the words of Merivale "the simpler habits of the Plebians and the Provincials prevailed over the reckless luxury and dissipation in which the highest classes had so long indulged." The trade with Rome was at low ebb from the days of Caracalla when Rome was a prey to confusion both internal and external and accordingly there have been few finds of coins belonging to this period. The occidental trade revived again though slightly under the Byzantine emperors. The locale of the coins suggest a brisk trade only in pepper and spices and accordingly when Alaric spared Rome in 408 A. D. he demanded and obtained as part of the ransom 3,000 pounds of pepper (Gibbon Ch. XXXI).

Let us now consider the articles of trade in detail. It is too well known that aromatics were consumed on religious and funeral celebrations in Rome. Incense was burnt at every worship. At the funeral of Sylla 210 loads of spices were strewn upon the pile. Pliny in his Natural History (XII. 7 (14) refers to the pepper and ginger of India and the great demand for them in Rome where they were bought by weight like gold and silver. The auther of the Periplus names Tyndis, Muziris,

Nelkynda and Bacare as the ports from which pepper was exported. Mommsen (Prov. of the Roman Empire Vol. II. p. 301) remarks—" In the Flavian period in which the monsoon voyages had already become regular, the whole west coast of India was opened up to the Roman merchants as far down as the coast of Malabar, the home of the highly esteemed and dear-priced pepper for the sake of which they visited the ports of Muziris and Nelkynda. Somewhat farther to the south, at Kananor numerous Roman gold coins of the Julian-Claudian epoch has been found, formerly exchanged against the spices destined for the Roman kitchens." Then there was the demand on India in Rome for silk, muslin and cotton-fabrics. Indian silk so allured the Roman ladies that it sold for its weight in gold. (Encyclopædia Britannica, Vol. XI. p. 459). Tiberius Caesar had to pass a law forbidding transparent silk as an indecent dress. In fact the demand for these luxuries was so great that it shocked the sober-minded citizens of Rome. Thus Petronius complains that fashionable Roman ladies exposed their charms rather too immodestly by clothing themselves in the "webs of woven wind" as he called the Indian muslins imported from India. Pliny says in the same strain "In no year does India drain our Empire of less than 550 millions of sestereces (about 80 lakhs of rupees) giving back her own wares in exchange which are sold among us as fully one hundred times their cost price." "So yearly do we pay for our luxuries and our women." Other articles in demand at Roman markets were precious stones, pearls and minerals which have been carefully noticed and described by Pliny (Natural History XXXII. C. I.). The most highly prized of these stones was the beryl found in the ancient world only in the mines of Podiyur in the Coimbatore District and it is curious to note that in its neighbourhood the largest number of Roman coins has been found. Besides, the pearl-fishery of the southern seas attracted from untold ages a large crowd of foreign merchants. "We are assured on undisputed authority that the Romans remitted annually to India a sum equivalent to £ 4,000,000 to pay for their investments and that in the reign of the Ptolemies 125 sails of Indian shipping were at one time lying in the ports whence Egypt, Syria and Rome itself were supplied with the products of India." [Life in Western India (Guthric) from Tod's Western India, p. 221].

The fact of this trade with Rome is further very satisfactorily established by the various references we find in the native literature of India. The references has been dealt with in the J. A. S. B. for 1906, New series Vol II. by Dr. Satish Ch. Vidyābhūson. Thus the Mahābhārata speaks of the Romaka or Romans coming to the Emperor Yudhisthir with precious presents on the occasion of the Rajsūya Yajna at Indraprostha or Delhi. (Sabhāparva Ch. 51). In the famous astronomical works named Paitāmaha, Vāsishtha, Sūryya,

Paulisa and Romaka Siddhantas, some of which were compiled in the third or second century A. D. Romaka is often mentioned as a Mahāpuri, Pattana or Visaya i. e., a great city, state or dominion. Lastly the Romaka-Jātaka describes a sham priest killing a pigeon to eat it contrary to Buddhist practices, evidently to show the contrast of a Buddhist ascetic with a Roman ascetic.

This trade is further corroborated by evidences from foreign works. We have already referred to the description of mineral products which India sent abroad by Pliny. Even as far back as 177 B. C. Agatharchides describes Sabaea (Yemen) as being the centre of commerce betweenAsia and Europe and very wealthy because of the monopoly of the Indian trade. He also saw large ships coming from the Indus and Patala. The evidences of the Periplus are more interesting and detailed.

Trade was also carried on with China in this period. The name China first appears in the Manu Samhitā X. 43-44 ; Mahābhārata, Anuśāsana Parba, Ch. 33, sloka 21 and Ch. 36, sloka 18. Manu mentions the Chinese as denationalised Kshatriyas. In the Mahābhārata the Chinese are spoken of as allies of Bhagadatta of Assam. These Chinese even faught in the Kurukshetra against the Pāndavas. The same Epic gives a list of presents sent by the Chinese to Yudhisthira.

The Chinese records tell us that foreign trade in China had for a long time been covered by the name of tribute for, the Chinese would refuse to trade unless it was done under their own conditions viz., the appearance of the offering of gifts as a sign of submission and admiration on the part of the distant monarch. In each case, the full equivalent was paid for these offerings in the shape of countergifts presented to the so-called ambassadors by the Chinese court. Such tributory countries were Arabia, Persia and India. Now T'iendu or T'ien-chu is the name by which India was known to the Chinese since the 1st century B. C. when Buddhism was introduced from India to China. But a more ancient Chinese name for India is "Shin-du". This name evidently rendering the Sanskrit Sindhu (river) which was taken for India, appears in the Chinese annals about 120 B. C., after the expedition of General Chongkien to western Asia, who reported on the country of Shin-du from hearsay" (Dr. Bretschneider, Mediæval Researches). Mr. G. Hirth in his "China and the Roman Orient" gives the following evidences from Chinese texts regarding transmarine commerce between India and China in this period :— (1) The inhabitants of Tats'in (Syria) traffic by sea with Au-hsi (Parthia) and T'ienchu (India) the profit of which trade is ten-fold—"Hon-hen-shu." (2) The inhabitants of Au-hsi (Parthia) and T'ienchu have traded with China, its profit is hundredfold—"Chin-shu" (written 265 A. D.) (3) The merchants of this country frequently visit

Funam (Siam), T'ienchu (India), Jih-nan (Annam), Chiao-chih (Tongking) — "Liang-shu" (date uncertain). (4) The country of Tats'in (Syria), also called Likan, is on the west of the great sea, west of Au-hsi (Parthia). They always wish to send embassies to China but the Parthians wanted to make profit out of this trade and would not allow us to pass their country. Further they are always anxious to get Chinese silk—" Win-lio" (composed 220-24 A.D.). (5) It also appears from " Wu-shih-woi-kuo-chuan" i. e., foreign accounts of Wu (222 A. D.) that " ships were provided with seven sails, they sailed from Kang-tiao-chou and with favourable winds could enter Tats'in (Syria) within a month." Dr. Bretschneider presumed that the city of Kang-tiao-chau was on or near the Indian west coast (See his article in the China Review).

The Milindāpaṇha informs us (pp. 127, 327,) that under Rudradaman (A.D. 143-158) the Kshatrapa dynasty of Kathiawar was at the height of its power and Indians of the Tientes (Sindu) brought presents by sea to China.

It may be noted in this connection that India in this period maintained a sort of politico-religious intercourse with China. Kushana Kadphises II was defeated and compelled to pay tribute to China. And the Chinese annals note that in the reign of the Emperor Ho-ti (89 A. D.—105 A. D.) the Indians often sent missions to China. Kanishka on the other hand succeeded in accomplishing the supremely difficult feat of conveying an effective army across the Pamirs and subduing the chiefs or petty Kings in the Khotan, Yarkand and Kashgar regions which had been tributory to China. Besides these political relations we find from an unauthenticated accouut that Indian missionaries had entered China as early as 227 B. C. and in 122 B. C. a Chinese expedition is said to have advanced beyond Yarkand and to have brought back a golden image of Buddha. Communion between India and China becomes very frequent from this date. Knowledge of foreign doctine entered the country and in 61 A.D. Emperor Mingti sent messengers to India to bring back Buddhist books and priests. The priests were brought and one of them Kashiap-madanga (Kāsyapa Mātanga) translated a Sutta in Layong. He is followed in the same year by Fa-lan like the other, a Śraman of central India.

India's trade with Eastern Turkisthan may be suggested by the expeditions of Kanishka. The recent researches of Dr. Sven Hedin and Sir M. A. Stein have conclusively proved this fact, the chief centres of trade being Samarkand, Kashgar and Khotan all situated in the oases supplied by Nature where the caravans stopped and settled. This is further corroborated by the accounts of a Macedonian merchant Maes or Titianus in the 1st century A. D. How Khotan received her culture and religion (Buddhism) from

India is narrated by Stein in his book "The Sandburied Ruins of Khotan." Dr. Sylvan Levi in his paper on the Hindu Civilisation in Central Asia notes how the Kucha Kingdom adopted Buddhism and Sanskrit literature, how before long Sanskrit works on Astronomy and Medicine were translated into the Kuchian tongue some of which are at Petrograd while others at Tokio.

That India traded with and even colonised Further India has been proved by Col. Gerini. Ptolemy informs us that in his time the coastline of Further India was inhabited throughout its length by the Sindoi (Hindus). This colonisation must have been of transmarine orgin. On the one hand the Hindus did not advance along the land route long hidden and leading through the Ganges delta and Assam, until the second half of the present millenium. On the other hand the proof of the fact that the Hindus made their way to Further India by sea is the predominance of the Hindus along the coast as remarked by Ptolemy. This colonisation cannot have started from southern India for the reason that Brahminism at this period had taken but little hold on the south and the transmission of civilisation from these shores is therefore extremely improbable. It was not until a much later period that the communication between southern India and Further India began, the results of which are apparent in the later temple-buildings of the latter. Further evidences of the northern origin of this colonisation are the names of more important towns of Further India which are almost entirely borrowed from Sanskrit names of the towns of the Ganges valley and also the desire of the rulers of Further India to retrace their origin to the mythical Solar and Lunar dynasties of Madhyadeśha.

The maritime route led straight to Burma but the Indian civilisation at the moment found that province less favourable to its development than that of the great and more hospitable Champā Kingdom in the central south. The Gulf of Ligor and the banks of the great rivers of Cambodia seem to have been the central points of Brahminical influence. According to M. E. Aymonier, most of the traditional names of the Kings of Cambodia are to be read in inscriptions in Sanskrit from the 3rd century A.D. to 1108 A.D. Inscribed memorials, carvings and buildings make it quite clear that immigrants brought with them gods of the Hindu Pantheon (Śiva, Goneśha, etc.) and the beautiful legend of the Rāmāyana. Professor Lacouperie in his Western Origin of Chinese Civilisation also maintains that Cambodia was colonised by the Hindus in the first century A.D.

India's trade with the Malaya archipelago has been proved by Mr. John Crawford but unfortunately the beginning of this commercial intercourse can be proved only by indirect evidence. John Crawford in this connection relies on the

on the North coast of Socotra (Periplus, Para. 30). Of the trade with the eastern coast of Africa called Zanzibar, Periplus gives us pretty full information. After enumerating the commercial stations on the coast as far as Rhapta, now called Delgado, which was the most southerly point of his geographical knowledge and after describing their merchantile relations with Egypt, he continues—"Moreover, indigenous products such as corn, rice, butter, oil of seasamum, coarse and fine cotton goods and cane-honey (sugar) are regularly exported from the interior of Ariaka (Konkon) and from Barygaza to the opposite coast" (Periplus p. 8). In fact, as pointed out by Dr. Vincent "in the age of the Periplus the merchants of the country round Barygaza traded to Arabia for gums and incense, to the coast of Africa for gold and to Malabar and Ceylon for pepper and cinnamon and this completed the navigation of the entire Indian Ocean" (Commerce and Navigation of the Ancients Vol. II. p. 404.). Nor in this all. Cornelius Nepos says that Q. Metellus Celer received from the King of Suevi some Indians, who had been driven by storm into Germany in the course of a voyage of commerce (McCrindle, Ancient India, p. 110).

Coming to the ports we find that according to the Periplus Bharoach was the principal distributing centre of Western India. Paithan and Tagara (modern Dharur in the Nizam's Territory) were two inland towns of great commercial importance, of which the former sent into Bharoach for export waggons containing large quantities of onyx stones and the latter ordinary cottons, muslins, mallow-coloured cottons etc. The other sea-port towns mentioned in the Periplus are Barbaricum (on one of mouths of the Indus) Souppara (Modern Supara), Kalliena (modern Kalyan), Semulla (Chembur or Chaul) Mandagora (Mandad) Palaipatamai (probably Pal near Mahad), Melzeigara (Jaigarh or Rajpur) Byzantium (Vizavrug), Togarah (Devgarh) and Auramnobos (Malavan). To the south three great emporia are mentioned, *viz.*, Tyndis, Muziris and Nelcynda from which were exported pepper, spices, pearls, ivory, fine silks and precious stones. Bacare is the roadstead where the ships anchor to take the cargo. Beyond Bacare are the harbours of Balife and Comarc (Cape Comorin). The harbours on the eastern coast are Camara (probably Karikal), Poduka (probably Pondicherry or Calicut), Supatma (Madras) and Tāmralipti or Sonargaon. Ptolemy's Geography also mentions among others the following ports and towns of commercial importance viz., Syrastra (Surat), Monoglosson (Mangrol) in Gujrat, Ariaka, Soupora, Muziris, Bakarei, Maisolia (Maslipatam) and Kounagara (Konaraka).

A very nice idea of the imports and exports of India in this period can be gathered from the Periplus. Thus the imports were—(1) thin clothing (2) figured linens (3) topas (gem) (4) coral (5) storax (धूना) (6) frakincense (7) glass (8) silver plate (2) gold plate (10) copper (11) tin (12) lead (13) wine (14) sweet (flower) clover (15) realgar (gum) (16) tincture for the eye (17) gold coin (18) silver coin (19) antimony and (20) orphiment (mineral used for colouring). The exports were—(1) costus (spice and perfume) (2) bdellium (incense) (3) lycium (medicinal herb) (4) nard (do) (5) turquoise (precious stone) (6) lapis lazuli (7) animal skins (8) cotton cloth (9) silk (10) indigo (11) spikenard (medicinal herb) (12) ivory (13) onyx stone (14) porcelain (15) pepper (16) pearls (17) malabathrum (leaf used for perfume) (18) transparent stones (19) diamonds (20) sapphires (21) tortoise shell and (22) muslin. The seaport of Barbaricum imported articles Nos. 1—10 and exported articles Nos. 1 10 (paras. 37—39.) The imports of Barygaza were 1, 3 5, 10 18 while its exports were 1—3, 8-9, 11—15 (Paras. 42—49). The imports of Nelcynda, Muziris and Bacare were 1—4, 7, 10—13, 15, 17—19. Their imports were 9, 11, 12, 15—21. (Paras. 54—56). The exports of Tāmralipti were 11, 16, 17, 22 (Para. 63). From paras. 35-36 we further learn that Barygaza exported to Apologus (near the mouth of the Euphrates) and Ommana (on the Persian Gulf) copper, sandal wood, timber of teak wood and logs of blackwood and ebony while it imported from these places pearls, wine, gold, slaves and clothing.

The Tamil literature of the times gives us a nice account of some of the south Indian ports and their exports and imports. Thus Muchere near the mouth of the Periyar is a thriving port which imported gold (from the Yavanas) and exported spices (Erukkaddar Thayanakanar-Akam 148; Oaranar-Pūram, 343). In Kaviripaddinam goods were stamped with the Tiger Stamp after the payment of customs duties and passed on to ware-houses (Paddinappālai, 134-136). Close by were the settlements of Yavana merchants where many attractive articles were always exposed for sale. Into this port "horses were brought from distant lands beyond the seas; pepper was brought in ships; gold and precious stones came from the northern mountains; sandal and aghil came from the mountains towards the west; pearls from the southern seas and coral from the eastern seas; the produce of the regions watered by the Ganges; all that is grown on the banks of the Kāveri; articles of food from Elam or Ceylon and the manufactures of Kalakan (in Burma)" [Paddinappālai 1-40]. Mr. Kanakabhai Pillay shows on the authority of Perumpada-arrupadai that around the Coromondol coast there were light-houses built of brick and mortar which exhibited blazing lights at night to guide ships to ports (The Tamils 1800 years Ago, p. 27).

It will not be out of place to mention here that according to the author of the Periplus there were three kinds of ships used in this period:—(1) the native vessels which make coasting voyages (2) the monoxyla, "with their foundation formed of a single timber, hollowed and then raised with tiers of planking till they contain 100 or 150 men" (Dr. Vincent, Commerce and Navigation of the Ancients Vol. II. p. 521). "Vessels of this sort are employed in the intercourse between the two coasts" (*Ibid*). (3) "Colandiophonta built for the trade to Malacca, perhaps to China were exceeding large and stout" (*Ibid*). Mr. Sewell says (Imperial Gazetteer of India, New Ed. Vol. II. p. 324)—"Pliny (Vol. VI). states that Indian vessels trading with Ceylon were so large as to be able to carry 3,000 amphoræ. On the east coast, the coins of the Andhra dynasty confirm this, many of them bearing the device of a two-masted ship evidently of large size."

When at the height of their power the Mauryas and the Selucid Empires were conterminous, intercourse by land between India and the Western World was unimpeded. But revolt in the Selucid Empire placed the overland trade routes in the hands of hostile powers while the invasions of the Śakas from Seistan a century later made trade impossible through these routes. Trade was resumed when order was restored in Central Asia by the strong hands either of the Roman or Kushan Emperors.

Hence trade was carried on with China along two routes *viz.*, (the overland route from China *via* N. Tibet, Turkisthan, Bactria to the Punjab (Periplus, paras. 64-65) or along (2) a short and a more direct route from China across Tibet to the borders of Sikkim (*Ibid.* 64-65). The over-sea routes were—(1) the coastal route from Egypt through the Red Sea along Arabia, Gedrosia, Indo-Scythia and the Indian coast (paras. 6, 26, 35-36), (2) from Cana on the south Arabian Coast straight across the sea to Barbaricum, (3) Berygaza, and (4) Nelcynda (para. 57) (5) from Cape of Spice (Cape Guard on the E. African Coast) straight across the sea to Barygaza (on the mouth of the Euphrates) and Ommana (on the Persian Gulf) [Paras. 35-36.]. (8) Before the time of the author of the Periplus (*i. e.*, middle of the 1st century A. D.) goods were sent from India through Aden to Egypt and *vice-versa* (Para. 26). This shows that "the Hindus did not always wait for others to come to them for goods."

Inland trade was carried on throughout N. India along the two main routes connecting Pātalipūtra (1) with Kabul and (2) the Indus Valley. "The main stages of the first route together with distances between the stages are known from ancient authorities who derived their information from the campaigns of Alexander and Selucus. The most complete record has been preserved by Pliny VI. 17 (21). Many of his measurements are no doubt correct when due allowance is made for the necessary *de tours* in Marches; but as others are evidently less exact, it will be more convenient to summarise here such information as is supplied by the Imperial Gazetteer and to estimate other distances approximately by straight lines drawn on the map" (Cambridge History of India, Vol. I):—

From Charikar (Alexander-under—the Caucasus) to Kabul 40 miles.

„ Kabul, S. W. to Kandhahar (Alexandrea-among-the Arachosians) 313 miles.

„ Kabul, S. to the Indus Delta 725 miles.

„ Kabul, S. to South Kathiawar 1000 miles.

„ Kabul E. to Jelalabad 101 miles.

„ Jelalabad, E. to Peshwar 79 miles.

The stages on the Royal Road which ran from Chārsadda (16 miles N. E. of Peshwar to Patna are:—

From Chārsadda (Puskalābatī) E. to Shahdheri (Taxila) 80 miles.

„ Shahdheri S. E. to Jhelum (Nicaca) 70 miles.

„ Jhelum S. E. to Sialkot (Sākala) 55 miles.

„ Sialkot to the Beas (Hyphasis) 65 miles.

„ the Beas S. E. to Sutlej at Rūpar 85 miles.

„ the Sutlej to the Jumna at Karnāl 100 miles.

The course of the second (central) route which joined the northern route at Kausāmbi was as follows:—

From Hyderabad in Sind to Ujjain 500 miles.

„ Broach N. E. to Ujjain 200 miles.

„ Ujjain E. to Besnagar (Vidisha) 120 miles.

„ Beshnagar N. E. to Bhārut 185 miles.

„ Bhārut N. E. to Kausāmbi 80 miles.

From Kausāmbi to Kaśī 100 miles.

„ Kaśī to Patna 135 miles.

From the evidences of Tamil literature we get the following inland trade-routes in S. India :—

From Kanchi to Trichinopoly via Tirukkoilur.

„ Trichinopoly via Kodumbai (in the state of Podukotta) to Neḍumgulam, then in three branches to Madura.

„ Madura along the banks of the river Vaigai up to Palnis, from Palnis it went up the hills and down, again along the banks of the Periyar to the town Vanji situated near its mouth.

„ Venji to modern Karoor and then to Tirukkoilur.

The Pali Mahābaṃśa mentions a great trunk road between Mahārāṣtra and Malwa which probably wound its way over the hills by way of Burhanpur into western Malwa. Besides these routes we find a large number of inland routes enumerated by the author of the Periplus. Thus, (1) from countries on the Upper Indus goods were carried up to Minnagara along the Indus. From Minnagara goods are sent to Barygaza (2) and Barbaricum (Paras. 37 and 41) (3) Goods are brought down from the upper country, for example, Kabul and the regions of the Upper Indus to Ujjain. From Ujjain they are sent to Barygaza (Paras. 42-49). (4) Goods from the regions along the Bay of Bengal are brought down to Paithan and Tagaṛa. From these two places they are carried by waggons and through great tracks without roads to Barygaza (Paras. 50-51).

From the above survey it will be seen that "instead of the rigid insolation apparently decreed to India by Nature we find a remarkably active intercourse with foreign countries. The great and almost impregnable barriers on the north are pireced by mountain passes which have been throughout used as the pathways of commerce and communication with the external world. Towards the south, the ocean itself was converted into a great highway of international commerce with the rapid development of national shipping". And a survey of the articles of exports supplied by the Periplus would show that "the old prosperity of India was based on the sound principle which is that after clothing and feeding your own people, then of your surplus abundance, give to the stranger" and that the "renowned art, industrial fabrics and exports were not multiplied on the reprehensible practice of depleting the the country of its foodstuffs" (Major J. B. Keith in the Asiatic Quarterly Review, July, 1910).

The merchants were organised into guilds which were of such authority that the King was not allowed to establish any laws repugnant to the rules of these trade-unions. The heads of guilds are mentioned next after the priests as objects of a King's anxious concern. The power of these guilds may be guessed from the fact that the Epic recommends the King to circumvent them by bribery and dissension since "the safeguard of corporations is union" (c. f. Mbh. III. 249, 16; XII. 54, 20; also Hopkin's India Old and New, p. 169).

Such a brisk and well regulated trade would invariably presuppose a stable currency which however underwent certain changes. Thus Kārshāpana according to Manu was a copper coin only, whereas we have seen it denoted silver and gold coinage also in the time of the Jātakas. Again Śatamāna in this period was a silver coin only, whereas in the Brāhmana period it was also a gold coin. The typical silver coin mentioned by Manu is Dharaṇa or Purāṇa. But this Dharaṇa is equal to 90 white mustard seeds, while according to Kautilya, it was equal to 88 white mustard seeds. But the most important change was due to the influence of Rome. As a result of active trade relations with the Roman Empire we find an unmistakable copy of the head of either Augustus or Tiberius on certain coins of Kadphises I; while Kadphises II. carried much farther his imitation of Roman usage by striking an abundant and excellent use of gold coins agreeing closely with the Cæsarian aurie in weight and not much inferior in fineness. The bulk of the considerable inflow of Roman gold into India as testified to by Pliny in 77 A. D. seems so far as N. India was concerned, to have been melted down and reissued as orinentalised auric first by Kadphises II. and afterwards by Kanishka, Huvishka and Vāsudeva. In peninsular India, the Roman auric circulated as currency just as the British sovereign passes current in many countries of the world. At Ozeni (Ujjain) the coins of the Bactrian Kings Menander and Apollodotus were found in this period (Vincent: Periplus II. pp. 363-65). The existence of golden coins is also corroborated by evidences from the Mahābhārata (Birāt Parva sl. 43-44; Drona Parba ch. 17, sl. 25; Aśvamedha Parba ch. 65. sl. 20; Sabhā Parba ch. 23. sl. 53).

In Periplus we find mention of the "silent barter" resorted to on the border of This (China) which is still practised by the Veddas of Ceylon. The goods to be bought are left in a place and the purchaser takes them, replacing them by their equivalent in value.

Among the instruments of credit we find references to debt-sheets in the Milindāpaṇha where the banskurpt makes a public statement of his assets and liabilities [Mil. 131 (text); c. f. 279].

But the most interesting feature of the system of exchange in this period is that guilds served roughly speaking the functions of modern banks. Thus No. 12 of the Nasik Cave Inscriptions records that Usavadāta, son-in-law of King Nahapana has bestowed this cave on the saṃgha generally, he has also given a perpetual endowment—3000 Kāhāpanas. Of these 2000 have been invested in a guild at Govardhana fetching interest at the rate of 1 pratika per 100 monthly. This interest is to be used as cloth money by the monks. The remaining 1000 was deposited in another weaver's guild fetching interest at the rate of $\frac{3}{4}$ padika for the hundred per month. This interest is to be used as pocket money (Ep. Ind. Vol. VIII. p. 82). Here we have a reference to two guilds of weavers which, like banks, received permanent deposits which they held as trustfunds, the principal of which they were to keep in tact and be responsible for and might invest in their own way subject to that responsibility, as banks do with their deposits but for the use of that money they had to pay interest at certain stipulated rates to the beneficiary named in the grant. The low rate of interest (12 per cent per annum and 9% per annum) is an index at once of the security and stability of the banks, their efficiency, permanence and prosperity which attracted to them even royal deposits and benefacations. Similarly No. 15 of the Nasik series (Ibid p. 89) records how in order to provide medicines for the sick of the saṃgha of monks, of whatever sect and origin dwelling in this monastery on mount Trirasmi, a perpetual endowment had been invested for all time to come with the guilds dwelling at Gobardhana viz., in the guild of kularikas (potters) 1000 kārshāpaṇs, in the guild of odayantrikas 2000, etc. One of the Junnar Buddhist Cave Inscriptions (Bühler-Burgess, Arch. Surv. W. Ind. Vol. IV. No. 24. p. 96) records the investment of the income of a field at Vadālikā for planting karanja trees and of another field for planting banyan trees by the lay worshipper Aduthuma, the Saka. Another inscription of the same series (No. 27) mentions the investment of money with the guild of bamboo-workers (vasakāra) and the guild of brazirs (Kāsākāra).

The national wealth of India must have been considerable if we look to the flourishing condition of her arts and crafts, the immense volume of her inland and international commerce and the immense output of her land and sea-mines. From her trade with Rome alone she received £400,000 (Mommsen's Provinces of the Roman Empire Vol. II. pp. 299-300). Hence the remark of Mr. R. Sewell. "The Andhra period seems to have been one of considerable prosperity" (Imperial Gazetteer, New Edition, Vol. II. p. 325).

The burden of taxation upon the people was not so heavy as some Western scholars think it to be. The following rates of taxes are given by Manu:—(1) $\frac{1}{5}$th on gold and cattle (VII. 130.) (2) $\frac{1}{6}$th, $\frac{1}{10}$th, or $\frac{1}{12}$th part of lost property (VIII. 34.) (3) $\frac{1}{6}$th of trees, meat, honey, clarified butter, perfumes, roots, medicinal herbs, substances used for flavouring food, flowers and fruits (VII. 131.) (4) a trifle on common inhabitants who live by traffic (VII. 137.) (5) $\frac{1}{6}$th on grain (6) $\frac{1}{20}$th on sums of money down to one Kārshāpaṇa. (X. 120). According to the Mahābhārata taxes there must be, because the people must be defended and this costs; but they must be light and vary according to need. The tax in kind is common. The merchant pays in kind, the ranchman pays in kind but the townpeople are fined in copper money. Śūdras, manual labourers and artisans render assistance to the King by labour. The following humane rules are worth noting:—(1) Though even dying a king could not tax any Śrotriya (Manu VII. 133). (2) A blind man, an idiot, a cripple, a man of 70 years were exempt from taxes (Manu IX. 201). (3) In times of distress only can the king take $\frac{1}{4}$ of (3) and (4) mentioned above (Manu X. 118). (4) The king was entitled to forced labour of mechanics and artisans for one day in the month (Manu VII. 138). (5) When the country was threatened with invasion special war-taxes can be imposed and war-loans raised (Mahābhārat, Śāntiparba, Ch. 97. 30-35.). (6) Nevertheless, the necessaries of life were to be exempt from taxation (Mahābhārat, Śāntiparba, Ch. 87. Sl. 14).

Moneylending was an approved line of business. Among the seven modes of acquiring wealth usury finds a place:—(1) inheritance (2) gift from a friend or depositor (3) purchasing (4) conquering (5) usury (6) labour (7) presents from the good (Manu X. 115.). Usury also finds a place among the ten approved means of livelihood enumerated in (Manu X. 116.). Nevertheless, a usurer was not to be invited to a Srādha (Manu III. 153) and a Brahmin is forbidden to take food from a usurer (Manu IV. 210). The following rules regarding interest are worthy of note :—(1) 5% a month is the highest rate of interest (Manu VIII. 142,152). (2) Interest on money if paid all at once and at the same time as debt should not exceed double the principal (Manu VIII. 151). (3) Interest on corn, fruit, wood or draught animals and debt (principal) should not exceed 5 times the principal (Manu VIII. 151). (4) Renewal of the principal was allowed (Manu VIII. 155). (5) When a debtor acknowledged in court that a debt is due, he deserves a fine of five in the hundred. (6) If he has denied the debt he should be fined twice as much. (7) A money-lender should take a monthly interest of 2%, 3%, 4% and 5% according as the debtor is a Brahmin, Kshatriya, Vaiśya and a Śūdra respectively. (8) Interest over a year was not permitted. (9) Nor interest unrecognised by law. (10) Wheel interest (compound interest ?), periodical interest, stipulated interest and corporal interest were also prohibited (Manu VIII. 153). (11) A witness to a loan transaction had to incur the whole of the debt and a tenth of the whole sum or fine if he failed to attend the court when summoned in suits for the debt (Manu VIII. 107).

These elaborate rules regarding interest, taxes, trade and wages of labourers all go to show that the economic organisation of India in this period was as complete as ever. The various professions mentioned in Manu's Code show the highly specialised and civilised life of the times. The various grains, spices and perfumes, the various mineral and industrial products show a highly cultivated and industrial country. The Code in general presents the picture of a peaceful and flourishing community. Gold, gems, silks, ornaments are spoken of as being in all families (Chap. V. 111-112; VII. 130).

The Gupta Period.

(320—500 A. D.)

The Golden Age of the Guptas is equally characterised by a remarkable economic development of the country. This was the period of the expansion of India and of much colonising activity towards the Farther East from Bengal, Kalinga and the Coromondol Coast. Parts of Burma and Malacca were colonised, chiefly from Kalinga and Bengal as shown in Sir A. P. Phayre's History of Burma and testified to by Burmese sacred literature and coins. The main evidences for the Economic History of this period are supplied by the accounts of Fa Hien, the Christian Topography of Cosmos, the Śukranītisāra, the Yājnabalkya Smṛiti, the Vishnu Smṛiti, the Nārada Smṛiti and the Purāṇas. Yule's Cathay and the Way Thither and the Chinese annals like the Kwai Yuen Cataloque of the Chinese Tripitaka have recorded many facts relating to early commerce between India and China.

The economy of India must have been based as in the previous periods on a system of Village Communities only with this difference that the degree of control from the central government was less than what existed under the Mauryas. The immense development of trade no doubt led to a vigorous growth of city-life in important centres of trade. Fa Hien says the towns of Magadha were large. But the majority of the people lived in the villages and agriculture was their principal industry. In Chapter IV, Sec. 4, lines 91-122 of Śukranītisāra we get some of the Agri-flori-horti-cultural ideas prevalent in those times. Ordures and dungs were recognised as good manure (*l.* 94). There were also arrangements for irrigation: Wells, canals, tanks and ponds should be made accessible (by staircases etc.) There should be many of these so that there may be plenty of water in the Kingdom (*ll.* 124-127). Water-reservoirs (নিপান) are also maintained (Chap. IV. Sec. 5, line 141). It is further laid down that "if people undertake new industries or cultivate new lands and dig canals, tanks, wells, etc., for their good, the King should not demand anything of them until they realise profit twice the expenditure (*ll.* 242-44). Sukra is thus definitely an advocate of the Young Industry Argument. The King shall take his due from the peasant in such a way that he be not destroyed. It is to be realised in the fashion of the weaver of the garland and not of the coal-merchant (*ll.* 222-23); the King should realise $\frac{1}{3}$rd, $\frac{1}{4}$th or $\frac{1}{2}$ from places which are irrigated by tanks, canals and wells; by rains and by rivers respectively (*ll.* 227-29). He should have $\frac{1}{6}$th from barren and rocky soils (*l.* 230).

Coming to Forest Produce we find mention of Udambara, Aśvatha, tamarind, Chandana, Bata, Kadamba, Aśoka, Bakula, Mango, Punnag, Champaka, Pine (সরল), Pomegranate, Walnut, Neem, Date, Tamāla, Likucha, Cocoanut, Plantain (*ll.* 95-102) which bear good fruits. Khadira, Teak, Śāl, Arjuna, Śami and many other large trees are mentioned (*ll.* 115-122). There were also Superintendents of parks and forests who had to know the causes of the growth and development of flowers and fruits, who knew how to plant and cure the trees by administering proper soil and water at the suitable time and who knew of their medicinal properties (Chap. II. lines 320-24).

In the arts and crafts there was a unique development. After going through the enumeration of 64 Kalās given by Śukrāchārya, Chap. IV. Sec. III. one can hardly believe that the Hindus were a race of abstract metaphysicians who were negligent of the actual needs of soceity and cultivated the art of preparing for the next life only. He would rather think that they knew how to enjoy life and supply its necessaries, comforts and decencies. The more important of the Kalās are mentioned below:—dancing (*l.* 133) playing on musical instruments (*l.* 134) decorations (*l.* 135) antics (*l.* 136) jugglery, magic, etc., (*ll.* 135-39) distillation of wines and spiritual liquors from flowers etc., (*l.* 141) cooking (*l.* 143) confectionery (*l.* 146) pharmaceutical preparations (*l.* 147) analysis and synthesis of metals (*l.* 148) alloys (*l.* 149) salt industry (*l.* 150) polishing stone, wood and metal vessels (*ll.* 167-68) watch and clock industry (*l.* 170) dying (*l.* 171) rope industry (*l.* 174) weaving (*l.* 175) preparation of artificial gold and gems (*l.* 178) enamelling of metals (*l.* 179) tailoring (*l.* 183) oil industry, *i.e.*, extracting oil from seeds and fats (*l.* 187) [Fa Hien also speaks of oil of cinnamon used in a funeral ceremony] cane industry (*l.* 190) glass industry (*l.* 191) iron implements and tools (*l.* 193) nursing (*l.* 195) pumping and withdrawing of water (*l.* 129). Leather industry was known in its two processes—the flaying of the skin (*l.* 181) and the softening of the hide or tanning (*l.* 180). In another passage Śukra enumerates a large number of arts and crafts. Says he—"Among the King's servants and attendants there should be musicians, poets, guards of honour, artisans, artists, fools, ventriloquists, dancers and harlequins, (*ll.* 390-92) those who construct parks, artificial forests and pleasure-gardens, builders of forts, gunners (*ll.* 393-94) those who make lighter machines, gun-powder, arrows, cannon-balls and swords and construct various tools and implements, arms, weapons, bows, quivers etc. (*ll.* 395-96);

those who prepare ornaments of gold, jewels etc., builders of chariots, stone-cutters, black-smiths and those who enamel metals, (*ll.* 297-98) potters, copper smiths, carpenters, road-makers, barbers, washers, and those who carry nightsoil (*ll.* 399-400) messengers, tailors, and bearers of royal emblems and ensigns (*l.* 401), weavers, (*l.* 407) those who prepare fragrant resins (*l.* 410), sailors, miners, fowlers and repairers of implements (*ll.* 404-405.)

Śukra also refers to horse-brush which is an instrument with seven sharp teeth to be used in cleansing (or rubbing) these animals (horses, bulls, camels etc.) [Ch. IV. Sec. 7. *l.* 346].

As regards the liquor industry which was a Government monopoly it was laid down that "The King should build the Ganja house outside the village and there keep the drunkards and should never allow drinking of liquor in his kingdom in day time" (Ch. IV. Sec. *ll.* 4. 89—90.)

All the mines belonged to the King. As regards the royalty on mines it was laid down that the King should daily receive (as duty) from the sales of silver ⅛th, ¼th, ⅓rd or ½ and not more (*ll.* 643-44). According to Śukra royalties on mines constitute non-temitorial income (*ll.* 671-72.)

The weaving of cotton, silk and wool was also carried on in this period. Fa Hien speaks of "fine white linen painted with gaudy colours." Śukrā-chārya (Ch. I. Sl. 180) not only refers to silk and woolen goods but also gives the method of cleansing them.

Yājnabalkya speaks of paper made of cotton etc.

Pearl-fishery was undoubtedly a very flourishing industry in this period. According to Garuḍa Purāṇa it was carried on throughout the Indian Ocean as far as the Persian Gulf. Garuḍa Purāṇa, Part I. Chapter 68 discusses corals and pearls while Chapter 69 discusses the pearls born of oysters and describes the pearls of the Palk Strait and of the Persian Gulf. The Barāha Purāṇa also relates how a merchant embarked on a voyage in quest of pearls. According to Śukrāchārya pearls grow in fishes, snakes, conches, hogs, bamboos, clouds and shells. Of these the greatest amount is said to come from shells (Sukranītisāra Ch. IV. Sec. 2. lines 117-18). The people of Ceylon could make artificial pearls like these (*Ibid*, Ch. IV. Sec. 2. *l.* 124.). Fa Hien says "Ceylon and the adjoining islands produce pearls and precious stones and the Maṇi-gem is also found in a district where the King placed a guard and claimed as royal share three out of every ten" (Beal, LXXII).

Jewellery was also in a highly developed condition. The classic drama of the Little Clay Cart speaks of "golden stairways inlaid with all sorts of gems" and of "crystal windows from which are hanging strings of pearls." Again "the arches set with sapphires look as though they were the home of the rain-bow." The Garuḍa Purāṇa (Part I. Ch. 72) mentions the blue stones found on the sea-coast of Ceylon while Chapters 77 and 79 describe various precious stones of Yavana, China and other lands. Chapter 80 mentions the Bidrume (a stone) of Romaka (Rome).

In the Little Clay Cart there is also mention of " the high ivory portals of a courtesan's house.

The Gupta artists and craftsmen were no less capable in the working of metals. Śukra enumerates the metals in order of their value, thus—gold, silver, copper, zinc, lead, tin and iron. Bronze is the alloy of zinc and copper, brass of copper and tin (Ch. IV. Sec. 2. *ll.* 173-176); of these the iron industry reached the high point of development. The Iron pillar of Chandragupta II (415 A. D.) at Delhi situated near the Kutb-Minār is 22 feet high with a diameter of 16·4 inches. According to the analysis of Sir Robert Hadfield the pillar contains the following :—

Iron	99·120
Angār	·080
Sulphur	·006
Sylicon	·46
Phosphorus	·113
Manganese	·000
	99·965

From this it is apparent that the pillar is made of pure wrought iron with no mixture of manganese.

Roscoe and Schorlemmer have rightly observed "It is not an easy operation at the present day to forge such a mass with our largest rolls and steam-hammers; how this could be be effected by the rude hand-labour of the Hindus, we are at a loss to understand." Ferguesson has remarked "Taking 400 as a mean date and it certainly is not far from the truth—it opens our eyes to an unsuspected state of affairs to find the Hindus at that age capable of forging a bar of iron longer than any that have been forged in Europe upto a very late date and not frequently even now." There is a still larger iron coloumn at Dhar (about 321 A. D.) over 43 feet 8 inches in length with a diameter of 10¼ inches. Jāḥāngir has written in his Memoirs "Outside the fort of Dhar there is a Jami Masjid and a square pillar lies in front of the Masjid with some portion imbedded in the ground. When Bāhādur Saha conquered Malava he was anxious to take the pillar with him to Gujrat. In the act of digging out, it fell down and was broken into two pieces (one piece 22 feet long and the other 13 feet)." If joined the Dhar pillar would the highest iron pillar in the world.

It is remarkable that the Delhi pillar though fully exposed to the weather has never rusted but retains its inscriptions as clear as when it was engraved. Dr. Panchānon Niyogi remarks in his memorable work entitled "Iron in Ancient India" "two explanations are possible of this remarkable power of ancient specimens of iron resisting corrosion—either there was something in the composition of the iron or that the beams were painted or both. To the author it appears that both the facts have operated in enabling the Indian iron pillars and beams to withstand the corroding influence of wind and rain............the one point remarkable regarding the composition of the Delhi iron, Sinhalese iron and other specimens of Indian iron is that all these specimens of iron are free from manganese and sulphur and contain a tolerably high percentage of phosphorus."

That much specialisation took place in this industry will be evident from the fact that in ancient India iron was divided into three classes—Munda, Tikshna, and Kānta. Munda in its turn was divided into three classes—Mridu, Kunta and Karar. Tikshna was subdivided into six classes—Khara, Sāra, Hrinnāt (হৃন্নাট), Tārābarcha (তারাবর্চ্চ), Bājir বাজ্জির) and Kālalouha. Kānta was divided into five classes—Bhrāmak (ভ্রামক), Chumbaka (চুম্বক), Karṣhak (কর্ষক), Drābak (দ্রাবক), and Romakānta (রোমকান্ত) From old Sanskrit texts like রসরত্নসমুচ্চয় and রসেন্দ্রসার সংগ্রহ we learn that Munda, Tikshna and Kānta iron are the modern cast iron, steel and wrought iron. The Hindu Āyurveda Śāstras make mention of hamatide (গৈরিক) and iron pyrites (তাপ্য). The Hindu Medical men knew the prepartion of Chloride of iron, Oxide of iron and Sulphide of iron (History of Hindu Chemistry by Dr. P. C. Roy). From the

Yuktikalpataru we learn that swords were manufactured in Benares, Magadha, Ceylon, Nepal, Anga, Mysore, Surat and in Kalinga. The Śukranītisāra also mentions the manufacture of small and large nalikās besides guns and cannon-balls already mentioned. Sivedasa in his commentary of Chakrapana quotes Pātanjali as an authority on Lohaśāstra or the Science of Iron. (History of Hindu Chemistry, Vol. I. p. 55).

The art of casting copper statues on a large scale by the *cire perdue* process was practised with conspicuous success. A copper image of Buddha about 80 feet high was erected at Nālanda at the close of the 6th century. The fine Sultanganj Buddha 7½ feet high (now in the Museum at Bermingham) dates from the reign of Chandgupta II.

From the Yuktikalpataru [which was probably compiled by Bhoja Narapati (Dr. Rājendralāl Mitra's Notices of Sanskrit Mss., Vol. I. No. CCLXXI) from works at least as old as the 4th or the 5th Century A. D.] we learn that the art of ship-building was carried by the ancient Hindus to a very high stage of development. After pointing out that the Kshatriya kind of wood (which is light and hard and cannot be joined on to other classes) as the best for ships, Bhoja an earlier authority on ship-building, points out that care should be taken that no iron is used in joining together the planks of the bottom of sea-going vessels for the iron would inevitably expose them to the influence of magnetic rocks in the sea. The author of Yuktikalpataru divides ships into two classes—special and ordinary. The special is further sub-divided into two—Dirgha (दीर्घ) and Unnata (उन्नत). There are ten kinds of Dirgha ships :—

Names of ships.		Length in cubits.	Breadth in cubits.	Height in cubits.
(1) Dīrghikā	...	32	4	$3\frac{1}{5}$
(2) Taraṇī	...	48	6	$4\frac{4}{5}$
(3) Lolā	...	64	8	$6\frac{2}{5}$
(4) Gatvarā	...	80	10	8
(6) Tarī	...	112	14	$11\frac{1}{5}$
(5) Gāminī	...	96	12	$9\frac{2}{5}$
(7) Jangālā	...	128	16	$12\frac{4}{5}$
(8) Plābinī	...	144	18	$14\frac{2}{5}$
(9) Dhāriṇi	...	160	20	16
(10) Beginī	...	176	22	$17\frac{3}{5}$

Unnata ships are subdivided into five classes :—

Urdhavā	...	32	16	16
Anūrdhavā	...	48	24	24
Swarṇamukhī	..	64	32	32
Garbhiṇī	...	80	40	40
Mantharā	...	96	48	48

Ordinary ships are divided into ten classes :—

(1) Kshudrā	...	16	4	4
Madhyamā	...	24	12	8
Bhīmā	...	40	20	20
Chapalā	...	48	24	23
Patalā	...	64	32	32

Names of ships.		Length in cubits.	Breadth in cubits.	Height in cubits.
Bhayā	...	72	36	36
Dirghā	...	88	44	44
Patraputā	...	96	48	48
Garbharā	...	112	56	56
Mantharā	...	120	60	60

Of these ships Lolā, Gāminī, Plābinī, Gatvarā, Tarī, Jangālā and Dhāriṇī, Anūrdhavā, Garvinī, and Mantharā, Bhīmā, Bhayā and Garbharā bring ill luck. The prow of ships may admit of the shape of the heads of lion, tiger, elephant, buffalo, serpent, duck, peahen, parrot, frog, man etc. Ships may be decorated with gold, silver, copper, the compound of these three, pearls and garland of gold. Again a vessel with four masts is to be painted white, that with three masts to be painted red, that with two yellow and that with one blue. According to the position of their cabins ships are Sarbamandirā (সর্ব্বমন্দিরা), Madhymandirā (মধ্যমন্দিরা) and Agramandirā (অগ্রমন্দিরা) Agramandirā ships are eminently fitted for long voyages and for naval warfare (History of Indian Shipping, pp. 20-26).

Fa Hien thus speaks of a fine piece of bamboo-work carried in procession in Magadha "On this occasion they construct a four-wheeled car and erect on it a tower of five stages composed of bamboos lashed together, the whole being supported by a centre-post resembling a large spear with three points, in height 22 feet and more. So it looks like a pagoda. They then cover it with fine white linen which they afterwards paint with gaudy colours. Having made figures of the Devas decorated with gold, silver and glass, they place them under conopies of embroidered silk. Then at the four corners of the car they construct niches (shrines) in which they place figures of Buddha in a sitting posture with a Bodhisattva standing in attendance. There are thus 20 cars prepared and differently decorated" (Beal, LVI—LVII). Similar processions of lifelike figures painted in diverse colours took place in Ceylon. At Toli says Fa Hien a skilful carver of wood carved a wooden image of Maitreya Bodhisattva, 80 feet in length.

Townplanning was also known. In the Śilpaśāstras the proper place for each kind of building was strictly prescribed as well as the measurements of actual buildings down to the smallest ones. The whole was planned in the model of a city in Heaven. Thus all building is traced back to the work of the divine architect Viśwakarmā. Thus architecture becomes a sacred calling with the master craftsman as priest. Hence Bāna of the next epoch comparies Ujjain to Kailāsh with its many peaks clear cut against the sky.

"The three closely allied arts of architecture, sculpture and painting" says Mr. V. A. Smith "attained an extraordinarily high point of development. The accident that the Gupta Empire consisted for the most part of the provinces permanently occupied at an early date by the Muhammadans who systematically destroyed Hindu buildings for several centuries obscures the history of Gupta Architecture. No large building of the period has survived and the smaller edifices which escaped destruction are hidden in remote localities away from the track of the Muslim armies chiefly in Central India and the Central Provinces. They closely resemble rock-cut temples (Oxford History of India, p. 160). Fa Hien noticed a huge stone saṃgha-rāma in the Deccan (in the modern Chanda District). "It is constructed out of a great mountain of rock hollowed to the proper shape. The building has altogether five stages. The lowest is made with elephant figures and has five hundred cells in it. The second is made with lion shapes and has four hundred chambers. The third is made with horse shapes and has three hundred chambers. The fourth is made with ox shapes and has two hundred chambers. The fifth has dove shapes and has 100 chambers in it. At the very top of all is a spring of water which flowing in a stream before the rooms encircles each tier and so running in a circuitous course, at last arrives at the very lowest stage of all, where flowing past the chambers it finally issues through the door. Throughout the consecutive tiers in various parts of the building windows have been pierced through the solid rock for the admission of light, so that every chamber is illuminated and there is no darkness. At the four corners of the edifice they have hewn out the rocks into steps as means for ascending". (Beal, LXVIII-LXIX). In Samkāsya "there are 100 small towers. A man might pass the day in trying to count them without succeeding. If any one is very anxious to find out the right number then he places a man by the side of each tower and afterwards numbers the men; but even in this case, it can never be known how many or how few men will be required" (Beal, XLII-XLIII.). "In old days" says Fa Hien "men bored through the rocks (10,000 feet high) to make a way and spread out side-ladders of which there are 700 steps in all to pass. Having passed the ladder we proceeded by a hanging rope bridge and crossed the river". The Viśwakarmā cave of Ellora has a hall which is 85 feet by 43 feet. The facade looks like an ordinary two-storied house with verandahs richly sculptured. At Ellora there are many monasteries attached to the Viśwakarmā cave. Three temples here *viz.*, the Do-tal, the Teen-tal and Daś-Avatār show the gradual merging of Buddhist excavations into Hindu. The temples of Ellora constructed in a later period (8th or 9th century A. D.) make Ellora one of the wonders of the world. The Kanheri cave on the island of Salsettee in the Bombay harbour was excavated early in the fifth century A. D. It copies the Karli cave (1st century B. C.) but the style is inferior.

The most important stone temple of this age is that of Deogarh in the Lalitpur subdivision of the Jhansi Destruct, U. P. the panels of whose walls contain some of the finest specimens of Indian sculpture. The larger brick temple at Bhītargāon in Cawnpur district which has been ascribed to the reign of Chandragupta II. is remarkable for vigour and well-designed sculpture in terra-cotta. Fragments including some beautiful sculptures indicate that beautiful stone temples of the Gupta age stood at Sārnāth near Benares. "The Gupta sculpture exhibits pleasing characteristics which usually enable a student familiar with standard examples to decide with confidence whether or not a given work is of Gupta age. The physical beauty of the figures, the gracious dignity of their attitude and the refined restraint of the treatment are qualities which are not to be found elsewhere in Indian sculptures in the same degree. Other obvious technical marks are the plain robes showing the body as if they were transparent, the elaborate haloes and the curious wigs" (Oxford History of India, p. 162).

Two of the finest caves at Ajantā Nos. XVI. and XVII. were excavated in this period (J. R. A. S. 1914, p. 335). A Danish artist thus speaks of the paintings in Ajantā caves "they represent the climax to which genuine Indian art has attained" and that "everything in these pictures from the composition as a whole to the smallest pearl or flower testifies to depth of insight coupled with the greatest technical skill" (Ann. Rep. Arch. Dept. Nizam's Dom. for 1914-15. App. H. by Axel Jarl). The worth of the achivement will be further evident from the fact that "much of the work has been carried on with the help of artificial light, and no great stretch of imagination is necessary to picture all that this involves in the Indian climate and in situations where thorough ventilation is impossible" (Griffith, The Paintings in the Buddhist Cave-temples of Ajantā). About the truth and precision of the work which are no less admirable than its boldness and extent, Mr. Griffith has the following glowing testimony "During my long and careful study of the caves I have not been able to detect a a single instance where a mistake has been made by cutting away too much stone, for, if once a slip of this kind occurred, it could only have been repaired by the insertion of a piece which would have been a blemish" (Ibid.). The closely related frescoes at Sirgiriya in Ceylon were executed in this period (between 479-497 A. D).

Some of these crafts were organised into guilds. Śukra mentions the guilds of cultivators, artisans, artists, usurers, the dancers and the ascetics (Ch.

IV. Sec. 5. *ll.* 35-36). It is further laid down that "that the leader or captain of those who combine to build a palace or a temple and construct canal or furniture is to get twice the share got by each" (606-07). The goldsmiths should get remuneration according to the labour undergone by each in cases where they combine (সম্ভূয়) to perform a work of art. Evidence of Yājnabalkya, Nārada and Vishnu tend to prove conclusively that the guilds were not only recognised as a part of the state fabric but also their authority was upheld by that of the state. Thus Nārada says "The King must maintain the usages of the guilds and other corporations. Whatever be their (religious duties), (the rules regarding) their attendance and (the particular mode of) livelehood prescribed for them, these the King shall approve of" (X. 2, 3). We are further told that "those who cause dessension among the members of an association shall undergo punishment of a specially severe kind; because they would prove extremetly dangerous, like an (epidemic) disease if they were allowed to go free" (X. 6.). The Yājnabalkya Saṃhitā also prescribes that if a man steals the property of a guild or any other corporation or breaks any agreement with it he shall be banished from the realm and all his property confiscated (II. 187-192). Similar injunctions also occur in the Instiutes of Vishṇu (গণদ্রব্যাপহর্ত্তা বিবাস্যঃ). Besides these, Yājnabalkya (chap. II. slokas 186-192) lays down that (1) the guilds could possess corporate property (2) that they could lay down rules and regulations corresponding to the Articles of the Association of the present day. Nārada (X. 1) refers to the Samaya which he defines as the aggregate of rules settled by the corporations; (3) that the duties arising from the rules and regulations (Sāmayika) not inconsistent with the injunctions of the sacred texts as well as the regulations laid down by the King must be observed with care, thus placing duty towards the guild on an equal footing with that towards the state; (4) some pure and virtuous men were appointed as the Executive officers (কার্য্যচিন্তকাঃ); (5) they often transacted business with the Court in their name and were held in high respect there. (6) They possessed executive authority over the members of the guild and could punish any one who disobeyed their decision (কর্ত্তব্যং বচনং তেষাং সমূহহিতবাদিনাম্). Yājnabalkya here makes no mention of the President of the guild but there must have been one as the frequent reference to Śreṣhthin in contemporary inscriptions show and as Śukra mentions the leader or captain of corporation in 606-07 quoted above; (7) they were, however, bound by the laws and usages of the corporation and if they violated them in the exercise of their authority and there was dissension between them and the general members, the King had to step in and make both parties conform to the established usuage. Mitrāmiśra [Viramitrodaya (edited by Jivānanda Vidyāsāgar) p. 428] goes further. He takes verse 187 of the second chapter of Yājnabalkya to refer to the Mukhyas and cites the following text from Kātyāyana as an illustration of the doctrine "মুখ্যদণ্ডেন সমূহস্যৈবাধিকার (the right of the assembly to punish its chiefs) :—

সাহসী ভেদকারী চ গণদ্রব্যবিনাশকঃ
উচ্ছেদ্যাঃ সর্ব্ব এবৈতে বিখ্যাপ্যৈব নৃপে ভৃগুঃ ।

Thus any of the Executive officers who was guilty of any heinous criminal act, who created dissension or who destroyed the property of the association could be removed and the removal was only to be notified to but not necessarily to be sanctioned by the King. When the removal could not be effected on account of the enormons power of the Executive officers, the matter was to be brought to the notice of the King who would hear both sides of the case and decide (Nārada X. 3 and Jagannatha's comment on it). Mitramiśra observes in the same strain (সমূহাশক্তৌ তস্য দণ্ডো রাজ্ঞা বিধেয়ঃ) "the King should step in only when the assembly found itself unable to punish the officers". He quotes as an illustration of this, Manu (VIII. 219-21) " If a man belonging to a corporation inhabiting a village or a district after swearing to an agreement, breaks it through avarice (the King shall banish him from his realm". He takes the whole passage as referring to the Mukhyas or Executive officers alone.

Some other cases of royal interference may be gathered from Nārada (X. 4, 5, 6.) where it is laid down that the King could forbid combinations of different associations (possibly of a hostile nature), arming of those bodies without due causes and the conflict between them. He could also prevent them from undertaking such acts as were either opposed to his wish or interests or of contemptible and immoral nature. Thus a King could interfere with them only in some specified cases but otherwise they were free to act in whatever way they liked and the King was bound to accept their decision.

According to Nārada regular rules were laid down for the attendance of members in the assembly and the King had to approve of them whatever they might be (X. 3.). It appears from Mitramiśra's comment on the passage that the sound of a drum or other instruments was a signal for the attendance of members in the guild hall for the transaction of affairs (Viram. p. 430).

These guilds also possessed judicial authority over its members. Thus Śukra lays down "The cultivators, the artisans, the artists, the usurer, the corporations, the dancers, the ascetics and thieves should decide their disputes according to the usuages of their guilds (ch. IV. Sec. 5, *ll.* 35-36). Thus the guilds could only interfere in cases which affected or had a tendency to affect the transaction of their business. The following passage from Śukra seems, however, to show that the guild also formed part of the ordinary tribunals of the country "The Kula (family) Sreṇi (guilds) and Gaṇas (republican communities) are the three successively higher organisations of self-adjudication. When and where these fail, the King with his officers is to interfere" (ch. IV. Sec. 5. *ll.* 59-60). According to Nārada also (107, p. 6) the guild formed the second of the four ordinary courts of justice from each of which an appeal lay successively to the next higher ones. This is supported by the recently published Damodarpur Copper Plates dated in the year 433 and 438 A. D. in the reign of the Gupta Emperorr Kumārgupta I, where we find a clear reference to courts presided over by the chiefs of different guilds of merchants and artisans (Ep. Ind. Vol. XV. p. 130).

The existence and organisation of the guilds is further corroborated by the inscriptions of this period. Thus the Indore Copper Plate Inscription of Skandagupta (Fleet, Gupta Ins. No. 16) dated 465 A. D. records the gift of an endowment, the interest of which is to be applied to the maintenance of a lamp which has been established in a temple for the service of the Sun-god. We are further told that "this gift of a Brahmin's endowment of (the temple of) the Sun (is) the perpetual property of the guild of oilmen of which Jīvanta is the head, residing in the town of Indrapura, so long as it continues in complete unity (even) in moving away from this settlement" (Ibid p. 71). Here we find "the custom of designating a guild by the name of its headman, the mobility of the body, greater importance being attached to the unity of the guild than the place where it settles". It should be noted that "none but a fully organised body could thus shift from place to place and yet retain its unity and public confidence". No less interesting is the Mandasor stone inscription of Kumārgupta and Bandhubarman (Fleet, Gupta Inscriptions, No. 18) which relates how a guild of silk-weavers, originally settled at Lāṭa, immigrated into the city of Daśapur attracted by the virtues of the King of that place. Here some of them learnt archery, some adopted the religious life, some learnt astrology and astronomy, some poetry, some became ascetics, while others adhered to their hereditary profession of silk weaving. It built in 436 A. D. a magnificent temple of the Sun at Daśapur and while it fell into disrepair the same guild repaired it in 472 A. D. This inscription shows that the guilds were not stereotyped close corporations of crafts busy alone with their own profession but that "through the autonomy and freedom accorded to them by the law of the land they became a centre of strength and an abode of liberal culture and progress which truly made them a power and ornament of the society." (Corporate Life in Ancient India, p. 68).

Combined with this widespread corporate regulation of industral life there was a very general but by no means cast iron custom for the son to follow the calling of the father. Thus it is laid down by Vishṇu (III. 2) and Yāynabalkya (I. 360) that the King should enforce the observance of the respective duties of the castes. Śukra says "every caste should practise the duties that have been mentioned as belonging to it and that have been practised by ancestors and should otherwise be punished by Kings (Ch. IV. Sec. 4, *ll* 82-83). But he also says "For Brahmins agriculture has been prescribed by Manu and others" (Ch. IV. Sec. 3, *l.* 37). Another instance of mobility of labour we find in the Mandasor Stone Inscription of Kumāragupta and Bandhubarman (mentioned above) where the silk weavers took to different pursuits with impunity.

In this connection it may be noted that according to Fa Hien the Chandālas who did not observe the rules of purity were obliged to live apart and were required when entering a town or bazaar to strike a piece of wood as a warning of their approach in order that other people might not be polluted by contact with them.

A very new and interesting feature of the rules regarding the labourers of this period is the existence of rules regarding *Bonus, Leave and pension* and something approximating to the *Provident Fund.* Thus it was laid down by Śukrāchārya that even a slight portion should not be deducted from the full remuneration of a servant who has been ill for half a fortnight. And if the diseased be highly qualified he should have half the wages (Ch. I. *ll.* 822-24). The King should give the servant 15 days a year respite from work (Ibid. *l.* 825). The King should grant half the wages without work to the man who has passed 40 years in his service (Ibid. *ll.* 826-27) for life and to the son if minor and incapable half the wages or to the wife and wellbehaved daughters (Ibid. *ll.* 828-29). He should give the servant ⅛th of the salary by way of reward every year and if the work has been done with exceptional ability ⅛th of the services rendered. He should keep with him as deposit ⅙th or ¼th of the servant's wages, should pay half of that amount or whole in two or three years.

A large number of rules regarding labourers and their wages has been laid down by Sukrāchārya. According to him remuneration can be paid according to time, work or according to both. It is to be paid therefore as arranged i. e., according to contract. According to the qualifications of the workers there should be the rates of wages fixed by the King for his own welfare (Ibid *ll.* 803-804). Wages are to be so fixed that the worker may maintain those who are his compulsory charges (Ibid. *ll.* 805-806). Thus the equitable rate of wages is that which considers not simply the absolute necessaries of life but also recognises the standard of life and comfort as implied in the care for family and dependents. Those servants who get low wages are enemies by nature (Ibid. *ll.* 807-808). Here Śukra is aware of the political and social effects of low wages and thus his equitable standard anticipates by centuries the socialistic cries for "higher life" to be lived by the working classes. The wages of the Śūdras are to be just enough for food and raiment (Ibid. *l.* 809). At the same time Sukra lays down that "you should not commit violence on any body in the matter of renumeration, duties or revenues by increasing them through slight or strength (Chap. I lines 617-18). This law prohibits exactions and undue enhancements of payment from the master in the shape of increased wages or salary, from merchants in the shape of augmented excise and customs and from the subjects in the shape of exorbitant revenues. Rates in all these cases should not be increased by threat of physical violence or by crafts of diplomacy. According to Śukra the goldsmith's wages is to be $\frac{1}{30}$th (of the value worked upon) if the workmanship is excellent, $\frac{1}{60}$th if mediocre, half of that if of inferior order (*ll.* 653-54). The wage of the goldsmith is to be half of that in the case of Kataka (bracelet), half of that in the case of mere melting (*l.* 655). The silversmith's wages is to be half if workmanship be of the highest order, half of that if mediocre, half of that if inferior and half of that in the case of Kataka (*ll.* 656-57). The wages is to be $\frac{1}{4}$th in the case of copper, zinc and jasada metal, half or equal or twice or 8 times in the case of iron (*ll.* 658-59).

It is evident from the various kinds of ships mentioned above that maritime intercourse was fully maintained in this period between India and the outside world. In fact in the 'spacious times' of Gupta Imperialism Indian traders carried the torch of civilisation into the hearths of the people of Java, Pegu, Cambodia, Siam, China and even Japan. The conquest of W. India by Chandagupta II. brought the Gangetic provinces into direct communication with the western ports especially those of Gujrat and so with Alexandria and Europe. Trade also followed the landroute through Persia. The Raghubaṃśha of Kālidās mentions the carrying into Persia of the victorious arms of Raghu by the landroute (পারসীকান্ ততোজেতুং প্রতস্থে স্থলবর্ত্তনা). This express reference to landroute implies that the water route was well known. The Sakuntalā also relates the story of a merchant named Dhanavṛidhi whose immense wealth devolved on the King on the former's perishing at sea aud leaving no heir behind. In the Yājnavalkya Saṃhitā there is a passage which indicates that the Hindus used to make sea voyages in pursuit of gain (II. 3). The Varāha Purāṇa (Ch. 171) mentions a childless merchant named

Gokarṇa who embarked on a voyage for trading purposes. In the same Purāṇa we are told of a merchant who went on a ship in quest of pearls with people who knew all about them. In a passage of the Mārkandeya Purāṇa we find a reference to the dangerous plight of the man sailing on the great ocean in a ship overtaken by a whirlwind. The Vishnu Purāṇa Book II. discusses the earth surrounded by the seas and the ocean tides. The Vāyu Purāṇa mentions King Bharat of the Vairāja dynasty as having conquered 8 islands of the Indian Ocean (c. f. also Bhāgabat Bk. V. Ch. 19).

From this time forward trade with Rome gradually declined. Already the trade with Alexandria had suffered much at the hands of Caracalla. The Palmyrine trade was ruined by the destruction of Palmyra itself in 273 A. D. Constantine weakened the Roman Empire by changing the seat of government in 330 A. D. Alaric sacked Rome in 410 and Attila ravaged her lands in 451. In 454 the huge wave of a Vandal invasion swept off her arts and crafts. She was again pillaged in 472 and 476. Thus Rome that eternal city—the mother of arts, civilisation and heroes—" stood childless and crownless in her voiceless woe like another Niobe all tears ! ! ! "

The powerful Sassanids of Persia now monosed the Indian trade.

According to Hamza of Ispahan the ships of India and China could be seen constantly moored at Hira near Kufa on the Euphrates (Yule's Cathay and the Way Thither I, LXXVIII). The ports of Sindh and Gujrat appear among the chief centres of this naval trade.

The Tamils in this period carried on their commercial relations with the people of Lower Burma or Pegu. According to Sir A. P. Phayre (History of Burma pp. 28 and 31) Pegu was conquered by emigrants from the Telegu Kingdom bordering on the Bay of Bengal and consequently the people of Pegu have long been known to the Burmese and to all foreigners by the name of Talaing. According to the same authority the people of Kalinga had commercial intercourse with Burma as the existence of some coins and medals in Pegu with Hindu symbols shows (History of Burma, p. 31).

Nor is this all. According to R. F. St. Andrew St. John (J. R. A. S. 1898) " somewhere about 300 A. D. people from the west coast of Bengal founded colonies on the coasts of the Gulf of Martaban, of which the principal appear to have been Thaton or Saddhamanagara." The inscriptions found in the French territories in Cambodia and Annam state that there were Brahminical Kingdoms and Sivism there in the 4th and 5th centuries A.D. In the Annandale Report for 1913, it is stated that there is clear evidence of the existence of a

Hindu Kingdom in Pagan. Dr. Annandale says that the Brahmins once held sway over the Malaya peninsula.

"That there was intercourse also with Malacca is evident from many words in the Malayan language which Marsden has traced to an Indian or Sanskrit origin. To this day there are Klings or descendants of settlers from ancient Kalinga at Singapore." The name of Klings is derived from Keiling whence they are said to come. With reference to this ancient trade Sir Walter Elliot observes "There is no doubt that the intercourse between the east coast of India and the whole of the opposite coast of the Bay of Bengal and the straits of Malacca was far greater in ancient times . . . It had attained its height at the time the Buddhists were in the ascendant *i.e.*, during the first five or six centuries of our era. The first great Buddhist persecution both checked it and also drove great numbers of the victims to the opposite coast. The Tamil and Telugu local histories and tradition are full of such narratives" (Quoted in History of Indian shipping, p. 147.)

Trade was also carried on in this period with the island of Java which the Hindus have long colonised in the early centuries of the Christian era. This trade is proved by the evidence of the Chinese pilgrim Fa Hien who in the end of the 4th century found Java entirely peopled by the Hindus and who sailed from the Ganges to Ceylon, from

Ceylon to Java and thence to China on board a ship containing in all 200 passengers and manned by crew professing the Brahminical religion. It is noteworthy that "astern of the great ship was a smaller one as a provision in case of the larger vessel being injured or wrecked during the voyage" (Beal, Buddhist Records of the Western World, Vol. II. p. 269).

Trade was also carried on with Sumatra as has been pointed out by Dr. R. G. Bhāṇdārkar in his article on the eastern passage of the Sakas [J. R. A. S. (Bombay Branch) XVII]. Certain inscriptions show a Māgadhi element which may have reached Java from Sumatra and Sumatra from the coast either of Bengal or Orissa. M. Coleman says "Mr. Anderson in his account of his mission to the coast of that island (Sumatra) has, however, stated that he discovered at Jambi the remains of an ancient Hindu temple of considerable dimensions and near the spot various mutilated figures, which would appear to clearly indicate the former existence of the worship of the Vedantic philosophy" (Hindu Mythology, p. 361). It is further observed in the Bombay Gazetteer (Vol. I. Part I, p. 493) that "the Hindu settlement of Sumatra was almost entirely from the east coast of India and that Bengal, Orissa and Masulipatam had a large share in colonising both Java and Cambodia cannot be doubted." In fact, notwithstanding the marvellous fertility of the soil and the wonderful industries that flourished in the country, India had to resort to colonisation of foreign lands to provide for her superabundant population. Professor Heeren rightly observes "How could such a thickly populated and in some parts overpeopled country as India have disposed of her superabundant population except by planting colonies?" (Historical Researches, Vol. I. p. 310).

It was also in this age that we find the field of Indian maritime trade in the eastern seas extending as far as China and Japan. This commercial intercourse with China began as we have already seen, at the commencement of the Christian era while "the Chinese did not arrive in the Malaya archipelago before the fifth century and they did not extend their voyages to India, Persia and Arabia till a century later" (Mr. G. Phillips in the J. R. A. S. 1895, p. 525). The first eminent Buddhist to come to India was Fa Hien. A little before him in 398 Amitodana went to China. After him the Kwai-Yuen-Catalogue as well as other Chinese works mention a series of names of Buddhist priests who sailed between S. India and China. Thus in 420 Saṃghavarmi a Sinhalese went to China. In 424 Guṇabarma went to China. In 429 three other Sinhalese went to China. From Bhikshuṇī Nidāna we learn that in 433 a party of Sinhalese nuns went to China on board a ship called Nandi. In 434, another batch of Sinhalese nun under the leadership of a certain Tissara went to China. In 435 Guṇabhadra reached Kau in China. In 442 Saṃghabarman reached China by the overland-route and returned to India by the sea. In about 488 Saṃghabhadra went to China. Mr. Kakasu Okakura has remarked "Down to the days of the Muhammadan conquest went by the ancient highways of the sea, the intrepid mariners of the Bengal coast, founding their colonies in Ceylon, Java, Sumatra and binding Cathay (China) and India in mutual intercourse (Ideals of the East, pp. 1-2). Thus the Tamils, the Sinhalese and the people of Bengal were the principal sharers in the trade with China [History of Indian Shipping, pp. 165-66].

The great trading centres of Bengal in those days were Satgaon, Champā, Sonargaon and Tāmralipti. Satgaon was called Tcharitrapoura in the time of the Chinese pilgrim's visit. Sonargaon was the greatest harbour of E. Bengal while Champā or Bhagalpur was the starting station for Subarṇabhūmi. Fa Hien when he visited India (399-414) found Tāmralipti as a great maritime settlement of the Buddhists and from its harbour he set sail for Ceylon. The ports of Sindh, Cutch and Gujrat, were famous for the volume of their trade with the East. Of these Sindhu or Debal and Orhet *i.e.*, Soratha or Veraval were the leading centres of trade with Ceylon (Yule's Cathay, I. CLXXVIII).

According to Professor Lacouperie (Western Origin of Chinese Civilisation) throughout this period the monopoly of the sea-borne trade of China was in the hands of Indian merchants who exported into China pearls, rubies, sugar, aromatics, peacocks, corals and the like. While we know from Sakuntalā that India imported from China Chinese silk—

"গচ্ছতিপুরঃ শরীরং ধাবতি পশ্চাদসংস্থিতং চেতঃ।
চীনাংশুকমিব কেতোঃ প্রতিবতং নীয়মানস্য।"

In the Indian exports to Europe dyes, cosmetics and artificial imitations of natural flower-scents bulked very largely and it is interesting to note that Varāhamihir who flourished in the sixth century alludes to the manufacture of these articles.

According to Śukrāchārya the regions of duties are the marketplaces, streets and mines (ch. II. Sec. 2, line 213). Duties are to be levied on goods only once (*Ibid. l.* 214). The King should receive the $\frac{1}{32}$nd portion from the seller or buyer. Even a $\frac{1}{20}$th or $\frac{1}{16}$th is a fair and legitimate duty (*Ibid. l.* 217). If the seller has to give the commodity at a loss, no duty is to be realised from him but it is to be realised from the buyer (*Ibid. ll.* 218-19). But we should remember that it is difficult to carry out this maxim of Public Finance. The king should realise $\frac{1}{32}$nd portion of the increase or interest of the usurers (*Ibid. l.* 255). He should also have land tax from shopkeepers (*Ibid. l.* 257). He should realise from minerals at the following rates: half of gold, one-third of silver, one-fourth of copper, one-sixth of zinc and iron, half of gems, half of glass and lead after the expenses have been met (*Ibid. ll.* 233—35). He should realise $\frac{1}{3}$rd, $\frac{1}{5}$th, $\frac{1}{7}$th, $\frac{1}{10}$th or $\frac{1}{20}$th from collectors of grasses and wood (*Ibid. ll.* 237—38). In the gambling houses where the king's guards kept order $\frac{1}{5}$th or $\frac{1}{10}$th of the winning was the King's dues (Agni Purāṇa). It is interesting to note that according to Sukra "That man is a good collector of taxes and duties who realise these from shophkeepers in such a way as not to destroy their capital" (Ch. II. *ll.* 351—52).

Levies were also made in kind. Thus it was laid down that the king shall take $\frac{1}{8}$th of the increase of goats, sheep, cows, buffaloes and horses, $\frac{1}{16}$th of the milk of she-buffaloes, she-goats and female sheep (*Ibid. ll.* 239—40). The King should make the artists and artisans work one day in the fortnight for him (*Ibid. l.* 241).

In the marketplace, stalls (পণ্যবেশনম্) or shops are to be placed according to the classes of commodities (Śukra Ch. I. line 516). And in determining the value of a commodity two points are to be noticed says Śukra :—(1) সুলভাসুলভ, ease or difficulty of attainment—referring to the cost of production determining supply (2) অগুণতাগুণসংশ্রয়, its utility or power of satlsfying wants etc, because of its properties—referring to the demand for it determined by its uses. (*Ibid. ll.* 718—19), And a merchant should fix $\frac{1}{32}$nd or $\frac{1}{16}$th part as profit in a business with due regard to the expenditure and to the conditions of the place (transport and freight) and not more (*Ibid. ll.* 628—29). According to Fa Hien

34

in Ceylon "at the time of traffic the demons did not appear in person but only exposed their valuable commodities with the value affixed. Then the merchantman according to the price marked, purchased the goods and took them away (Beal, LXXII).

There are certain regulations regarding trade and industry which betray surprisingly modern features. Thus it is laid down that if wealthy men of good manners are ruined in a business, the king should protect them and suchlike men (Ch. V. *l.* 180 f.). This is a notable instance of State Intervention in Industry. Further, the seller of bad (adulterated) food is punishable like a thief (*l.* 641). Again, according to Yājnabalkya "for traders combining to maintain a price to the prejudice of labourers and artisans although knowing the rise and fall in prices the fine shall be the highest amercement. For traders combining to obstruct tht sale of a commodity by demanding a wrong price or for selling i', the fine is the highest amercement." The sale or purchase should be conducted at the price which is fixed by the king. The surplus made therefrom is understood to be the legal profit of business. Nor is all. It is laid down in Śukranītisāra that without the permission of the king, the following things are not to be done by the subjects:--gambling, drinking, hunting, use of arms; sales and purchases of cows, elephants, horses, camels, buffaloes, men, immovable property, silver, gold, jewellery, intoxicants and poisons, distillation of wines, the drawing up of deed indicating a sale or gift or loan, and medical practice (Ch. I. lines 603—08). "Here is a mention of those practices and professions which for public safety, social peace and future interests of the parties concerned should be endorsed by the state and receive a royal patent, character or license to testity to their bonafide charter. In all these cases the state according to Śukrāchārya must interfere even on the principle of individualistic minimum. Here the hoary Śukra and the modern Sidgwick are on common ground."

Coming to the trade orgainisations we find that both Nārada (III. 1—9) and Yājnabalkya (II. 262 ff.) have laid down rules for the transaction of joint business (सम्भूयसमुत्थानम्). Nārada expounds the fundamental principles of joint stock business thus :—"Where traders or others carry on business jointly, it is called partnership which is a title of law. Where several partners are joitnly carrying on business for the purpose of gain, the contribution of funds towards the common stock of the association forms the basis (of their undertakings). Therefore let each contribute his proper share. The loss, expenses and profit of each partner are either equal to those of the other partners or exceed them or remain below them according as his share is equal to theirs or greater or less. The store, the food, the charges (for tools and the like), the loss, the freight and the expense of keeping valuables must be duly paid for by each of the several partners, in accordance with the forms of their agreement." [(Nārada III. 1—4); S. B. E. Vol. XXXIII. p. 124]. It thus appears that an agreement was drawn up among partners, intending to carry on business together, in which the general principles upon which the business would be managed were clearly laid down. Śukrāchārya called this business deed as সাময়িকপত্র and defined it as "one which individuals frame after combining their shares of capital for some business concern (*ll.* 627—28) According to the comments of Chandeśvara on Nārada III. 4 quoted above, a partner if necessary could draw from the common fund an amount regulated by the share he paid (Vivādratnākar p. 112). From Nārada III. 3 quoted above we find that losses, expenses and profit of each partner are proportionable to the amount contributed by him to the joint stock. Yājnabalkya, however, lays down that the profit etc., may be either in proportion to the amount contributed by each or as originally agreed upon among the partners. Thus by virtue of this previous agreement, some of the partners probably on account of their greater skill and special knowledge, might enjoy a greater share of the profit, than was warranted by the amount of money contributed by them. The relation of the individual to the corporate body was also clearly laid down. Thus, Nārada III. 5 lays down that when a partner injures the joint property through his negligence by acting without the assent or against the express injunctions of the other partners, he must compensate for the loss. Yājnabalkya (II. 265) says that if a man is guilty of fraud he should be expelled from the company, paid his capital but deprived of profits. Yājnabalkya (II. 263) and Nārada (III. 6) however refer to special rewards being given to worthy members. It is no less interesting to find that the joint stock company also looked after the interests of the individual even after his death (Nārada III. 7; Yājnabalkya II. 267). It is also worthy of note that priests carried on sacrificial acts and ceremonies on the same principle of partnership (Yājnabalkya II. 268 and Nārada III. 8 and 9).

Such an immense volume of trade would necessarily presuppose the existence of a good system of exchange. And we find from Yājnabalkya (I. 361ff.) that there existed in this period also a large variety of gold, silver and copper coins. Thus there were the golden dīnār and suvarṇa, the māshas and kṛishnālas which were both silver and copper coins. According to Nārada (App. 57ff) in the south the currency consisted of subarṇa and dīnār, māshas, kakani and silver kārshāpaṇas. According to Mr. V. A. Smith "the coinage bears an unmistakable testimony to the reality of Roman influence and the word dīnār, the Latin denarius, was commonly used to mean a gold coin" (Oxford History of India, p 162).

Nor is this all. We find from the inscriptions of the period that the guilds performed the functions of of modern banks by allowing investment of money and property in it and giving interest thereon. Thus the Indore Copper Plate Inscription of Skanda-gupta (Fleet, Gupta Inscriptions No. 16) dated in the year 465 A. D. records the gift of an endow-the ment, the interest of which is to be applied to the maintenance of a lamp which has been established in a temple for the service of the Sun-god.

We shall now touch on a few rules regarding loans and interests which are undoubtedly of great economic importance. According to Śukra money-lending was an approved line of business (Śukra III. *ll.* 365-67) and the following points are to be noted with regard to a loan transaction:—(1) The business qualifications of the debtor are to be studied. (2) There are to be pawns or securities (বন্ধ). (3) There must be men who stand bail (প্রতিভূ). (4) There are to be witnesses. (5) Receipts for value received as well as documents mentioning other conditions should be prepared (গৃহীত লিখিতম্) (III. *ll.* 384-85). It is further laid down that when the amount drawn from the debtor in the form of interest has reached twice the principal, then the king shall make the debtor pay only the principal to the creditor and nothing more than that (*ll.* 631-32). If four times the value have been received by the creditor from the debtor, the former is to receive no more (Ch. V. *ll.* 192-95). Again, it is said that creditors take away people's wealth by compound interest. So the king should protect the people from them (*ll.* 633-34). But if somebody does not return the money to the creditor when he is able, the king should make him pay that back by the methods of Sāma (সাম), Daṇḍa (দণ্ড) etc. (*ll.* 635-36).

We have now seen the wonderful achievements of the period in the various arts and crafts the immense development of foreign trade which was not satisfied with the markets of Europe and Egypt alone but also found vent in a regular traffic in the eastern waters between Bengal and Ceylon, Kalinga and Suvarṇabhūmi embracing the islands of Java, Sumatra and Malacca, Cambodia, China and even Japan. The result was the growth of the proverbial wealth of India and "those great monuments of art which India was enabled to erect after clothing and feeding her own people." Hence we find the immense stress laid upon wealth by Śukrāchārya "In this world wealth is the means to all pursuits. So man should try to acquire that by good ways and means e.g., by good learning, good service, valour, agriculture, usury, store-keeping, arts or begging." (III. *ll.* 364-67). "Even defects are regarded as merits and even merits become defects of the wealthy and the poor respectively. The poor are insulted by all." (III. *ll.* 370-71). And again "man is the slave of wealth, not wealth of any body; so one should always labour for wealth. Through wealth men get virtue, satisfaction and salvation" (Ch. V. *ll.* 77-79).

The Age of Harsha.

(600-647 A. D.)

The break-up of the stately fabric of the Gupta Empire effected by the nomadic hordes from Central Asia who swarmed across the N. W. passes must have told heavily upon the foreign trade of India. But at the same time we should bear in mind that among all the political deluges that have overflooded the soil of India, the Indian village system always served as the veritable Noah's Ark in which the village ploughman and craftsman could easily carry on their peaceful avocations. Hence it is that we hear of the considerable economic development and prosperity of the kingdom of Valabhi, hence it is that we hear of the maritime activities of the Jats and the Gurjaras, hence it is that we find the people of Gujrat on a fresh colonising expedition to Java and Cambodia in this period. And if there be any lack of material for the Economic History of the 6th Century, it is no longer felt when the story of the 7th is to be told. The invaluable description of India by Hiuen Tsang or Yuan Chwang, I-Tsing and others, his Biography written by his friends, the official Chinese historical works and an historical romance called Harṣhacharit composed by Bāna who enjoyed the friendship of King Harṣha, when combined with a considerable amount of information derived from inscriptions, coins and other sources supply us with knowledge surpassing in fullness and precision that available for any other period of early Hindu History, except that of Gautama Buddha.

The enormous growth of trade and industries must have led to a vigorous growth of city life, at least in the ports and important centres of trade (which will be enumerated in their proper place). According to Hiuen Tsang the imperial capital of Kanauj was a magnificent, wealthy and well-fortified city, nearly four miles long and a mile broad with many tanks and gardens. Hiuen Tsang gives us an account of about forty-five small kingdoms which he troversed and their important towns at most of which he touched. He also speaks of Nālanda and other places which were centres of learning and the arts. Besides, the Chinese account of the conquering progress of a Chinese army from Magadha to Bamian in A. D. 645-50 mentions the Chinese conquest of 580 cities in N. India.

But nevertheless the bulk of the people lived in the villages and the King was the ultimate owner of the soil. The existence of King's ultimate ownership and a whole village owned by one man is evident from the following lines of Bṛihaṣpati:

"Suppose land is taken from a village belonging to one man and transferred to another man by (either the action of) a river or by the King. To which man does it belong? It belongs to him who gets it from the river or from the King." Again, Bṛihaṣpati says that the reason why the King becomes heir to property left intestate without another heir is that he is "the owner of all". Nārada who wrote his Code a little earlier says "The real estate held for three generations cannot be estranged except by the King's will."

The chief industry of the people was agriculture. Kashmere was famous for its suffroon (called Kashmere in Sanskrit for this reason) and rice. Government dues were paid in kind and it is interesting to note that the Kashmere Government gave rice naturally to its servants as pay (c. f. Konkan before the English conquest). But the rice of Magadha was no less good. According to Hiuen Tsang it is the "rice for the great" (Beal, Vol. II. p. 82). In Pāryātra (100 miles W. of Mathurā) a strange kind of rice is grown which ripens in 60 days. Lampaka (in Afganisthan) and Kausāmbi also produced rice. Besides rice and corn, ginger, mustard, melons and pumpkins are grown. Onion and garlic are little grown.

The usual food of the people according to Hiuen Tsang was—milk, butter, cream, soft sugar, sugar-candy, cakes and oils; mutton, deer, gazella, and fish are taken fresh.

Hiuen Tsang says, that it is difficult to mention the various fruits—Āmla, Kapitthya, Madhuka, Bhadra, Amalā, Tindaka, Udambara, Mochā, Pansya, cocoanut, date, chestnut, loquat, persimmon, pear, wild plum, peach, apricot, grapes etc. Kashmere he says is famous for fruits and flowers. Udyana is famous for grapes and scented shrub called turmeric. In Chināpapi (between the Rāvi and the Sutlej) peach was introduced by the Chinese hostages. Hence peach is called Chīnani (চীনানি) and pear is called Chīnarājaputra (চীনরাজপুত্র Sugarcane was grown in Lampaka (in Afganisthan) and in Kausāmbi. The Malabar Ghats (mountains South of Malayakūta) are famous for white sandalwood and the karpur tree (Beal, Vol. II. p. 232).

According to Hiuen Tsang "The young of seven and more are taught five Vidyās and the second of these is Silpa-Sthāna-Vidyā which treats of arts and mechanics (Beal, p. 78.)

The weaving industry was in a very flourishing condition. Cloths were woven from cotton, silk and wool. According to Hiuen Tsang there were (1) cotton fabrics (2) silk fabrics (কৌষেয়, Kiau-she-ye) (3) fabrics manufactured from hemp (ক্ষৌম, T'so-mo) (4) cloths woven from the fine hair of goats (কম্বল, Kien-po-lo) and (5) Karāla fabrics manufactured from the fine hair of a wild animal. It is seldom that this can be woven and therefore the stuff is very valuable and it is regarded as fine cloth (Beal, p. 75). The cotton and cotton fabrics of Broach were still famous as in the days of the Mahābhārata. This perfection of the art of weaving can be gathered from a description by Bāna of pieces of cloth collected on the occasion of the marriage of Rājaśri "The Palace was strewn with Kshauma (silk) Bādra (cotton), Dukula (linen) Lālātamtuja (?), ansuka (?), Naitrā (?), cloths glistening like serpent's skin, fit to be blown even by a breath and inferrable only by touch, of all colours of the rainbow." Hunter remarks "shut out as Orissa was, from the general polices of India, it boasted of fabrics which it could send as valuable presents to the most civilised monarchs of the interior. So fine was the linen which the Prince of Kalinga sent to the King of Oudh, that a priestess who put on the gauzy fabric was accused of appearing naked" (Cosma's Analysis of the Dulva, Journal of the Asiatic Society of Bengal, Vol. VI. 1837).

The metal industries were highly developed. Hiuen Tsang refers to a copper statue of Maheśwar 100 feet high. Its appearance is grave, majestic and lifelike (Beal, vol II. 45). Sung-yun who came to India in 518 A. D. says "within the Pagoda (in Gāndhār) there is contained every sort of Buddhist utensil. Here are some gold and jewelled vessels of a thousand forms and vast variety to name which even would be no easy task. At sunrise the golden disc of the vane are lit up with dazzling glory whilst the gentle breeze of morning causes the precious bells (that are suspended from the roof) to tinker with a pleasing sound" (Beal CV). Hiuen Tsang also mentions golden, silver, copper and iron vessels not to speak of wooden and stone ones (Beal, 77). Hiuen Tsang also frequently mentions Teou-ship which is a compound of equal parts of copper and calamine (silicate of zinc) [Beal 166 f. n.]

We shall now refer to the wonderful achievements in applied chemistry that took place in this period. Thus Varāhamihir in his Vṛihat Saṃhitā mentions "several preparations of Vajralepa", cement strong as the thunderbolt which was used in the architecture of the times whose remains still testify to the adamantine strength of these cements ; (2) the "tempering of steel" in a manner worthy of advanced metallurgy a process to which the mediæval world owes it Damascus sword" (Dr. B. N. Seal's thesis or "The Chemical Theories of the Ancient Hindus"). Hence the Broach lance-shafts were famous in this period and were prized abroad ; (4) the extraction of the principle of indigotin from the indigo plant by a process "which however crude is essentially an anticipatian of modern chemical method" ; (5) the preparation of fast dyes for textile fabrics by the treatment of natural dyes like manjishtha with alum and other chemicals. Hence Mr. Bancroft gives much praise to the "natives of

India for having so many thousand years ago discovered means by which the colourable matter of the plants might be extracted, exygenated and precipitated from all other matters combined with it." Even Mill is constrained to say "Among the arts of the Hindus that of printing and dying their cloths has been celebrated ; and the beauty and brilliancy as well as durability of the colour they produce, are worthy of particular praise" (Mill's India vol. II. p. 21.) (3) the prepation of cosmetics and even artificial imitation of natural flower scents which bulked so largely in the Indian exports to Rome.

Pearlfishery was another flourishing industry of this period. According to Varāhamihir, Garuḍa Purāṇa and Bhoja, pearlfishing was carried on in the whole of the Indian Ocean as far as the Persian Gulf and its chief centres were at the coast of Ceylon, Pāralaukika, Sourāṣtra, Tāmraparṇi Pārasava, Kaurava, Pāndyavātaka and Hoimadeśha. The industry was mainly in the hands of the Tamils who gave to the Gulf of Mannar the name of Salābham " the sea of gain."

No less important was the salt industry. According to Hiuen Tsang salt is found in Malayaketu and in Surāstra. In Broach they boil the sea water to get salt (Beal vol. II. 259) Again "They find here (in Sind) a great quantity of salt which is red like a cinnabar, also white salt, black salt and rocky salt. In different places both far and near this salt is used for medicine" (Beal II, 272).

In the fine arts the most unique achievement of this period was the magnificent temple of Borobudur in Java whose beautiful sculptures show in splendid relief ships in full sail and scenes recalling the history of the colonisation of Java by Indians. Of one of them Mr. Havell thus speaks in appreciation "The ship magnificent in design and movement is a masterpiece in itself. It tells more plainly than words the perils which the Prince of Gujrat and his companions encountered on the long and difficult voyages from the west coast of India. But these are over now. The sailors are hastencing to furl the sails and bring the ship to anchor." (E. B. Havell, Indian Sculpture and Painting, p. 124). No less magnificent were the sculptures on the Ajantā caves Nos. 1-5 which are placed between 525-650 A. D. Hiuen Tsang's is the earliest recorded reference to these caves. He heard that "on the stone walls are painted different scenes in the life of Tathagata's preparatory life as Bodhisattva. These scenes have been cut out with the greatest accuracy and finish" (Beal's Buddhist Records of the Western World II. p. 257). We are further told by Hiuen Tsang that "In the great temple of Gayā the utmost skill of the artist has been employed; the ornamentation is in the richest colours (red and blue). He also found the doors, windows and the low walls (of the Saṃgha-rāma) painted profusely (Beal, 74). He also refers to painted mats (Beal, 75) and to painted figures of Buddha in Gāndhāra. Of the Topes which are erected to mark some sacred event or site or to preserve some relic of Gautama Buddha, the Sarnath Tope near Benares is a solidly built structure of this period. Yuan Chwang saw the Jarāsandha Baithak a tope 28 feet in diameter and 21 ft. high and the Dagobā (central tope) of Amaraoti, now no more. Pallava art reached its zenith in this period. Mahendra-barman I. (600-25) is memorable for his public works which include rockcut temples and caves, the ruined town of Mahendravādi and a great reservoir near the same. His successor Narasiṃgha-barman (625-45) founded the town of Māmalla-puram or Mahābalipuram and caused the execution of the wonderful Rathas or Seven Pagodas at that place, each of which is cut out from a great rock boulder. His artists also wrought the remarkable relief sculptures in the rocks at the same place.

As regards jewellery we find that the ornaments of kings and grandies are extraordinary. Garlands and tiaras of precious stones are their head ornaments and their bodies are adorned with rings, bracelets and necklaces. Wealthy merchantile people have only bracelets (Watters, I. p. 51). Armlets or angadas have not been noticed by Hiuen Tsang though they are by Bāna as also kuṇḍalas and Keyurs or ear-rings (See Bāna's description of

Kumāragupta and Mādhavagupta in Harshacharit pp. 197-198). Bāna also describes a black horse thus "Upon its forehead dangled rings of fine gold and it was adorned with trappings of gold." Hiuen Tsang also refers to gem-decked caps (Beal, p. 75) and he found in the temple of Gayā a statue of Buddha which was of cast gold and silver decorated with gems and precious stones.

Ivory work was also carried on and ivory puppets are mentioned in the Kāmasūtra and in the Mālatīmādhava.

Townplanning was also highly developed in this period specially in the Deccan. The Pallava capital of Kanchi was constructed on a nice plan. "Here" writes Professor Geddes "is not simply a city made monumental by great temples and rich and varied innumerable minor ones; what rejoices one is to find the realisation of an exceptionally well grouped and comprehensive town plan and this upon a scale of spacious dignity combined with individual and artistic freedom to which I cannot name any equally surviving parallel whether in India or elsewhere" (Quoted by C. P. Venkatarāma Aiyar in "Town Planning of Ancient Deccan" p. 78.)

Some of these crafts were organised into guilds. The literature of the period throws interesting side-light on the nature and origin of these guilds. Thus regarding the origin of guilds Bṛihaṣpati (XVII.

5-6) says "A compact formed among villagers, companies of artisans and associations is called an agreement; such an agreement is to be executed to provide against dangers and for the purpose of discharging their duties. When a danger is apprehended from robbers or thieves and irregular troops, it is considered as a distress common to all. In such a case, it is the united body, not a single indivudal, whoever (*i.e.*, however great) he may be that is able to repel the danger." The programme of work of these guilds included various things besides the strictly professional business and Bṛihaspati (XVII. 11-12) preserves a specimen of such items of business in the following lines :—

"সভাপ্রপদেব গৃহতড়াগারামসংস্কৃতিঃ।
তথানাথদরিদ্রাণাং সংস্কারো যজনক্রিয়া॥
কুলায়নং নিরোধশ্চ কার্য্যমস্মাভিং রশতঃ।
যত্রৈতল্লিখিতং সম্যক্ (পত্রে) ধর্ম্যা সা সময়ক্রিয়া॥"

Thus it was fully realised that the value of co-operation lay in the facilities it affords for preventing common danger and for performing a variety of objects of public utility such as the construction of a house of assembly, of a shed for (accomodating travellers with) water, a temple, a pool and a garden and the helping of poor people in the performance of the saṃskāra or sacrificial acts enjoined by the Śāstras.

We learn also from the same authority some of the formalities which accompanied the formation of a new guild. Says Bṛihaspati (XVII. 7) :—

"কোষেণ লেখক্রিয়য়া মধ্যস্থৈ বা পরস্পরম্ ।
বিশ্বাসং প্রথমং কৃত্বা কুর্য্যুঃ কার্য্যাণ্যনন্তরম্ ॥"

"Mutual confidence having first been established by means of (the ordefal by) sacred libation, by a stipulation in writing, or by umpires, they shall set about their work" (S. B. E. Vol. XXXIII, p. 347). Thus the first step towards the organisation of a guild was to inspire mutual confidence among the intending members. This was done by one of the following means :—

Kosha.—This no doubt refers to the ordeal described in detail in Yājnabalkya II. 114-115 and Nārada I. 329-31). The person to be tested was "to drink three mouthfuls of water in which (an image of) the deity whom he holds sacred has been bathed and worshipped. If he should meet himself with any calamity within a week or a fortnight (after having undergone this ordeal) it shall be regarded as proof of his guilt (here unfitness for membership) otherwise he would be considered pure (and fit to be a member of the guild).

2. *Lekha-kriyā.*—This probably refers to an agreement, laying down the rules and regulations of the guild to which all must subscribe.

3. *Madhyastha.*—It perhaps refers to the practice of a well-known man standing guarantee for the faithful conduct of another.

The executive of the guild was to consist of a President assisted by two, three or five officers. They are to be selected from persons who are honest, acquainted with the Vedas and their duty, sprung from noble families and skilled in every business (*Ibid.* XVII. 9). Persons not deserving of these posts are also mentioned (*Ibid.* XVII. 8) in detail :—

"বিবেষিণো ব্যসনিনঃ শালীনালসভীরবঃ
লুব্ধাতিবৃদ্ধবালাশ্চ ন কার্য্যাঃ কার্য্যচিন্তকাঃ"

These executive officers could deal with an offending member in whatever way they liked beginning from mild censure upto expulsion (Bṛihaspati, XVII. 17). Thus if an individual member falls out with his associates or neglects his work, he is to be awarded a fine amounting to six nishkas of four suvarṇas each. If he injures the joint stock or breaks the mutual agreement, though able to do the same, he was to be punished by confiscation of his entire property and by banishment from the town. Thus in the prosecution of their official duties, the hands of the executive were unfettered for Bṛihaspati states explicitly " whatever is done by those (heads of the association) whether harsh or kind towards other people, in accordance with prescribed regulations, must be approved of by the king as well, for they are declared to be the appointed managers (of affairs). [*Ibid.* XVII. 18].

Inspite of this exercise of high authority by the executive officers the demorcatic element was quite a distinguishing feature of the guild organisations of the period. We have already seen that the executive officers were ultimately responsible to the assembly of the guild and that when the assembly found itself unable to bring them to book, the king should step in. Bṛihaspati (XVII. 20) speaks in in the same strain :—

"মুখ্যৈঃ সহ সমূহানাং বিসম্বাদো যদা ভবেৎ।
তদা বিচারয়েৎ রাজা স্বধর্ম্মে স্থাপয়েচ্চতান্ ॥"

"When a dispute arises between the chiefs and the societies, the king shall decide it and shall bring them back to their duty (S. B. E. Vol. XXXIII. p. 349). Several other features also clearly bring out the democratic feeling that pervaded these institutions. Thus, we learn from Bṛihaspati that there was a house for the general meeting of the guild (Bṛihaspati XVII. 11) where the idea of "liberty of speech" was probably not unknown. Thus Chandeśvara quotes the following passage from Kātyāyana in his Vivādaratnākar—

"যুক্তিযুক্তঞ্চ যো হন্যাৎ বক্তুর্যোনাবকাশদঃ।
অযুক্তঞ্চৈব যো ব্রুয়াৎ প্রাপ্নুয়াৎ পূর্ব্বসাহসম্ ॥"

and adds the comment [যো ব্রুয়াৎ কার্য্যচিন্তকেষু (Bib. Ind. p. 179). Thus the executive officer who injures another for having said reasonable things, interrupts a speaker (lit. gives no opportunity to the speaker to continue) or speaks some thing improper is to be punished with 'Pūrvasāhasadaṇḍa'. Further says Bṛihaspati (Virāmitrodaya p. 432) :—

"যত্তৈঃ প্রাপ্ত রক্ষিতং বা গণার্থং বা ঋণম্ কৃতম্।
রাজপ্রসাদলব্ধঞ্চ সর্ব্বেষামেব তৎসমমিতি ॥"

"Whatever was acquired (such as a field or a garden acquired in course of a boundary dispute in a law court) or preserved (from a thief) by them (the officers of guilds) and whatever debt is incurred by them (for the purpose of the guild) or whatever is bestowed upon the guild as a mark of royal favour, all this is to be divided equally among all the members". And again—

"গণমুদ্দিশ্য যৎকিঞ্চিৎ কৃত্বর্ণং ভক্ষিতস্মবেৎ।
আত্মার্থং বিনিযুক্তং বা দেয়ং তৈরেব তদ্ভবেদিতি ॥"

"If however the money borrowed by them is spent for their own individual ends and not for the interest of the guild, they were liable to make good the amount". It appears from the comments of Mitramiśra that the admission of new members in a guild and the exclusion of old members from its fold depended upon the general assembly. He also quotes a passage from Kātyāyana to show that the new member would at once share equally with others, the existing assets and liabilities of the guild and enjoy the fruits of its charitable and religious deeds, whereas the man who was excluded from the guild would at once cease to have any interest in any of them. Chaṇḍeśwara also quotes the same passage (Virāmitrodaya p. 432) and informs that it required the consent of all to become the member of a guild, but one might give up the membership of his own accord.

We have already seen that the guild could sit in judgement upon its members in cases which affected or had a tendency to affect its transaction of business. But the following passages from Bṛihaspati (I. 28,30) show that the guild also formed part of the ordinary tribunals of the country. "Relatives, guilds, assemblies (of co-habitants) and other persons duly authorised by the King should decide law suits among men excepting causes concerning violent crimes (sāhasa); when a cause has not been duly investigated by meetings of kindred, it should be decided after due deliberation of guilds; when it has not been (duly) examined by guilds, it should be decided by assemblies (of co-habitants); and when it has not been (sufficiently) made out by such assemblies, (it should be tried) by appointed (judges)" [S. B. E. Vol. XXXIII. p. 281]. The Chapter in which these passages occur deals generally with the constitution of the courts of justice and there is nothing to show that the judicial functions of the guilds noticed here related to its members alone or simply with reference to its own proper business.

The very fact that Bṛihaṣpati has noticed these latter functions separately in a later chapter, seems to prove that in the passage quoted above, reference is made to the guilds as ordinary courts of law. The exception noticed in Ch. I. verse 28 (just quoted) *viz.*, causes concerning violent crimes (sāhasa) also proves that the writer had in view only the ordinary cases to be tried by ordinary courts of justice.

Besides the craft guilds, there was another form of co-operative production carried on under joint stock principles. The basis of partnership in these cases consisted not of the capital money contributed by each, but of the skill and technical knowledge which each brought to the work. As this naturally varied in different persons the share of profit which each enjoyed was also different. Thus Bṛihaṣpati says (ch. XIV. 28ff.) "when goldsmiths or or other artists (*i. e.*, workers in silver, thread, wood, stone or leather) practise their art jointly, they shall share profits in due proportion, corresponding to the nature of their work" (S. B. E. Vol. XXXIII p. 340). On the same principle, "the headman among a number of workmen jointly building a house or temple or digging a pool or making articles of leather is entitled to a double share (of the remuneration)" [*Ibid.* p. 341] and among the musicians "he who knows how to beat the time shall take a share and a half but the singers shall take equal shares" (*Ibid.*). Even among thieves and freebooters "four shares shall be awarded to their chief, he who is (specially) valiant shall receive three shares; one (particularly) able shall take two and the remaining associate shall share alike". (*Ibid.*). On the other hand, if any one of them is arrested, the money spent for his release shall be shared by all alike (Kātyāyana, quoted in Vivādratnākar, p. 126.). It may also be noted that the priests carried on sacrificial acts and ceremonies on the same principle of partnership (Bṛihaspati, XIV. 15). Thus of 16 priests at a sacrifice, the four chief officiators who receive about half, and the second, third and fourth groups, respectively half, $\frac{1}{3}$rd and $\frac{1}{4}$th of that. The commentator explains that if, for example, the sacrificial fee consists of 100 cows, each of the first group would receive 12, each of the succeeding groups 6, 4, and 3 respectively (Virāmitrodaya, p. 387).

We shall now advert to caste in its occupational aspect and the first important remark to make in this connection is that while the occupation of the first two castes remained much the same as in the days of Manu, the occupation of the Vaiśyas had undergone a change. "কৃষিগোরক্ষা বাণিজ্যং বৈশ্য-কর্ম্মস্বভাবজম্" says the Bhāgavat Gita but agriculture and cattle-breeding had ceased to be the occupation of the Vaiśyas and had now become the occupation of the Śūdras; so that the Vaiśyas were now only traders. The spread of Buddhist sentiment (specially under Harṣha) with its aversion to the taking of life must be held responsible for this change of occupation. The ploughing of land in which action worms and insects are inevitably killed were gradually looked upon as sinful and eventually prohibited to the Dwijas: a prohibition which is also noticed in Manu. These classes hence withdrew from agriculture and left it in the hands of the Śūdras. In the Punjab and elsewhere, however, several communities did not mind this prohibition and hence their sinking in public estimation to the rank of the Śūdras. Another important change in occupation can be gathered from another statement of Hiuen Tsang. Thus in Watters Vol. I. page 170 we find that "sovereignty for many successive generations has been exercised by the Kshatriyas alone. Rebellions and regicides have occasionally arisen, other castes assuming the distinction." Hiuen Tsang does not even make the greet Harṣha, his own benefactor and patron a Kshatriya but a Vaiśya, a fact which is also indicated by the suffix 'bardhana' assumed by many Kings of the family and also the suffix 'bhuti' in the name of Pushyabhuti, its founder mentioned by Bāna. We might in this connection refer to the existence of untouchables at that time who are now called Panchamas or the fifth class. "Butchers, fishermen, public performers, executioners and scavengers have their habitations marked by a distinguishing sign" (Watters, Vol. I. p. 147).

According to Hiuen Tsang, the people are not subject to forced labour. When the public works require it, labour is exacted but paid for. The payment is in strict proportion to the work done.

The evidences of the foreign trade of India in this period are numerous. The representations of ships and boats furnished by Ajantā paintings are mostly in cave No. 2 of which the date is placed between 525-650. And these representations afford a vivid testimony to the ancient foreign trade of India as Griffiths has rightly remarked. The contemporary literary works also hint at the flourishing condition of shipping and ship-building and the development of sea-borne trade. Thus one passage in the Vṛihat Saṃhitā (4. 8.) refers to the existence of shippers and sailors as a class whose health is said to be influenced by the Moon. Another (7. 6) refers to the stellar influences affecting the fortunes of traders, physicians, shippers and the like. The third (9. 31) also mentions a particular conjunction of stars similarly affecting merchants and sailors. The fourth (10. 3) refers to the existence of a class of small shippers who probably are confined to inland navigation. The fifth (10. 10) mentions the causes which bring about the sickness of passengers sailing in sea-going vessels on voyages and of others. The sixth (44. 12) recommends as the place for an auspicious sea-bath the seaport where there is a great flow of gold due to multitudes of merchantmen arriving in safety, after disposing off exports abroad, laden with treasure The popular drama of Ratnābalī which is usually attributed to King Harṣha relates the story of the Ceylonese Princess, daughter of King Vikramabāhu being shipwrecked in mid-ocean and brought thence by some merchants of the town of Kausāmbi. In the Daśakumārcharit of Dandī there is the story of a merchant named Ratnobhava who goes to an island called Kālavana, marries there a girl, but while returning home is shipwrecked; and another of Mitragupta who goes on board a Yavana ship and losing his way arrives at an isle different from his destination. These evidences are corroborated by the accounts of Hiuen Tsang. According to him the people of Surāstra derived their livelihood from the sea by engaging in commerce (Beal, Buddhist Records, Vol. II. p. 269).

About this time, swarms of daring adventurers anticipating the enterprise of the Drakes and Frobishers or more probably of the Pilgrim Fathers sailed in search of plenty till the shores of Java arrested their progress and gave scope to their colonising ambition. Mr. Sewell says "Native tradition in Java relates that about the beginning of the 7th century (603 A. D. according to Ferguesson) a Prince of Gujrat arrived in the island with 5000 followers and settled at Mataram. A little later 2000 more immigrants arrived to support him. He and his followers were Buddhists and from his time Buddhism was firmly established as the religion of Java. (Antiquarian Notes in Java in J. R. A. S. 1906, p. 402).

Nor is this all. "When the Chālukya Prince, brother of the King of Kalyan was founding a new kingdom at Rajmundry, which involved the rooting out and dispersion of the pre-existing rulers, nothing is more probable than that some of the fugitives should have found their way to Pegu. One Tamil MS. refers to a party of Buddhist exiles, headed by a King of Manda flying in a ship from the Coast" (Sir A. P. Phayre's History of Pegu in A. S. J. 1873) Mr. Ferguesson remarks (Indian Architecture, p. 103). "The splended remains at Amarābatī show that from the mouths of Krishnā and Godāvari the Buddhist of N. and N. W. India colonised Pegu, Cambodia and eventually Java."

There was a brisk trade with China in this period. Thus we are told (1) 'As regards Tat'sin and Tienchu (India) far out on the western ocean, we have to say that although the envoys of the two Han dynasties, Chang Chieu and Panchlao have experienced the special difficulties of this road, yet traffic in merchandise has been effected and goods have been sent out to the foreign tribes, the force of winds driving them far away across the waves of the sea'—Sung-shu (about 500 A. D.) (2) '(in the west of it (Tienchu, *i. e.*, India) they carry on much trade by sea to Tat'sin and Auhsi, specially in the articles of Tat'sin such as all kinds of precious things, corals, amber, chimpi (gold jadestone) chuchi (a

that during the period between Cheng-Kuan (A. D. 627-650) and T'ien-Shon (A. D. 690-692) of T'ang dynasty, the people of Tein-chu (i.e., India) sent envoys with tribute to China (J. R. A. S. 1896. p. 490). In the 7th century A. D. the Indo-Chinese intercourse was a little disturbed. Matouanlin states that Yangti the first emperor of the Sui dynasty (605 A. D.) sent Feitou to summon the Tibetans, Indians and other people to pay him homage. Many princes responded to this but the Indian Kings alone refused to enter into such a subsidiary alliance. The emperor was highly enraged at this.

With the accession, however, of the Tang dynasty in 626 A. D. the troubles were over and the Indo-Chinese intercourse revived. In 641 A. D. Harṣhabardhan hearing of the glories of China and its the then emperor Tai-tsoung from Yuan Chwang sent some ambassadors and a letter to the Chinese emperor. In reply, the Chinese emperor sent an officer under Li-i whom Harṣha received at the head of his ministers and again offered as presents some mica-laminæ, some perfumes and a tree called Bodhi-druma (The tree of Intelligence). The mission sent by the Chinese emperor in return for this embassy reached Magadha in 648 A. D. when the latter had died and the throne been usurped by his minister Arjunāswa. The usurper gave the mission a hostile reception and plundered its property, Wang-hiuen-tse who was in charge of the mission fled to Tibet and came down with a Tibetan army, reinforced by an army of 7000 horsemen from Nepal and inflicted a disastrons defeat upon Arjunāswa. (L. A. Waddell's "Tibetan Invasion of India in 647 A. D. and Its Results" in the Imperial and Asiatic Quarterly Review. Jan. 1911 pages 37-65). In the same century different parts of India sent commercial expeditions to China in 667, 668, 672, 690-92 (Montouanlin; Panthier p. 53; Julien p. III.).

An interesting sidelight has been thrown by Tao-Sün 595-667 and I-Tsing (who came to India in 673 A. D.) on the trade-routes between India and China with their convenient halting places. Thus Tao-sün (An account of Buddhist regions, Part I. 10. 6.) mentions three routes from China to India. The first is to the S. W. of lake Lop to Tibet and Nepal. The second is from Shan-shen to Khotan and so on. The third is the outward one followed by Hiuen Tsang. I-Tsing has recorded the itenaries of about 60 Chinese pilgrims who visited India in the 7th century A. D. from which it is clear that the whole coast of Farther India from Burma to China and also of the islands of the Malaya Archipelago was studded with prosperous Indian colonies and naval stations which ships regularly flying in the Eastern waters between India and China used as convenient halting places. I-Tsing refers to more than ten such colonies

38

where Indian manners, customs and religious practices prevailed together with Sanskrit learning. These were Sri-Bhoja in Sumatra, Kalinga in Java, Mahasin in Borneo and the islands of Bālī, Bhojapara etc. In these naval stations passengers often changed their ships, though many would come direct to Bengal like I-Tsing who disembarked at the port of Tāmralipti, while others would halt at Ceylon, to reship themselves for Bengal like Fa-Hien.

As regards the trade with Japan following as in the case of China, in the track of religious intercourse between the two countries which developed during the period, we have a few evidences to adduce. Japanese tradition records the names of many Indian evangelists who visited Japan to propagate the religion of Lord Buddha. Thus Bodhi-Dharma after working in China came to Japan and had an interview with Prince Shotoker (A. D. 573-621). Mr. Havell in his Indian Sculpture and Painting remarks " From the seaports of her eastern and western coasts India sent streams of colonists, missionaries, and craftsmen all over Southern Asia, Ceylon, Siam and for distant Cambodia. Through China and Korea Indian art entered Japan about the middle of the 6th century." For a fuller account of the economic relations between India and Japan in the year following the death of Harṣha, the reader is referred to (1) Rev. Daito Shimaji's article on " India and Japan in Ancient Times " and (2) Dr. Taka-kusu's article on " What

Japan owes to India" in the Journal of the Indo-Japanese Association for January, 1910).

We should bear in mind that her trade in Eastern waters alone was not able to give full scope to India's throbbing international life in this period. We have already seen in the evidences of Cosmos Indicopleustes (535 A. D.) that trade was carried on in this period between India and the coasts of the Persian Gulf, the Red Sea and Ethiopia. Already in this period, taking advantage of the anarchy and chaos that followed the disruption of the Gupta Empire and the Hun inundations, the Arabs invaded Sind and the Punjab both by sea (637 A. D.) and through Persia (650-660). From Reinand's Memoire Sur l'Inde, 170, 176 we learn that the Arabs in 637 invaded Thana from Oman and Broach and Sindh from Bahrein. King Khusru II of Persia in the 36th year of his reign (625-26 A. D.) received a complimentary embassy from Pulakeśhi II. The courtesy was reciprocated by a return embassy from Persia which was received in the Indian court with due honour (V. A. Smith. E. H. I. 384-385). There is a large fresco-painting in the cave No. 1 at Ajantā which is still easily recognisable as a vivid representation of the ceremonial attending the presentation of their credentials by the Persian envoys. As a result of this trade with Persia a large contingent of Indian merchants settled in Persia and we are told by Hiuen Tsang that in the chief cities of Persia, Hindus were settled enjoying the full practice of their religion (Reinaud's Abulfeda, CCCLXXXV). After the destruction of Rome in the latter half of the 5th century Constantinople became the centre of Indo-European trade which flew in not only through the Oxus and the Caspian but also along the Red Sea and the Nile. But the rise of Islam soon proved a wet blanket to Indo-European trade which was forced to resume its old and tedious route. Goods were carried up the Indus; thence on camels to the banks of the Oxus; thence to the Caspian Sea; thence through Volga and Don to the Black Sea whence ships carried them to Constantinople.

Some idea of the trade of Ceylon in this period can be gathered from the accounts of Cosmos. He says "From all India, Persia, Ethiopia, between which countries it is situated in the middle, an infinite number of vessels arrive at, as well as go from, Ceylon. From the interior of the continent as for instance from China and other commercial countries, it receives silk, aloes, cloves and other productions, which it exports to Malabar where the pepper grows and to Calliene (near Bombay) whence is brought steel and cloth, for the latter is also a great port. It likewise makes consignments to Sindh on the borders of India and also to Persia, Yemen and Adule. From all these countries it receives articles of produce which again it transmits into the interior, together with its own productions. Selandie (Sinhala Dwipa) is consequently a great emporium and being situated in the middle of the Indian Ocean, it receives merchandise as well as sends it to all parts of the world" (quoted in Heeren's Historical Researches Vol. II. p. 298). Professor Heeren adds "during a space of a thousand years, that is, from 500 B. C. to 500 A.D., the island of Ceylon so conveniently situated for such a purpose, continued to be the great emporium of the Hindu carrying trade from Adule on the east of Africa, Yemen and Malabar and the Ultra-Gangetic Peninsula, even to China." He also says "Ceylon was the common mart of Australian Commerce" (Historical Reserches Vol. II. p. 426). The enormous wealth of Ceylon due to this commerce made Ceylon—the Golden Lankā, a trite phrase in the historical and fabulous writings of India and Ceylon.

Coming to the chief centres of trade with their articles of import and export we find that Cosmos Indicopleustes in his Christian Topography speaks of Mala or Malabar as the chief seat of the pepper trade and mentions the five pepper marts of Poudapatana, Nalopatana, Salopatana, Mangarouth and Parti and also other ports farther northward on the western coast such as Kallyan and Gujrat. In 526 he found Sindhu or Debal and Orhet *i.e.*, Soratha or Verabal as leading places of trade with Ceylon (Yule's Cathay I. CLXXVIII.) About this time as Ferguesson has pointed out, Amarāvatī, at the mouth of the Krishnā was superseded as the port for the Golden Chersonese by the accomplishment of the direct voyage from Gujrat and the west coast of India. Maritime trade was also carried on in the important seaports of Gujrat viz. Broach, Cambay and Prabhāsa (as noticed in the Gujrat Gazetteer). Teakwood and bamboo of Sindan (Sanjan) were largely exported. Broach lance-shafts were also exported as also the shoes of Cambay. Broach cotton and cloths must have been exported and import of horses came from Persia and Arabia. According to the Arab historians of the 8th century "formerly Yavanas were imported and now Tapan girls and emarelds were exported for Arab chiefs." According to Hiuen Tsang Thaneśwar and Kānyakubja were great inland centres of trade. The Sanskrit drama Ratnābalī refers to Kausāmbi as a great resort of merchants and traders one of whom rescued the Ceylonese princess, a daughter of Vikramabāhu from a watery grave. Hiuen Tsang also speaks of Malayakūta (Beal II. p. 231) and Ceylon (Beal II. p. 239) as great centres of trade. On the west coast are Tamluk and Puri. At this time, Pulakeśhi reduced Puri "which was the Mistress of the western seas" (Dr. R. G. Bhāndārkar's Early History of the Deccan, Ch. X.). At the time of Hiuen Tsang, Tamluk was still an important Buddhist harbour. It was "situated on a bay, could be approached both by land and water and contained stores of rare and precious merchandise and a wealthy population." According to I-Tsing

" Tāmralipti is 40 Yojanas south from the eastern limit of India. The people are rich .... this is the place where we embarked when returning to China " (Taka-kusu's I-Tsing XXXIII, XXXIV). The Daśakumārcharit of Dandī written in 7th century A. D. mentions it. So also does the Buddhist work Dasa-Bhumiśvara. It continued to be an important port even in later times. In 1276 some Buddhist monks of Tamluk went to Penang and reformed Buddhism there. About 1495 Rāmachandra Kavi-Bhāratī went to Ceylon from that place. But soon after as Sir W. W. Hunter remarks in his " Orissa " p. 315 the "harbours were left high and dry by the landmaking rivers and the receding sea. Religious prejudices combined with the changes of Nature to make the Bengalees unenterpresing upon the ocean."

In the town of Thaneśwar, the stalls are arranged on both sides of the road with appropriate signs. Those who cultivate the royal estates says Hiuen Tsang had to pay $\frac{1}{3}$rd of the produce. The river passages and the roadbarriers are open on payment of a toll. Again "the private demesne of the crown are divided into four parts ; the first is for carrying out the affairs of state and providing sacrificial offering. The second for providing subsidies for the ministers and chief officers of the state. The third for rewarding men of distinguished ability. The fourth for charity to religious bodies whereby the field of merit is cultivated. In this way *the taxes* of the people are *light* (Beal, p. 87).

Coming to the trade organisations of the period we find that trade was carried on under joint stock principles. Hiuen Tsang refers to companies of sea-merchants with merchant-chiefs (Beal, vol. II. 125, 253) Bṛihaspati (XIV. 1-32) has laid down rules for the joint transaction of business (সম্ভূয় সমুত্থানম্). As the success of the "joint stock company depends upon the individuals that form it" Bṛihaspati lays down in detail persons unworthy of a joint stock business. Says he "Trade or other occupations should not be carried on by prudent men jointly with incompetent or lazy persons or with such as are afflicted with an illness, ill-fated or destitute. A man should carry on business jointly with persons of noble parentage, clever, active, intelligent, familiar with coins, skilled in revenue and expenditure, honest and enterprising" (S. B. E. vol. XXXIII. p. 336). Besides their duties concerning the joint business the company also looked after the interests of the members after their death. Thus says Bṛihaspati "should any partner in trade happen to die through want of proper care his goods must be shown and (delivered) to officers appointed by the King" (S. B. E. vol. XXXIII p. 338).

Coming to the constitution of the Joint Stock Company we find that they had their chiefs referred to by Hiuen Tsang. The democratic character of the company is shown by the following rules and regulations :—"whatever property one may give (or lend) authorised by many or whatever contract they may cause to be executed, all that is (considered as having been) done by all" (S.B.E. vol. XXXIII p. 337). Again Bṛihaspati endorses the view of Nārada who says "loss, expenses and profits of each partner are proportioned to the amount contributed by him to the joint stock." Coming to the relation of the members to the corporate body, we find that "when any one among them is found out to have practised deceit in a purchase or sale, he must be cleared by oath (or ordeal)". They are themselves pronounced to be arbitrators and witnesses for one another in doubtful cases and when a fraudulent act has been discovered unless a (previous) feud should exist between them (S. B. E. vol. XXXIII p. 337). If after this his guilt was established he should be paid his capital and expelled from the company, his profits being forfeited to it as Yājnabalkya had already laid down (II. 268). Again according to Bṛihaspati when (a single partner acting) without the assent (of the other partners) injures (their joint property) through his negligence or against their express injunctions, he must by himself give a compensation to all his partners (S. B. E. Vol. XXXIII. pp. 337-8). But "that partner, on the other hand, who by his own efforts preserves (the common stock) from a danger unapprehended through fate or the king, shall be allowed a tenth part of it (as a reward) [Bṛihaspati, XIV. 10].

Besides a regular system of metallic currency we find on the authority of Hiuen Tsang that cowries and beads were used as media of exchange in Kong-tutu (Ganjam) [Beal, Vol. II. p. 207]. According to the same authority gold coins were used in Nepal (*Ibid.* p. 80). According to Arab historians the Roman dīnārs were used in Gujrat. We do not know whether the guilds performed the functions of modern banks by accepting endowments and giving interest as they have done in the previous periods but we have got an inscription at the Vailla-bhaṭṭa-Swāmin Temple of Gwalior which shows that as late as 877 A. D. endowments were made with the guilds as of old. Thus it records an endowment made with the guilds of oil-millers and gardeners who should give one palika of oil per oilmill every month and fifty garlands every day respectively for the temple out of the interest of the endowments (Epigraphia Indica, Vol. I. p. 159 ff.).

Yuan Chwang found India prosperous and the reasons are not far to seek. A judicious distribution of lands among all classes of people is the root of a country's welfare and India is blest in this respect from the earliest times, Moreover, we have already seen that India in this period cultivated commercial relations with Pegu, Cambodia, Java, the islands of the Malaya Archipelago, China, and even Japan in the east and with the provinces of the Roman Empire, Arabia, Persia, Ethiopia and the coasts of the Red Sea in the west. She had trading settlements in southern China, in Java, Sumatra, Borneo, Bālī, Bhojapara, in all the chief cities of Persia and even on the coasts of the Persian and Bahrein Gulf. In the sixth century, apparently driven out by the white Huns the Jats from the Indus and tho Cutch occupied the islands of the Bahrein Gulf. Thus both the East and West become the theatre of Indian commercial activity and gave scope to the artisans and merchants. As a consequence, she had the balance of trade clearly in her favour as of old, a balance which could only be settled by the export of precious metals from the countries commercially indebted to her. For, a genial climate and a fertile soil, coupled with the industry and frugality of her people made India virtually independent of foreign nations in respect of the necessaries of life while the ideal of simple living and free thinking must have rendered the secondary wants of the mass of the people very limited in number. Thus has she been for many centuries the final depository of a large portion of the metallic wealth of the world. It was this flow or "drain" of gold into India which as we have seen, so far back as the 1st century A. D. was the cause of alarm and regret to Pliny. It was probably also the same flow of of gold into the country, that even earlier still in the fifth century B. C. enabled the small Indian satrapy of Darius to pay him 360 Eubolic talents of gold, worth fully £ 1,290,000 and constituting about one-third of the total bullion revenue of the Asiatic Provinces (Herodotus III).